Yemen

D1220457

The principal sights

< Lift flap for map

Yemeni coastguard in the Red Sea at Loheya (19th-century engraving)

Peter Wald

Yemen

Translated by
Sebastian Wormell

PALLAS GUIDES

Front and inside front cover: Village in the Hadramawt (Photographs: Monica Fritz)
Back cover: A bar in San'a (Photograph: Monica Fritz)
Inside back cover: By the Great Mosque in San'a (Photograph: Monica Fritz)

Contributors:

Sebastian Wormell studied art history at Heidelberg, Cambridge, and the Courtauld Institute, and has lectured for the University of London

Michael Field is a journalist and consultant, whose most recent book is Inside the Middle East, *published by John Murray and Harvard University Press (1995/1996)*

Richard Porter is the Director of BirdLife International and has made many expeditions to Yemen and Socotra

Barbara Fyjis-Walker studied at the Sorbonne and learnt Arabic at Shemlan, Lebanon; she has spent many years in the Middle East

Monica Fritz lives and works in Milan; she is presently completing a new book of photographs of the Yemen

Special thanks to our sponsors: Shell International Petroleum Company Limited, Lufthansa and Universal Travel

This book is part of the Pallas Guides series, published by Pallas Athene.
If you would like further information about the series, please write to:
Dept. Y, Pallas Athene, 59 Linden Gardens, London W2 4HJ

Series editor: Alexander Fyjis-Walker
Series assistants: Barbara Fyjis-Walker and Lynette Quinlan
Series designer: James Sutton
Maps editor: Ted Hammond

German edition first published by DuMont Buchverlag GmbH & Co., Cologne 1980, 6th edition 1992. All rights for all countries reserved by DuMont Buchverlag GmbH & Co., Limited partnership, Cologne, Germany. The title of the German original is, Der Jemen by Peter Wald.
© 1980, 1992 DuMont Buchverlag, Köln

English edition published by Pallas Athene London, 1996
Translation, adaptation, updatings, revision and all additional material © Pallas Athene 1996
All rights reserved

ISBN 1-873429-11-8

Printed through World Print, Hong Kong

Contents

Plates

Foreword

The notes and photographs taken by the late Angela Wald were indispensable for the first edition of this book twelve years ago and have remained so for the later revised and expanded editions. We are indebted to Professor Walter W. Müller's comments for the correction of some errors. Our contact with Professor Horst Kopp has contributed much to the revision of the book.

In Yemen itself we have also received much help from our Yemeni friends and others. In particular, Kinga and Heiner Rudersdorf and Martin Weiss gave us much productive and inspiring support. Our thanks also go to the authors of *Djambija*, the journal of German development workers in Yemen. Their reports from all parts of the country provided us with valuable information and thought-provoking comment. The same is true of many articles in *Jemen-Report*, published by the Deutsch-Jemenitisher Gesellschaft.

We must also thank Professor Jürgen Schmidt, the Director of the San'a branch of the German Archaeological Institute. Through his published writings and through personal communication he has deepened our understanding of the history of South Arabia.

In 1987 in San'a we met again Jeffrey Meissner, now Director of the American Institute for Yemeni Studies. About ten years earlier his work with Angela Wald laid the foundations for this book.

Edith and Peter Wald
Cologne, Spring 1996

Translator's and editor's note

We are very proud to be publishing the first English edition of Peter Wald's celebrated guide to Yemen. As well as the extraordinary beauty, and riches, that gave Yemen the name of Happy Arabia, Arabia Felix, the country glories in ten thousand years of history. Peter Wald's explorations of this heritage are based on key places; readers should co-ordinate these with the chronology on page 303.

Any book about an Arabic-speaking country has to face the perplexities of transliteration. Like many others we have kept to traditional forms where they exist, and we have avoided using the complete panoply of strangely placed dots and commas which will confuse the lay person without seriously helping the expert. We have however kept both the ayn (') and the khamsa ('), except at the beginning of words, since they indicate major elements of pronounciation. For the same reason the mutations of the definite article are shown (ie Salah ad-Din, not al-Din, for Saladin). We have nevertheless stuck with the traditional transliteration using J in such words as *jambiya*, although the actual sound produced in Yemen is closer to a hard G.

For this English edition we owe many thanks to Julian Paxton and Olav Ljosne of Shell Petroleum International for their generous sponsorship; to Michael Field for his contribution and advice; to Richard Porter for his photographs, contribution and great patience; to Monica Fritz for her photographs; to Marco Liviadotti of Universal Travel for his considerable help and cooperation; to the British Yemeni Association for constant interest; to Murad Boutros for his kind help with typesetting in Arabic; and to Barbara Fyjis-Walker, James Sutton, Ted Hammond and Lynette Quinlan without whom this book would not have been possible.

Sebastian Wormell
Alexander Fyjis-Walker
London, Spring 1996

The Exploration of Yemen

It is now just over 25 years since Yemen opened up, at least in part, to foreign travellers. The civil war in the Yemen Arab Republic (also called North Yemen and by far the more populous of the two states that united in 1990 to form the present Republic of Yemen) ended in 1969 with a compromise between the warring factions. It was not long before visitors started arriving in San'a from all over the world to discover North Yemen for themselves. If there were only a few thousand a year at first, this trickle eventually became a respectable stream of ten to twenty thousand a year. During the centuries of the theocratic rule of the Imams, until 1962, only a few foreigners - diplomats and urgently needed specialists - had been allowed in. Now the republic opened up even to independent travellers, drawn only by curiosity about this mysterious country and its people.

Yemen had already attracted European explorers in the 18th and 19th centuries. Since 1762, when the German explorer Carsten Niebuhr reached the land of the Imam in the south-west corner of the Arabian Peninsula, around 30 names have been added to the list of great traveller-discoverers. These pioneers managed to penetrate into the interior of Yemen only with the greatest difficulty; some explorers paid for their curiosity with their lives. As late as the 1960's aid workers and researchers were making their way into Yemen only at high, sometimes fatal, risk to themselves.

It often took the European discoverers of Yemen years to reach their goal; today's traveller can reach San'a by plane in a single day. The most important towns of North Yemen can now be covered in a few weeks using good overland roads and tracks, though a visitor wishing to gain anything more than a superficial knowledge of Yemen will have to turn off the main routes. The larger towns, San'a, Sa'da, Hudayda and Ta'izz, together with the Ma'rib oasis and the coastal town of Mukalla, can be easily reached by bus. There is much more to travelling in Yemen than the simple journey, however. The trip up to San'a (which is on a plateau at an altitude of about 2400 m) along the Chinese-built road is breathtaking in itself; but one has to get out and stay a while to appreciate the achievements of the local architects who built whole towns on the mountain summits, with tall houses constructed of finely hewn ashlar laid without mortar. The further journey from Hudayda to Ta'izz, a fast trip on a road provided by the Soviet Union, will reveal the African influence in the

THE EXPLORATION OF YEMEN

Yemeni coastal plain, the Tihama; but the most lasting impressions will come from visiting the Tihama markets, which in the smaller towns are only just off the road. Finally the journey up from Ta'izz to San'a, this time on a road built with aid from West Germany, is impressive for the magnificent panorama as the road crosses three passes. The most interesting towns and valleys lie, however, beyond the road. And that is where the real adventure begins.

On most minor roads the independent foreign traveller can use the local communal transport: shared taxis run between almost all towns, even if they are linked only by a stony path or a sandy track. The drivers set off as soon as they have enough passengers. Since many of the tracks are suitable only for four-wheel-drive vehicles, one should not expect too much comfort. The adventure is not so much to do with sharing a car designed for about eight persons with as many as twelve or fourteen, nor even with the fearsome curved dagger worn by most of them. (Men carry the *jambiya*, especially in the more tribal north of the country, not so much as a weapon as a status symbol; the quality of its craftsmanship is very variable.) The adventure lies in the journey itself. Often the overloaded car climbs to giddy heights on a narrow unmetalled road and then descends 800 or 1000 m in sharp twists and turns. Strong nerves are needed to enjoy the superb views of the mountain slopes with hundreds of terraced fields, while the driver stops the vehicle with difficulty and then has to reverse to take the next hairpin bend. The subtropical natural beauty at the bottom of the valley, the splendour of bananas, palms, papayas, bamboo and coffee trees can only be really appreciated if one faces danger with the same equanimity as the Yemeni passengers or can recover one's composure quickly.

The modern explorer should try to travel through some at least of Yemen on foot. There are some paths that even cross-country vehicles cannot cope with, and on them one sees Yemen as it has been for many thousands of years. The tourist will pass caravans carrying firewood which look not so very different from many of the caravans which made their way from the South Arabian coast northwards to the shores of the Mediterranean long before the birth of Christ. The shelters for livestock and herdsmen, built of layers of roughly hewn stones with round or pointed arches supporting an enormous roofing slab, may go back to the early Islamic period (see the illustration on page 27). Even the people the traveller encounters could come from another millennium, unless they are bodyguards of a tribal chief and armed with sub-machine-guns.

The early discoverers of Yemen almost always began by encountering the people of the coastal regions after arriving by boat at Aden or a Red Sea port. **Carsten Niebuhr**, who was a member of the Danish expedition to Arabia Felix (or 'Happy Arabia', the name by which Yemen was known to classical geographers, a mistranslation of the Arabic name meaning nothing more than the 'country on the right-hand side' of the Red Sea), landed on 29 December 1762 at the small Yemeni port of

Carsten Niebuhr, dressed in the Yemeni costume presented him by the Imam. In the background Yemenis fighting with the jambiya

Loheya. He and his companions had already visited Egypt, the Sinai Peninsula and the Arabian port of Jeddah. They knew that at Loheya they would be entering the domain of the Yemeni Imam. The governor of the province where they landed, Emir Ferhan, a Yemeni of African origin, proved very helpful and gave the foreigners support during their first steps in the country. 'We parted from this good governor with real regret', wrote Niebuhr in his journal when the group left Loheya on camels and horses for the difficult journey to the town of Bayt al-Faqih in the Tihama; the modern traveller can follow their steps in a four-wheel-drive car in a few hours. By the time Niebuhr and his companions arrived at Bayt al-Faqih almost two months had passed since their landing on the Yemeni coast. They made the town their base and set to work. The six members of the party, all specialists in different fields, set about gathering material for a comprehensive study of the country. Niebuhr concentrated on the groundwork for a map of Yemen. His efforts resulted in a work which was to guide European explorers in Yemen for about a century.

The Danish expedition had stayed too long in the coastal plain, then still badly infested with malaria. The party was delayed partly by the first signs of the illness and partly by the conditions laid down by the local chiefs for their departure for

Ta'izz and San'a. By the time the group finally entered the Yemeni capital on 16 July 1763 two of its members had already died on the way, and the four who remained had malaria in their blood. In the first half of August 1763 British sailing ships were to set sail from the port of Mokha, and Niebuhr and his companions decided not to miss this chance of leaving a country that had proved so dangerous to them. So in the end they stayed only sixteen days in San'a, although the journey from Copenhagen had taken two and a half years.

During this short stay, Niebuhr attempted to draw a plan of the city. There were difficulties, as he noted in his journal: 'wherever I went, the mob crowded after me so, that a survey was absolutely impossible.' Nonetheless he was able to give a description of the Yemeni capital. 'The city-gates are seven,' he wrote in another passage from his journal. 'Here are a number of mosques, some of which have been built by the Turkish pashas. San'a has the appearance of being more populous than it actually is; for gardens occupy a part of the space within the walls. In San'a, are only twelve public baths: but many noble palaces, three of the most splendid of which have been built by the reigning Imam. The palace of the late Imam El Manzor [al-Mansur], with some others, belong to the royal family, who are very numerous.' The four foreigners were received twice by the ruling Imam, al-Mahdi Abbas, before they set off on the difficult journey back to Mokha. On 23 August 1763 they set sail for India in the British ship.

A Yemeni from the Tihama (19th-century engraving)

Although the Danish expedition to Yemen was ill-fated - Carsten Niebuhr returned to Europe as the only survivor - the enterprise seems to have stimulated other explorers to set off for Southern Arabia. In 1810 **Ulrich Jasper Seetzen**, a Russian scholar of German descent travelled through Yemen. Thanks to his efforts manuscript copies of early Arabian inscriptions first arrived in Europe, but Seetzen himself never returned. When he had been in Yemen for about seven months he wrote his last recorded report in Mokha on 10 November 1810, saying that he was going to travel once more to San'a and from there head out to Ma'rib and Hadramawt. After his departure from Mokha there is no reliable information about the explorer. According to one story he was found murdered by the roadside on the way to Ta'izz, but there was also a rumour that he had been poisoned in San'a.

Over the next 50 years five archaeologists, a pharmacist, a missionary, two botanists and a naval officer all attempted to lift the veil that lay over this

The harbour at Mokha in the mid-19th century

mysterious land. **Joseph Wolff**, an Austrian Jewish convert to Anglicanism, travelled extensively carrying the Bible to Jewish communities, and indeed to all others in the Yemen in the 1830's, undergoing gruelling experiences which were written up on his return. The first European to succeed where Seetzen had failed, in reaching Ma'rib, was a French pharmacist, **Joseph Arnaud**. He was perhaps the first development aid worker in the whole region. In the late 1830's and early 1840's he worked as a pharmacist in the service of the Imam, French medical practicioners being popular in Southern Arabia. When his contract ended he was encouraged by the French consul to undertake an expedition to the ruined city of Ma'rib. The detailed preparations for the journey had to be made in secret, to keep them from the Imam's knowledge. Arnaud recruited a bedouin as guide, and so benefited from guarantees of safety given by a tribe to anyone under the protection of one of its members, and when he set off for Ma'rib on 12 July 1843, he was himself in Yemeni bedouin dress. The journey there lasted six days, but Arnaud was only able to spend two days in Ma'rib and the area around it; the inhabitants of the town and its environs turned out to be so unfriendly that the traveller could only take a hasty look at the ancient ruins and could not give much attention to the numerous Sabaean inscriptions. Nevertheless 56

An audience with the Imam (19th-century engraving)

copies made by him of the latter reached Europe, where they caused a stir in scholarly circles. Once translated and analysed, this little group of inscriptions provided the basis for an understanding early South Arabian Semitic script and language.

Another Frenchman, **Joseph Halévy**, was also responsible for great advances in South Arabian research. Under the auspices of the Academy of Inscriptions in Paris he made a journey across Yemen in 1869-70, dressed as a poor oriental Jew. In this guise he met with contempt and condescension, but he still managed better than a Christian would have done. Halévy came home with almost 700 copies of inscriptions.

Modern research on Yemen was given a considerable boost by the Austrian **Eduard Glaser**, who made four exhaustive journeys through the country between 1882 and 1894. Glaser visited the most important places in the highlands, the coastal plain and the region between the cities of Ta'izz and Aden as well as Ma'rib, and he described them to interested readers in Europe in more detail than any traveller before him. He advanced the study of South Arabian script by making plaster and cotton squeezes of inscribed slabs, but the use of this new technique was only a small part of his contribution: here for the first time was a researcher who knew his Yemeni environment so well and could fit in to it so exactly that it left him time for thorough research. Glaser was an explorer, scholar and journalist, and published the results of

Travellers in the Arabian desert in the 19th century

his archaeological, philological, ethnographical and geographical studies in the leading scholarly journals of the day. His work pointed the way for all subsequent students of Yemen, and many recently published studies are still building on it.

Some of Glaser's writings remain relevant to the traveller in Yemen to this day. For instance, in his journal in 1884 he comments on the importance of meal times to the Yemenis: 'Without breakfast no South Arab will do even the slightest piece of work, since to him meal times are paramount. When the *wagt al-rhadda*, i.e. the time of the midday meal, approaches, he drops everything and goes off to the *rhadda*; and in planning any journey he works out in advance where he will have his lunch-break. The Turks, who do not stick so precisely to meal times, are regarded by the South Arabs in this respect as simple barbarians.' Today's visitor will find the same attitude still prevails; at the time of the midday meal hardly a taxi, bus or even donkey leaves its place.

In Eduard Glaser's day the area under Turkish control was limited essentially to San'a; outside the capital and a few fortified towns, the power of the Ottoman Empire did not extend very far. Nevertheless the Austrian managed to travel to the tribes in the highlands, who were practically autonomous, without the agreement of the Governor of San'a. Since it seemed advisable, to pretend to be a Muslim, Glaser dressed accordingly, though this meant that he was often taken for a Turk, which could also be dangerous since the occupying power was in constant conflict with the native Yemeni ruler, the Imam. Glaser's command of Arabic was a boon in these difficult situations and his sharp powers of observation quickly enabled him to adapt himself to the mentality of the tribal Yemenis and the sheikhs. He soon acquired a comprehensive knowledge of tribal law and would use it to call on the services of the most influential mediator whenever a situation threatened to turn ugly.

When **Hermann Burchardt**, a German, made his third journey to Yemen in 1909, there was a truce between the Turks and the Imam. This meant that Burchardt travelled under the protection of both powers. Their letters of recommendation were of no use, however, when on 19 December 1909 he and his Italian companion Benzani were attacked by robbers and killed with shotguns. The attack took place in a high valley with luxuriant subtropical vegetation between the towns of al-Udayn and Ibb, a place that is now a popular with tourist excursions; the valley is reached by an unmetalled road with terrifying hairpin bends (see page 178ff).

Hermann Burchardt started life as an office worker in Berlin, but soon developed a love of travel. Islamic countries were his main interest, and at the age of 33 he began

Hermann Burchardt, pioneer of photography in Yemen

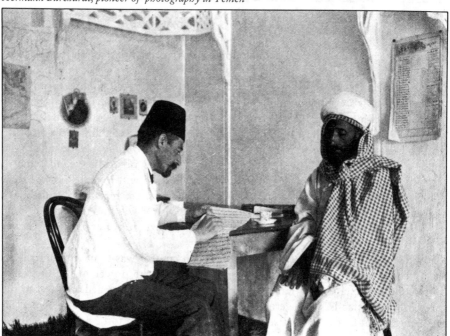

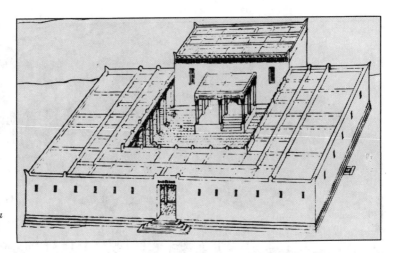

*The Sabaean
temple at Huqqa
(reconstruction
drawing)*

to study Arabic. Two years later he moved to Damascus and used the Syrian capital as a base for explorations. Tragically, he never got round to writing a comprehensive account of his journeys in the Arab world with his impressions and discoveries, but his executors did discover extensive notes and photographs. Burchardt took a complete set of photographic equipment with him on three Yemen journeys - in those days a vast amount of baggage. He left us the first great photographic documentation of northern Yemen.

In the 1920's two German Yemen researchers, **Carl Rathjens** and **Hermann von Wissmann,** successfully built on the work begun by Eduard Glaser some 50 years earlier. They too were not afraid of what were then still dangerous and exhausting journeys to Yemen and into the interior of the country. Publication of their findings made a wider audience aware of the existence of the archaic society in the southwest of the Arabian Peninsula. Rathjens and Wissmann were responsible for excavating the Sabaean temple at Huqqa, north of San'a, and for producing the first accurate plan of the old quarter of the capital, based on aerial photography.

The early exploration of southern Yemen was as difficult as that of the north. Aden, the capital of the former Popular Democratic Republic of Yemen (known as South Yemen), was the starting point for exploration in both directions. The first European account of the interior of Yemen is by the Italian adventurer **Ludovico di Varthema,** who landed in Aden in 1502. Varthema was taken prisoner and removed to the vicinity of San'a, but eventually he was released and permitted to travel through parts of Yemen. He left a record of his observations, as did an English merchant by the name of **John Jourdain,** who had landed in Aden 99 years later. After experiencing customs difficulties with the governor of Aden, Jourdain had

The harbour at Mukalla (photograph taken by Freya Stark in the 1930's)

finally sought help from the Ottoman pasha in San'a. In 1611 another English merchant-adventurer, **Sir Henry Middleton**, spent several months in San'a as a prisoner; a hundred years passed before two French merchants risked the same dangerous journey from Aden to San'a. Serious exploration did not begin until 1842 when **Adolph von Wrede**, a German, arrived in Aden. His goal was not the Yemeni highlands but the tomb of the revered pre-Islamic prophet Hud in Hadramawt. Travelling in disguise he managed to penetrate into the interior of South Arabia, but he often failed to understand what he saw, and his account was greeted with incredulity in Berlin. As the next pathbreaking traveller in Hadramawt, **Leo Hirsch**, wrote in the introduction to the account of his own journey: 'An early and not inconsiderable stimulus to my undertaking I owe to von Wrede's travel work, which is based on observation; the accusation that it is implausible is certainly unjustified. Although von Maltzan [the editor] claims that his hero has complete mastery of Arabic, it seems to me that it is von Wrede's deficient linguistic training that is responsible for many of the conspicuous howlers he makes in names, as well as other mistakes, while his lack of judgement is responsible for statistics he gives that are often far removed from reality...'

For his part Leo Hirsch not only had a full command of Arabic but also of Hebrew. On the basis of these two Semitic languages the Berlin-born scholar began his studies of South Arabian dialects. However, his real aim was the exploration of Wadi Hadramawt, which he began in the winter of 1892-93. His starting point was Aden, which at that time had been for more than 50 years under British colonial rule. From Aden Hirsch first made his way by boat to some towns on the South Arabian coast. Although he brought good, British, letters of recommendation with him for the local rulers in Mukalla and Shihr, the way to the interior remained barred. Making the most of the situation he visited the coastal towns one after another and came close to the region that now forms the southwestern part of the Sultanate of Oman. Everywhere he came across the same problem: the local authorities welcomed him in a friendly manner but their responses to his wish to to travel to the north ranged from polite evasion to curt refusal. If asked persistently enough the governor or sultan would finally reveal the reason for the passive or open resistance: he was bowing to the wishes of the bedouin of the hinterland that foreigners be kept from entering Wadi Hadramawt. Leo Hirsch attributed the difficulties to a mixture of religious fanaticism, shrewd business sense and political rivalries. The explorer was perhaps too much a man of his time to recognize that the attitude of the bedouin arose from bitter experience of several earlier clashes with imperialism. The tribal warriors of the hinterland still had clear memories of the conquest of coast by the Portuguese in the 15th century; they knew what trouble it had cost their ancestors to prevent the 'infidel' from penetrating into the interior. They also knew that a foreign power had established itself in Aden and so suspected that every explorer was a spy scouting for new conquests.

It took Hirsch more than six months before he had soothed the mistrust of the bedouin and persuaded the rulers of the coastal region to support his enterprise. On 1 July 1893 he was finally able to set off from Mukalla into Wadi Hadramawt. At first his own party was part of a caravan which made its way by night marches because of the summer heat. Hirsch joined it reluctantly because the darkness made it difficult for him to examine the terrain. During the second part of the twelve-day journey to the town of Hajjarayn he resorted to day marches, though his men protested. In any case, as Hirsch wrote in his journal, 'we had the dazzling sun in our eyes almost incessantly; it is almost impossible to make out the objects.' Nevertheless the explorer discovered in this section some ruins under the sand which he took to be a 'large town', and the 'fragments of a light-coloured limestone covered with Himyaritic characters' which he gathered there seemed a strong indication that this was once a city of ancient South Arabia.

Hirsch stayed for 38 days in Wadi Hadramawt. He made the the town of Shibam his base for exploring the interior and he also managed to visit the cities of Say'un and Tarim. Though he makes almost no mention of the appearance of Shibam and Tarim, which later travellers have so much admired for their architecture, his journal

Hans Helfritz, the German pioneer traveller in the 1930's

contains appreciative comments about Say'un: 'The streets of Say'un are wider and cleaner, and are kept free of the outflows from the houses, which open into walled corners. Inside the mud walls surrounding the town are well-tended and considerable palm gardens, most of which belong to mosques. The latter are indeed numerous and in good condition; the most important of them were pointed out to me during our wandering through the town by my volunteer retinue, which behaved in a somewhat irritating but by no means unfriendly manner and seemed to be pleased that I was showing interest in their sanctuaries.'

Hirsch's achievement was that he was able to make his journey of exploration at all and that he left a reliable description of it. He travelled armed and was not afraid to use his weapon as a threat if it seemed necessary, though his perfect knowledge of Arabic enabled him to manage almost all situations by persuasion. He did have to draw his revolver in Tarim, however, when some of its pious inhabitants forced him to leave the town prematurely and saw him out with hostile gestures. A thorough knowledge of the Yemeni mentality enabled him to distinguish between false and genuine piety. During his stay at Shibam his journal contains the following passage: 'Of my medicines the one that most interested my friend Shemah was *berendi* (brandy). He extolled it as a panacea and made urgent enquiries as to whether I had any - a small indication of how the folly of his local piety was built on a very liberal view of the world. Poor Shemah! I had to leave his pains unalleviated, since I never drink spirits in the tropics.'

The pioneer of a new type of exploration of Yemen was **Hans Helfritz**. Although his visits to Hadramawt and part of the Yemeni kingdom in 1932-33 and 1935 had a scholarly purpose, his difficult journey was in fact more influential in encouraging 'adventure tourism'. As a young musicologist his expeditions to the southwest of the Arabian Peninsula were necessarily undertaken on a small budget. As well as wax cylinders for recording folk music he also equipped himself with a still camera and a cine-camera. He was a talented travel writer, able to turn his daring travels into exciting books with titles such as *Chicago of the Desert* and *Land Without Shade*, which aroused interest in Yemen among a wider public in the 1930's and 1940's; they remained useful to the traveller well into the 1970's. Helfritz travelled first in 1932 through Hudayda, and then in the domain of the Imam. To his own surprise he was given permission to visit San'a and he made the journey from the Red Sea coast to the capital by mule in eight days.

Helfritz was allowed to stay about two weeks in San'a, but was sent back to Hudayda for 'immediate deportation' after his interview with Imam Yahya. A ruler who worked tirelessly to keep radios, gramophones and even musical instruments out of his country could hardly have been sympathetic to this ethno-musicologist and his equipment. On a later visit Helfritz managed to reach the Yemeni capital again, though from a quite different direction. From Aden he travelled first by boat to Mukalla, but like Hirsch before him he at first found the way from the port to the interior barred. He was, however, able to set off on a march into Wadi Hadramawt from Shihr, the next town on the coast. The subsequent journey of discovery, though begun in the first third of the 20th century was no less impressive than the great pioneer journeys of the 19th. At first Helfritz followed in Hirsch's footsteps, but from Shibam he headed westwards, that is, through parts of the feared Rub al-Khali or 'Empty Quarter', to reach the sultanate of Bayhan. He thus found himself at the back door of the Imam's territory. With the greatest efforts he managed to engage some bedouin as guides for a journey from Bayhan to Harib. At Harib, a town in the heart of the ancient Sabaean empire, Helfritz was once again in the domain of Imam Yahya. He was promptly imprisoned for three weeks until permission was received from the ruler in San'a for him to continue his journey. As had happened when Helfritz first penetrated into Yemen, his route to the capital was precisely laid down.

A bedouin from Wadi Hadramawt (historical photograph)

However, as he wrote: 'The route which I had to take had the advantage of passing through a part of the Yemen as yet unknown, but it was long and had the reputation of being extremely difficult.' When at last he had put this arduous stretch behind him, he was immediately taken into police custody in San'a. After five days in the office of the chief of police, interrupted only by a walk through the town to visit two of his countrymen, Helfritz - who had a knack for irritating his hosts - was once again served with a deportation order and taken to Hudayda. Now an experienced explorer, Helfritz made use of his journey to the Red Sea under escort to gather further impressions of Yemen.

Helfritz's third great journey of discovery in South Arabia concentrated on the Hadramawt. The young German scholar now came into competition with two influential British travellers. In 1935 **H. St. John Philby** (father of the spy),who had formerly been a British agent in the Near East but was now the adviser and favourite of Ibn Saud, founder of the kingdom of Saudi Arabia, planned an expedition to Shabwa. Since this remote place was thought by scholars to be the centre of the ancient kingdom of Hadramawt, closer inspection of it would be of great interest. Meanwhile, **Freya Stark,** was using the help of influential friends in Aden and her own considerable experience to reach Shabwa. She had previously been involved in political and literary work in Baghdad, where Britain had become the 'Mandatory Power' after the First World War. Her journey had a number of aims: to increase the influence of the British government in Hadramawt, to make her the first European to reach a site in southwestern Arabia that was shrouded in mystery, and not least to find new material for travel books. However, a serious illness detained her in Shibam, while Philby was still busy with general travel preparations. The young German - of whose doings Stark heard frustrating news on her sickbed in Shibam - could not rely

Freya Stark, the British writer and traveller Hadramawt in the 1930's

on influential political sponsors and had only modest savings. Nevertheless, after having passed close by Shabwa two years before, he now became the first European to reach the town that had been so important in antiquity. Although Helfritz was only able to stay one night and a few daylight hours in Shabwa before he was driven from the town in his usual way by distrustful inhabitants, this journey in 1935 has gone down as a great event in the history of the opening of South Arabia. It was left to Philby, however, who finally made it to Shabwa two years later, to make a properly detailed survey of the region.

Shabwa remained difficult in the following decades. **Wendell Phillips**, the American explorer who followed Helfritz, could do no more than boast of having flown over it. 'Traditions of

Wendell Phillips with a find at Ma'rib

sand-covered temples, palaces, and buried treasures have made this one of the best-known and most sought-after spots,' he wrote in the early 1950's. 'We were the first Americans to see the old ruins, even from the air.'

This achievement seems tame compared with the efforts of Helfritz, Philby and Stark, but Phillips, a mixture of scholar, adventurer, agent and journalist always knew how to make the most of his failures. Any explorer aiming to follow unconventional routes has to be something of an adventurer, but Phillips' verve and brashness in trying to remove difficulties often landed him in still greater trouble.

Nonetheless today's archaeologist has much to thank Wendell Phillips for. In 1949 and 1950 he organized extensive campaigns of excavation in the South Arabian sultanate of Bayhan, then still under British protection. Phillips, ever the reverse of the lone, dogged traveller, worked with lavish funds and a team of first-class specialists, including experts in epigraphy, and his findings were correspondingly substantial. In Wadi Bayhan the American team uncovered the ruins of the ancient city of Timna and made many finds of statues, fragments of statues, bronze figures and utilitarian objects. Some of these finds carried inscriptions, and the Americans discovered further inscriptions on rock faces. Scholarly evaluation of these scraps of writing and classification of the artworks made it possible to provide almost precise dates for events in the history of the town and so draw up a much-needed chronology of the kingdom of Qataban. Phillips came to the conclusion that 'the most important period in the history of Qataban fell between about 350 and 50 BC', when in his view it was the most important single state in South Arabia.

During the Timna campaign Wendell Phillips had also had a look at Ma'rib, which was presumed to be the capital of the ancient kingdom of Saba. The distance between Bayhan and Ma'rib by desert tracks is only about 60 km, but between them, running through the desert sand at Wadi Bayhan, was then the scarcely marked border that separated a world empire from a backward Arab state still jealous of its independence: Bayhan was part of the British Aden Protectorate and Ma'rib belonged to the Kingdom of Yemen. The King of Yemen, as the Imam had been styled since the re-establishment of his authority, had made historical territorial claims in the British-controlled area, resulting in years of smouldering border conflict that occasionally flared up, with the British pitting air force planes against the Imam's tribal warriors. It was no wonder then that when Phillips left Bayhan secretly and headed for Ma'rib, he was stopped and sent back by armed Arabs. Phillips also used a supply plane from his Timna expedition to make an unauthorized flight over Ma'rib and take aerial photographs, and so put himself in danger of being shot at by the Imam's soldiers. Despite this experience he did finally apply to the Imam for permission to undertake archaeological work in the Kingdom of Yemen. To his surprise in the spring of 1951 he was requested to go to Ta'izz (the Imam's capital) for negotiations, and by April of that year he was able to conclude a contract with the Yemeni government for excavation work at Ma'rib. The then ruler, Imam Ahmad, had granted permission to the American - representing the 'The American Foundation for the Study of Man' - and his companions after their first audience. In retrospect we can assume that political considerations lay behind his willingness to ease Phillips's path. It is likely that he no more believed in the scholarly character of the project than did his advisers, seeing it rather as a screen for Washington to promote its own national interests against the British who had predominated in South Arabia up until then. (American involvement in the region extended to border clashes in the Empty Quarter, in which US military personnel attached to the Saudis fought against British troops.) Imam Ahmad presumably believed for a time that he could inflict damage on his British enemy if he allowed the Americans some influence in Yemen. So once the contract had been signed the main concern of the Yemenis was to keep comprehensive control of the archaeological enterprise.

The American team stayed for about nine months in Ma'rib in 1951-52; Wendell Phillips spent part of this time outside Yemen raising more funds to enlarge the expedition. For the archaeologists working in Ma'rib under their leader Frank Albright the nine months were a nightmare. Their every step was shadowed by officials of the Imam, and the uncertainty and inexperience of the Yemeni officials hindered every phase of the archaeological fieldwork. A steady conflict developed over taking

A shelter for livestock and herdsmen built of rough-hewn rocks

squeezes of Sabaean inscriptions, which were of enormous scholarly interest but no material value. The government soldiers stationed in Ma'rib, urged by their superiors to be vigilant, came to be regarded by the hard-pressed archaeologists as intolerable intimidation. When finally the expedition's leader, after waiting in vain two weeks in Ta'izz for an audience with the Imam, returned to take over command in Ma'rib, it was too late. Even his personal commitment was no longer any help. Wendell Phillips, the genius of organization, had no alternative but to organize the team's withdrawal. On 12 February 1952 the American expedition managed to flee over the border region of the Kingdom of Yemen to the sultanate of Bayhan in the British Protectorate in two lorries, leaving behind nearly all their finds, the greater part of the archaeological yield and most of their personal belongings.

In the months after their escape the propaganda war that developed between the Yemen government and Wendell Phillips revealed the extent of mutual misunderstanding. Yet all this could not undo the significant achievement of the expedition: at Ma'rib Sabaean temple complexes had been excavated for the first time in the history of modern archaeology. For over three decades this was to remain the only excavation of any importance in the region, and it is the source of a considerable proportion of the archaeological collection in the National Museum in San'a to this day.

More recently archaeological investigation of the north of Yemen has made some progress. In 1984 construction began on a new dam in Wadi Adhanna near Ma'rib and the area southwest of the building site was made available to archaeologists for fieldwork. The San'a branch of the German Archaeological Institute immediately started excavations. Italian and American archaeologists were also active in the region between Ma'rib and Sirwah. There was no expectation here of grand projects with sensational discoveries but the work of the German archaeologists cast a great deal of light on the origin and later development of Sabaean high culture. In the autumn of 1988 the Italian archaeological mission was able to begin excavating in Baraqish (Ma'in kingdom) with the aim of reconstructing parts at least of the ancient town and its irrigation system.

The findings of field research up to now have led to the realization that long before the formation of a Sabaean state there were well-organized small communities in the region between Ma'rib and Sirwah. At the margins of the wadis, which often carried water, a large number of individual families and clans were apparently settled in the 3rd millennium BC and they were able to undertake communal projects such as irrigation schemes, remains of which were found in the mid-1980's. At the beginning of the 1990's digging began at the temple of the moon god Almaqah near Ma'rib and on the town hill of Old Ma'rib.

Southwest of this great oasis German archaeologists have come across buildings with a religious function, which they date to the early historical periods before the foundation of the Minaean state. Italian archaeologists have discovered remains of settlement west of Sirwah, which they have been able to place fairly accurately between 1980 BC and 1750 BC using carbon dating methods.

Kingdoms of the Traders

*Though we were always looking about for monuments of antiquity, the most ancient
and lasting memorial of far past ages lay beneath our feet in that little narrow path
winding over Akaba and Wadi, and polished by the soft feet of millions of camels
that had slowly passed over it for thousands and thousands of years.*
Theodore and Mabel. Bent, Southern Arabia, 1900

The Greek historian and geographer Herodotus (born c. 484 BC) seems to have been
sure of his facts when he wrote: 'To the south Arabia is the last of the inhabited
lands; it is the only place where frankincense grows and myrrh and cassia and cinnamon and ladanum.' We cannot be so certain about the origin of most of the
frankincense on which the wealth of the Sabaean Empire and the other ancient kingdoms of Southern Arabia was based, though we know that for centuries frankincense
and other incense as well as spices and other trading commodities were carried over a
number of caravan routes through Yemen to the Mediterranean and Red Sea coast
before being shipped on to Egypt and Europe. Frankincense was certainly cultivated
in the coastal region of South Yemen, but it is doubtful whether the greater part of
the much sought-after substance was actually grown in southern Yemen. Indeed,
there is much evidence that great quantities of frankincense were obtained from the
north of the present-day Republic of Somalia and from India. The South Arabians
would have operated mainly as middlemen - and, because of their convenient
commercial and political position, their profits were considerable. The question
whether the South Arabians were more active as merchants or as producers is not
insignificant, since the predominant economic orientation would have influenced the
character of the country. Merchants would be constantly coming into contact with
foreign cultures and were mobile, whereas agricultural producers - such as were
certainly to be found in the Sabaean heartland around Ma'rib and in Wadi Hadramawt - must have created a static element in South Arabian culture. The cultural
evidence that has come down to us clearly indicates that strong external influences
were constantly being adopted.
     It is true the people who lived in the six kingdoms of ancient South Arabia over a
period of 1500 years were not entirely or even predominantly traders, but these kingdoms could only be created and maintained because they were foreign trading
partners of the established''industrial countries'. Egypt was surely the earliest
customer for frankincense, myrrh and other incense. Such aromatic substances played
an important part in the daily liturgy before the image of the sun god Amon-Re and
at funeral rites. The Babylonians too burned frankincense as a part of religious rites
for prayer and when consulting the oracles. Frankincense entered religious rites of

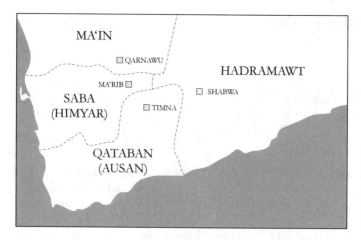

The six kingdoms of South Arabia. These did not all exist at the same time but were spread over a period of more than one and a half thousand years

the Jews even before the Babylonian Exile (586-538 BC); there it gained such important that the Mosaic scriptures prohibited, on pain of excommunication, the personal use of incense, which was reserved for religious purposes (Exodus 30: 37-8). In the 8th century BC the Greeks began to burn incense as a protection against demons. Frankincense and myrrh were important for the Romans for public and private sacrifices in front of the gods and later also in the imperial cult, while the Christian church introduced the use of incense in its ceremonies from the 4th century onwards.

But it was not only with Egypt and Europe that the South Arabians conducted their trade in frankincense; their convenient location soon brought them into contact with the great Persian Empire. After the military superiority first of the Assyrians and then of the Persians was apparent, the South Arabian rulers began to send frankincense and myrrh as tribute to Persia. Thus there was already a link with the Persian kings when, in the final phase of the independent trader kingdoms in South Arabia, a Himyarite prince called on them for help against the Ethiopians.

In the 1500 years between the founding of the Sabaean state and its final collapse its main concern was always the control of the trade routes. Since almost all the early trade routes were caravan roads the camel must have played a major role in the creation of the states of South Arabia. Research has shown that only after the domestication of the camel and its use as a beast of burden did it become possible to cross the Arabian Peninsula from from south to north and from north to south within time limits that were economically viable. It was not really possible to use donkeys to cover the distance of 2500 to 3000 km, but the camel could manage the sections of the journey where a donkey would have died for lack of water. The Sabaeans probably first came to notice as camel-drivers. Along the route that ran from the South

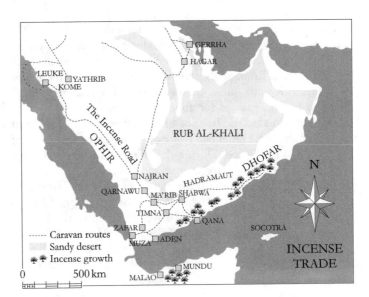

The most important caravan routes from southern to northern Arabia, showing the incense-producing regions

Arabian coast into the Yemeni hills and further north, there sprang up stageposts, bases, villages, eventually organized into federations which were maintained to protect the caravan routes. On about the first 500 km - measured from the south - of the desert way there grew up first the Sabaean state, then the kingdom of Ma'in, which had been the northern province of Saba and a South Arabian outpost towards central Arabia.

Not only did the South Arabians make use of the camel for transporting merchandise before the Egyptians and others, they also knew the secret of the monsoon wind before their customers did. They found the sea route to India long before the Egyptians and the northern Arabs, or the Greeks and the Jews. It was through South Arabia that spices from the Far East - including cinnamon - reached the Mediterranean. Textiles, precious stones, oils, furs and grain seem also to have been obtained from India by the South Arabians. So it can probably be assumed that they obtained perfumes, perhaps of lower quality, from their Indian trading partners in order to sell them on together with their home-produced frankincense and myrrh. The rise of the South Arabian traders meant that their demand for merchandise increased. They therefore soon established trading settlements on the East African coast and on the African side of the Red Sea. The settlements in present-day Eritrea developed into strong colonies, whose inhabitants played an important part in the founding of the state of Aksum.

Two developments in the field of maritime travel were later to bring about the decline of the South Arabian states. The inhabitants of the northern shores of Red Sea finally mastered the art of navigation along the coasts with their treacherous reefs, currents and pirates. This was a considerable setback for the Arabian caravan trade since the more the sea route was used, the less attractive the land route seemed. Later the Greeks and Romans also discovered the secret of the monsoon winds and took the trade with India into their own hands. The trading monopoly which the South Arabians had maintained for about 700 years was thus completely broken. On the South Arabian side the balance of power shifted in favour of those states which controlled the Bab al-Mandab (Gate of Tears) at the southern entrance of the Red Sea from the Gulf of Aden. During the reign of the Emperor Augustus two military expeditions were conducted against the Himyarite-Sabaean state. On each occasion the Romans came onto the scene mainly because the Himyarites were impeding sea traffic at the straits. First Augustus sent the governor of Egypt, Aelius Gallus with land troops into the Arabian expanses to conquer the heart of the Sabaean state. However, the expedition foundered outside Maryab (Ma'rib) because the Roman troops and their auxiliaries could not cope with the heat and the lack of water. Later a Roman fleet appeared at the southern exit to the Red Sea, destroyed a few harbours

The arrival of a caravan at Petra (19th-century engraving)

and seems to have forced Himyar to form an alliance with Rome and Hadramawt.

It is possible that already around the beginning of the Christian era the trade of the South Arabian landlocked states with the Mediterranean had come to an end, since by then almost all goods could reach the northern end of the Red Sea by boat. In the north the most important trading partners of the South Arabians were the Nabataeans, who had shifted the frontier of their state a long way southwards. From around 400 BC until perhaps AD 50 the Sabaeans were always accompanied through history by the Nabataeans as commercial partners. When the Jews were led into the Babylonian Captivity (587 BC) there followed a small migration of peoples: the Nabataeans, a desert people, poured in from Central Asia to occupy a region which had previously been inhabited by the Edomites, who had for their part taken possession of vacant Jewish territory. The Nabataeans settled in the region of the mountains of Shera around Petra in what is now Jordan. The migration there took place around 550 BC. The newcomers are thought to have made their living initially mainly by attacking caravans from the Arabian south. But as soon as they had constituted themselves into an ordered state, they began to make their profits from trade traffic though more regular channels: customs, duties and tolls took the place of straightforward robbery. Eventually the Nabataeans started organizing caravans of their own. From the 3rd century BC they appear to have controlled the northern section of what became known as the 'Incense Road' from South Arabia to the Mediterranean. Around the beginning of the Christian era the Nabataean Empire had attained its widest extent. The southern frontier of this caravan empire ran between the towns of Hegra and Hayil, from which it was just thirty days' march to the border of the Sabaean Empire. The estimated time needed for the whole journey from the Mediterranean coast to the South Arabian coast was around ninety days.

The Sabaeans maintained a trading station in the Desan oasis on the Nabataean territory, the border town of Hegra. Between the Nabataeans and the Sabaeans therefore there was a vigorous exchange not only of merchandise but also of ideas, cultural achievements and artistic influences. The Nabataeans had come into direct contact with Hellenistic culture when they conquered Damascus in the 1st century BC, and many of the Hellenistic influences in South Arabian art must have been transmitted by the Nabataeans. This cultural influence continued into the Roman period. There is evidence that the bronze statues of two Himyarite kings now in Sanʿa, were made by a sculptor and a South Arabian bronze founder in the 3rd century AD. Identical in type to portraits of Roman Emperors, the figures are identifiable as South Arabian only from the Himyaritc inscriptions, which are cast with the figures.

South Arabian influence can also be seen in the Nabataean architecture in North Arabia, such as the typical battlement decoration of the tombs at Petra. They also came to adopt the monumental architecture and monumental tombs common in South Arabia at a much earlier date.

The Script

The main evidence for the culture of the ancient South Arabians is the rich body of inscriptions to be found in present-day Yemen. The South Arabian characters are found carved on the walls of temple ruins and the stone fragments scattered on the ancient sites. One of the pleasures of the explorer is spotting stones with inscriptions built into the walls of more recent houses.

The characters are usually very simple and clear. Only in the late period of the Himyarite-Sabaean Empire did they lose these virtues, when diagonal strokes, decorative forms and emphasis on curves were added. In the final phase of the ancient culture of South Arabia the carved lines of script became to some extent a form of decorative art. In Islamic Arab culture calligraphy is of course the highest form of artistic expression, but the situation was not quite the same in the societies that came before Islam. For one thing, there was no religious prohibition of images. Since, however, nothing could be done by the Sabaeans without the blessing of the gods, their stone inscriptions had an important cultural and political function in recording the invocations and preserving them for posterity.

With the rediscovery of Yemen the inscriptions aroused the interest of students of dead cultures, and the explorers of the 18th and 19th centuries and the first half of the 20th regarded it as an important duty to collect copies of them. About 4000

Phonetic value	Sabaic script	Early Ethiopian script
'	𐩱 𐩱	አ አ
b	⊓ ⊓	ጠ ∏
g	ๅ	ๅ ๅ
ḏ	⋈ ⋈	ዘ
d	◁⍩	⊠ ꝑ 𐌷
h	ᖴᖶᖶᖴ	‹ ᐯ ᐀ ᖴ
w	⊕ ∞	⊙ ▽ ∞ ↓
z	⊢ ⵅ ⊢ ⵅ	⊢ ⊢ ⵕ
ḥ	↴ ᖴ	rh
ḫ	ᗡ ᖶᖳ	ᖳ ᖳ
ẓ	ꝑꝑꝑ	
ṭ	⊡	⋒ ⋒
y	ꝑ	⁹ ꝓ ꝓ ꝑ
k	𐩫𐩫𐩫	ሕ ሕ ሕ ⵁ
l	1ʃ	Λ
m	⌶⍩⍩	⌇⌇⌂
n	𐩬ꝑꝑ	ᖳ ᖳ ᖳ
s	⊓ ⵅ	⊓ ⵅ
ʿ	ꞁꞁ	
ġ	° ◊	° ◊ ▽
p	◊ ◊ 0	ᐊ 𐌻 𐌻 ᐊ
ḍ	⊟	
ṣ	ꝑꝑꝑꝑꝑ꞉	ꞁⵅꝑꞁ
q	◊ ◊	◊ ◊ ✦
r	) › ‹ (	ᘰ ᘰ ᘱ ᘰ
š	‹ › ›	ᗯ ᘮ ᗯ ᶄ ᵤ
t	ꝑ	+ ✗ + ✗ +
t	✗ ✗	

Sabaean script compared to early Ethiopic script

Ma'rib, a stone with an ancient inscription used as a door lintel

South Arabian texts have been accumulated in this way and their decipherment has provided much information about the history of the South Arabian kingdoms. On the other hand we still know little about the inhabitants' daily life and thinking. As in all areas of research into early South Arabia, there are great gaps in knowledge about the script and literature. Another considerable drawback is that no writings apart from the stone inscriptions have been found; no literature on perishable material such as leather, textiles or paper has so far come to light. Moreover, no numerical figures have yet been discovered and since it is unthinkable that a trading people like the South Arabians could have operated without system of numbers, we must assume that this is a lacuna in the evidence available.

The alphabet of the early South Arabians consists of 29 characters and has no signs for short vowels. The origin of the alphabet is unclear; according to one theory the system of writing which originated in the Syrio-Palestinian region also reached South Arabia and the characters were remoulded into the well-proportioned and linear script typical in the south. Another theory has it that the South Arabians received influences from the land between the Tigris and Euphrates for developing their own alphabet. Inscriptions in this early alphabet go back about 2700 years. In the 7th century BC the South Arabian script was still being read boustrophedon, that is the lines were read alternately from left to right and from right to left. From about the 6th century BC the South Arabian characters were read from right to left - like

Ma'rib, an architectural fragment with a Sabaean inscription

modern Arabic and Hebrew. The analysis of inscriptions collected from various places revealed that the same language, although in widely differing dialects, was spoken in all the kingdoms. Researchers believe they can recognize in the Sabaean dialect features that point to northern Arabia as the place of origin. In oases and ruins along the old trade road from South to North Arabia inscriptions have been found scratched or painted on the rock that show a mixture of the southern and northern Arabian dialects.

Sabaean, Minaean and Himyarite emigrants in the last 400 years before the beginning of the present era brought the script and language of South Arabia to Ethiopia. At first they became established in their original forms, particularly in the regions that are now Tigre and Eritrea. Later the plain, tall South Arabian characters were transformed into an almost cursive script. Every consonant was given a vowel sign, which the South Arabians did not originally use in their language. And not only the way of writing but the language itself changed: the South Arabians living on the African side of the Red Sea did without some consonants which were no longer necesto adopt the monumental architecture and monumental tombs common in South Arabia at a much earlier date.sary in their dialect. This led to the gradual development of a new written language known as 'Geez', whose script has been adopted for Amharic, now the main language of Ethiopia. Consequently more of the South Arabian script survives in the Amharic alphabet than in the letters of modern Arabic.

Ma'rib

Mistress of cities and diadem on the brow of the universe
Pliny

Recent research has shown that Sabaean culture began to flourish as early as around 1000 BC. An irrigation system built of massive ashlar uncovered in 1983-84 by German archaeologists 2 km southeast of the great Ma'rib dam at the foot of the Jabal Balaq al-Awsat can be dated to that period. However, this work should be seen as the private initiative of a community of peasant-farmers. The earliest inscriptions giving evidence of a Sabaean state date from the 8th century BC. The biblical account of the visit of the Queen of Sheba (Saba) to King Solomon (965-926 BC) in Jerusalem is therefore an anachronism. If a South Arabian queen visited Solomon her journey would have had to have taken place around 950 BC, but the present evidence indicates the Sabaean state only emerged some decades after the Solomon's death. The first indication of this is found in the annals of the Assyrian king Tiglathpileser III (745-727 BC) which mention the tribute that the Sabaeans had to send to Mesopotamia.

Did the great queen of ancient South Arabia really exist at all? She certainly has a place in the imagination of most Yemenis as 'Malika Bilqis' (Queen Bilqis); indeed the Awwam Temple dedicated to the moon god Almaqah, which was partly uncovered by Phillips, is attributed to her by the Yemenis. It seems to have been built in the 8th to 7th centuries BC, but neither in this period nor indeed in the whole history of the Sabaean Empire is there any evidence of a ruling queen. H. St. John Philby and other scholars have therefore suggested that the 'Queen of Sheba' was merely a tribal princess who arrived with Sabaean Arabs from Mesopotamia to pursue a nomadic existence in the region that is now Syria. At that time, says Philby, every tribal association of any size called its leader king or queen. Thus the leader of the Sabaeans in Syria came to Solomon in Jerusalem as the 'Queen of Sheba' to pay tribute. Another group of Sabaeans, who had migrated to South Arabia and settled there, then preserved the memory of 'Queen Bilqis' through the centuries. In the Islamic tradition she appears in the Koran (sura 37), when the hoopoe reports to Solomon: 'I come to thee from Sheba with sure tidings. Lo! I found a woman ruling over them and she has been given an abundance of all things and hers is a mighty throne.' To this day many Yemeni girls are called Bilqis.

The construction of the famous dam of Ma'rib (or Maryab as it was then called) began in the early 6th century BC. The dam extends for more than 680 m and completely closes the Wadi Adhanna. The storage and irrigation systems were given overflow channels. The ashlar used for the building represents a very high achievement in masonry, the joins between the blocks being barely visible although the individual blocks are joined inside with lead and copper pins. Some experts estimate that the system was sufficient to irrigate about 9600 hectares under cultivation. The Arab historian al-Mas'udi (d. 958) declared that 'a good horseman could not ride over the cultivated grounds around this city in less than a month.'

Irrigation is a symbol of a settled and advanced society. The dam at Ma'rib was the basis of her prosperity, and it was only when the permanent irrigation system and the dam installations had been built that Ma'rib became the capital of the Sabaean Empire and the 'Paris of the ancient world'. Before then the political and cultural centre of the young state was Sirwah, situated about 35 km to the west. The importance of Sirwah is still unclear. Except for a few superficial inspections no archaeological work has been possible there. Yet whatever future excavations and surveys bring to light, it is evident from its geographical situation that Sirwah could never have attained the importance that Ma'rib was later to achieve. The site is almost completely surrounded by high mountains; the Wadi Rada (Ghada) which provides its water bears no comparison with the broad Wadi Adhanna (also called Wadi as-Sadd) which feeds the Ma'rib oasis (enormous two millennia ago). Sirwah was excellent from the point of view of defence, but its immediate environs were not suitable as the heartland of a population of a growing empire that owed its power and prosperity more to the high duties and tolls it exacted from trade caravans than to a highly developed

The story of the Queen of Sheba as depicted in Ethiopian folk art. There was once in Ethiopia a terrible dragon which had to be fed every day with many animals. The Ethiopians therefore agreed that whoever killed the dragon would be given the throne. From left to right: A man prepared poison (1) and fed it to a goat (2), which was given to the dragon to eat (3). The dragon died, and the wise man was made king (4). But because he was so old, he presented his daughter Mekkeda to the people (5), and after his death she became the Queen of Sheba (6). One day Tamrin the merchant told her of the famous King Solomon (7), and she decided to send Tamrin to him with gifts (8). After his return (9) Tamrin told her about the power and wisdom of Solomon (10), and the Queen decided to visit him. After a long journey (11) she arrived at Jerusalem (12). The Queen of Sheba was received by Solomon, and one evening after a highly spiced meal (13), Solomon extracted from her the promise that she would take nothing which belonged to him. But tormented during the night by a raging thirst, she asked for a glass of water (14). When the King saw this, he took the opportunity to obtain her favours in love (15). The Queen of Sheba resolved to return to her own country and took leave of Solomon (16). Then she bore him a son, Menelik (17). When Menelik grew older he asked his mother who his father was. She showed him Solomon's seal (18), and the son decided to visit Solomon (19). Menelik was received by Solomon (20) and was then brought up by him (21). Eventually Menelik wished to return to Ethiopia, and took the tables of the law with him (22). Happily back home in Ethiopia (23) he was crowned Emperor of Ethiopia by his mother, the Queen of Sheba (24)

Taking a latex squeeze of a Sabaean inscription on the Temple of Awwam

agriculture. The Wadi Adhanna on the other hand was the ideal refuge for people and beasts who had just come out of the desert with its continual threat of drifting sand.

The Sabaeans' greatness was based their technological skill and their control over a large part of the South Arabian trade with Egypt, the states at the edge of the eastern Mediterranean, and Europe; consequently when advances in shipbuilding and navigation techniques (especially the discovery of the monsoon patterns by Hippalus) enabled Egyptians, Greeks and Romans to divert their trade with South Arabia to the sea route under their own management, the power and strength of the Sabaean empire faded away. Moreover, several neighbouring states had grown up over the centuries to compete with Saba, the oldest of the South Arabian kingdoms. Around 410 BC two vassal states managed to escape from Sabaean supremacy: Ma'in, the state of the Minaeans, to the north of Saba, and Qataban to the south, with coastlines on both the Red Sea and the Gulf of Aden. These two states formed an alliance with Hadramawt; this deprived the Sabaean Empire of a large part of its territory, and the Sabaean heartland was henceforth hemmed in by the three rivals in close alliance. A life-or-death struggle was inevitable. In 343 BC the Sabaeans succeeded in defeating

American archaeologists uncover the hall of the Temple of Awwam in 1951-2

Qataban and subjugating it again for a time. In 120 BC the Minaean state was reconquered, and Qataban, which by this time had recovered its independence, split into two provinces, Himyar and Radman. The Sabaeans supported the renegadism of these two provinces, which were thus able to constitute themselves as separate states; but they were rewarded only by the contribution made by the Himyarite state to the eventual downfall of Saba itself.

Even before the larger provinces on the edges of their empire broke free around 410 BC, the Sabaeans had conquered the kingdom of Ausan and annexed it to their vassal state Qataban. Ausan had been a coastal state on the Gulf of Aden, with a strong position in South Arabian trade, based on close connections with Africa. It had maintained trading settlements and stations on the East African and Ethiopian coast. The 'Ausanian Coast' on African territory was still known as such for centuries after the state itself had been destroyed by the Sabaeans, and Ausan itself had not been forgotten when at the end of the 1st century BC the state of Aksum (named after its capital city) emerged on the North Ethiopian plateau. An inscription carved on a stone throne dedicated in the 2nd century AD by an unnamed Aksumian

Ma'rib, at the south sluice of the Sabaean dam

king to his deity, announces the foreign policy aims of the new state: expansion as far as the White Nile in one direction, and the incorporation of South Arabia, the former Ausan, in the other. For about 400 years the Aksumites struggled to keep a foothold in South Arabia. In 570, traditionally the year of the Prophet Muhammad's birth, King Kaleb of Aksum sent his South Arabian governor Abraha - a Christian - with an army against the city-state of Mecca.

Shifts in the caravan routes, the moving of trade to the sea route, continual conflicts with the three, sometimes four neighbouring states, Persian, Roman and Ethiopian invasions all weakened the ancient Sabaean Empire. From the 3rd century AD it lived on only in the Himyar-dominated Himyarite-Sabaean state. Its capital was no longer Ma'rib but Zafar, which the Himyarites had founded in the central Yemeni highlands. It is probable that from this time onwards the population of the artificially irrigated Sabaean heartland diminished drastically, the irrigation systems and the great dam of Ma'rib were neglected and the mud and detritus which were always being washed down by the fast-flowing streams of Wadi Adhanna were no longer removed from the reservoir. This may have blocked the drainage and overflow channels so that eventually the water overflowed the top of the dam. There is evidence of breaks in the dam in the middle of the 5th and 6th centuries. A disaster occurred in

542 when the dam broke, but the governor Abraha was able to use soldiers and tribes to bring the situation under control again. The date of the last dam-break, which brought about the abandonment of the Ma'rib oasis, and hence the end of a thousand years of history, is not known, but it can have been only a short time after the catastrophe in 542. At any rate no date of any later disaster is known. Mention of the final dam-break is found in the Koran, which was published by the Prophet Muhammad in Mecca and Medina 80 or 90 years later. In sura 34 we read: 'For the natives of Saba there was indeed a sign in their dwelling-place: a garden on their left and a garden on their right. We said to them: "Eat of what your Lord had given you and render thanks to Him. Pleasant is your land and forgiving is your Lord." But they gave no heed. So We unloosed upon them the waters of the dams and replaced their gardens by two others bearing bitter fruit, tamarisks, and a few nettle shrubs. Thus We punished them for their ingratitude; for We punish none save the ungrateful.'

Religion

The ancient South Arabian inscriptions mention a large number of gods. At the centre of the Sabaean pantheon, however, is a trinity of celestial deities: the moon, the sun and Venus. The moon god Ilumquh (Almaqah) was the most important of these. It was to him the main temple in Ma'rib, which also served as a refuge in emergencies, was dedicated. The sun was a goddess and bore the name Shams - the Arabic word for sun. The god of Venus was, confusingly for us, male and was called Athtar; at Ma'rib he had particular importance as an irrigation god connected with fertility.

Sacrifice and prayer were the most important cult activities, as well as pilgrimages to religious centres. The inscriptions indicate that animal sacrifices and drink offerings predominated, and gods were also offered perfumes. Penance and repentance played a certain part. People prayed for health, fertility of the soil, for forgiveness for past transgressions. Public confessions of sins followed a breach of the conventions of purity. These were particularly clearly defined with regard to sexual relations and ritual observance. Depending on the rank of the deceased, graves would be simply framed with stones and covered with a heap of stones, or constructed in caves, which could sometimes be extended to form mausolea. Like the Egyptians, the Sabaeans believed in life after death; the deceased person still had claims on equipment and services, and was given jewellery, vessels, stelae, figures either carved or of fired clay in the grave. Since almost all activities were placed under the protection of the gods, the priests played an important role. Building work, agricultural labour and warfare were all accompanied by ceremonies, as were birth, marriage and death; indeed, whenever the Sabaeans undertook anything they recommended themselves to the gods and tried to curry their favour. Under these circumstances the priesthood must have become the dominant class in the state. Closely linked with the priests were the

Early Sabaean funerary stele with (above) the symbol of the moon god (now in the National Museum, San'a)

administrators who formed part of the temple staff, and men and women who had been consecrated to the gods. Until about 525 BC the Sabaean rulers called themselves *mukarrib* which has the approximate meaning of 'priest-king'. From this one can probably assume that the priesthood and the mukarribs were closely connected; in all probability the priests served the ruler as officials and advisers. Scholars suggest that the early Sabaean state was based on acceptance of a covenant between the deity, the mukarrib and the tribes.

Art

Today's traveller will probably have his first direct contact with Sabaean art in the Yemeni National Museum in San'a. Although the American excavation organized by Wendell Phillips in 1952 had to be discontinued while it was still at an early stage (see pages 25ff.), it had considerably enriched the collection of the museum. Tribal chiefs and politicians have made donations to the museum either from their private collections or from chance finds. But for an impression of the architecture of the Sabaeans, one has to go to Ma'rib and other ruined sites. A visit to Ma'rib, the economic and cultural centre of the vanished Sabaean Empire, gives an idea of the remarkable irrigation technology of the time, and the observant visitor will also make an acquaintance with Sabaean script (see pages 34ff.) and relief sculpture.

Any assessment of the artistic legacy of the Sabaeans is limited by the small number of finds. A comprehensive excavation in Ma'rib and Sirwah might multiply the number of Sabaean works of art known, and new finds would prepare the way for new analyses. As research stands at present, however, it seems that Sabaean art can be divided into two principal phases. During the first, an indigenous religious art flourished which was in keeping with local conditions and ideas; in the second, the art of the Sabaeans came under the influences of Assyrian, Egyptian, Phoenician, Greek and Roman art. What is presumed to be autochthonous Sabaean art, as found above all in statues made of alabaster and marble, did indeed continue in the second phase, but the styles that arose later show the overriding impulses and direct influences coming along the caravan and sea routes from the north and east. Some of the works of art that belong to the second phase may in fact have been imported from abroad.

The statues made from alabaster or marble by Sabaean sculptors have been seen by historians and art historians as votive gifts to honour the gods. In the same way depictions of human heads were set up in the temples. Stelae and panels with bas-reliefs were used mainly in the cult of the dead, and often the names of the donors of votive gifts or the names of the dead are still to be seen carved on the base of the figure or the shaft of the stele.

One widely respected theory suggests that in the Sabaean territories only small pieces of alabaster and marble could be found to use as raw materials, and consequently the sculptors were obliged to cut away as little as possible. This restricted the representational possibilities, and there was little or no scope for sculptors to develop their creative imagination. The statues are indeed stiff and stylized in appearance, and almost all the Sabaean sculptures from the first phase is of a standard size. The bent elbows, clenched fists and placing of the feet also seem to follow fixed norms. Yet this schematic approach may be due to circumstances other than the limited availability of materials: like the 'utilitarian art' in ancient Egypt, standardization in the Sabaean Empire could be the result of mass production. For centuries statues must have been consecrated to the gods, and quantity may have taken precedence over quality. These panels and stelae were sufficient for their religious purpose without any artistic individualization, just as in our culture gravestones have been standardized by tradition and religious convention.

It cannot be said with certainty when the second phase in Sabaean art started. Influences from other cultures were probably already making themselves felt soon after the establishment of trading relations between Saba and the Middle Eastern coast of the Mediterranean and between Saba and Egypt. The greater part of cast

Sabaean stele commemorating a dead woman

metal sculpture so far found seems to belong to the second phase. A possible link between the two phases may the bronze statue of a high dignitary found by the American Ma'rib Expedition. In Wendell Phillips' words: 'The outstanding piece was a three-foot bronze statue of a man walking in a rather stiff-kneed fashion. The head was held erect, eyes looking fixedly ahead, while both fists were directed to the front, elbows bent. The right hand probably held at one time a staff or sceptre which was now missing, while the left hand held the official seal, as if ready to stamp an important document. The man wore a short rectangular skirt held up by a broad belt, while draped over his head was a lion skin, fastened by clasped front paws around his neck.'

The figure, dated by archaeologists to the 6th century BC, is now one of the prize exhibits of the museum in San'a. Wendell Phillips's description places it in the first phase, but scholars have now suggested that it is a portrait, and that the striding posture with the left foot forward and the position of the hands indicate Egyptian influences.

The uncertainty that hangs over many aspects of Sabaean art can be seen in the work of Brian Doe, who was Director of the Department of Antiquities at Aden in the 1960's. In his book *Southern Arabia*, published in 1971, he illustrates several important pieces in the San'a museum including one particular small figure: 'A

Early Sabaean bronze statue of an important dignitary excavated in 1951 by Wendell Phillips's team (now in the National Museum, San'a). (See also page 105-6)

bronze seated cherub which appears to have been fitted at one time on an inscription stone. The head now merely rests on the torso and its original position is not known. Possibly of the third century AD, the piece evidences western influence in its workmanship.'

While the age of the figure is given only approximately, the western (presumably Graeco-Roman) influence seems unmissable. Doe is slightly less definite when it comes to the photograph of a bronze male head: 'This finely cast male head may well be a portrait. Despite the formalized treatment of the hair, the moustache and the beard have been suggested in a naturalistic manner. The sensitivity of the face may indicate the influence of a western artist.'

What is unmistakeable in both pieces is that they deviate strongly from the stylization we regard as typically Sabaean. They are therefore works belonging to the second phase, when the influences from other cultures - though not necessarily 'western' cultures - gained the upper hand. The head illustrated in Doe's book, if one ignores the hair style, in fact bears a strong similarity to the heads of Parthian statues. The close contacts between South Arabia and Iran in the first centuries of our era very probably brought Persian artistic influences to Saba, and hence western influence too, indirectly by way of the mixed Hellenistic-Iranian culture. Similarly Graeco-Roman influence was apparently transmitted to Sabaean art through Egypt,

The longest stele at Aksum, 33.3 m long, now in pieces

Horizontal frieze of ibex heads at Sirwāh

Nabataean Petra or Palmyra.

Sabaean architecture too can be divided into two phases: an autochthonous phase and a period of strong influences from other cultures. There is clear evidence of the artistic achievement of the Sabaeans themselves in the highly developed techniques used in the construction of their temples and irrigation systems. Research has shown that even before the 8th century BC the Sabaeans were carrying out grand building projects, though the art of constructing round and pointed arches and of vaults, at which architects in Yemen today are so outstanding, is a later phenomenon. The Sabaeans used stone beams for the lintels of windows and doors and as roof supports. For the construction of temples or large houses limestone ashlar was preferred; the blocks were almost always worked so precisely that they could be laid without mortar. For halls and courtyards they used monolithic columns. Many of these rested

Roof support and water spout from a Himyarite temple, in the form of a bull's head (now in the National Museum, San'a)

directly on slabs, while others had proper bases which were joined to the upper parts with lead or bronze pins.

There are still unanswered questions regarding architectural decoration, including the origins of one common and distinctive ornament described thus by Doe: 'Enhancing the rather severe, trabeated architectural form, this decorative style consists of the use of three-dimensional geometric patterns. With square or rectangular panels and recessed planes, cubistic patterns were produced by contrasts of light and shade.' Doe continues by postulating an Assyrian source, transmitted to South Arabia via the countries of the Mediterranean. If this theory is correct then the decorative forms underwent increasing refinement in the Sabaean culture. Here we come up against a new problem. The ornamental panels with rectangular and geometric patterns are generally thought to be depictions of South Arabian house façades. Doe, however, refers to the theory of another archaeologist, G.W. van Beek, who offers a quite different interpretation. He suggests that the relations between the the ornamental panels and known buildings are not clear enough for the the decoration to be described as pictorial stylization of house façades; instead, he claims, by simply rotating the illustrations one can make them into depictions of furniture, so that what were thought to be roof towers become the feet of tables or chairs. It is possible therefore these decorative panels once formed the walls of sarcophagi and stone chests or the arms of benches.

Further field work in Yemen will presumably provide evidence for a definitive clarification of this question. The conventional view of scholars (against which van Beek levelled his 'furniture theory') is based on the giant stelae which the descendants of Sabaean immigrants erected at Aksum in Ethiopia. The great majority of scholars accept that the decoration of these stelae reproduces the façades of South Arabian tower houses. The views of the French Ethiopian specialist Jean Doresse can here stand for the whole group: 'The decoration of the stelae ... consists of a stylization of the architectural features of the high façade, each section treated on a broad scale and as a separate unit. At the base of the column there is a representation of timber; above this a row of low windows, followed by a series of tall ones separated from one another by the ends of the beams that support each storey of the edifice ... There is no doubt that this make-believe is highly evocative of the numerous storeys, one on top of the other, piled up in ancient palaces belonging to Sabaeans or Himyarites, the source of this artistic inspiration.'

One element very frequently found in Sabaean architectural decoration is the bull's head, the symbol of the moon god. Bulls' heads carved in limestone are used as water spouts on temple roofs; bulls' heads with drainage channels formed part of the slabs for blood sacrifices in the temples. On grave stelae too the bull's head crops up, usually in frontal view. Between its horns there are sometimes symbols such as vines or a thunderbolt. Ibexes are almost as common a decorative feature as the bulls' heads; whole friezes of ibexes have been found, presumably used as cresting for walls.

From Ma'rib come alabaster revetment panels with side views of recumbent ibexes carved in relief. Building blocks with friezes of strongly stylized ibex heads are also common. From a later period, when Sabaean art was already greatly influenced by other cultures, the ibex seems to come to life: on one red marble fragment there is even an ibex caught in mid-leap. A frieze discovered at Timna shows ibexes turning with their front legs towards a stylized tree, which is to be interpreted as the tree of life. Other decorative features of Sabaean architecture include snakes, goats, birds, lions, camels, horses, fish and panthers, besides foliage scrolls, vine-leaves and meanders.

Visiting Ma'rib

Until the beginning of the 1980's visitors to Ma'rib could never spend long enough on site. Arnaud, and later Glaser and Phillips, all found themselves pressed for time, as did numerous tourists who followed in their footsteps. Yet Ma'rib lies only about 120 km east of San'a, across terrain that admittedly is difficult - but not so as to hinder anyone seriously intent on reaching the capital of the vanished Sabaean Empire, whether by camel or by car. The human terrain, however, was more intractable. Originally it was the mistrust, superstition and xenophobia of the inhabitants that drove almost all outsiders away. By 1975, when Ma'rib itself became more amenable to tourists, the difficulties lay rather with the militant independence of the tribes living between San'a and Ma'rib, who made the journey an unpredictable adventure.

Since 1984 Ma'rib has been easily reached by a well-made asphalt road 135 km long. As had happened before at Sa'da, the reduction of the journey time between the capital and the province to a few hours has ensured peace in the region. The road follows a great arc across the volcanic highlands northeast of San'a, crossing the Bin-Ghaylan pass (2300 m high) and the al-Fardah pass (2200 m). From the al-Fardah pass in particular there is spectacular view over deep wadis and the desert stretching away to the north and east. At the eastern end of the pass the asphalt road curves north to Baraqish and Ma'in (see p. 61). As you enter the Ma'rib Oasis, on the right of the road, opposite the airfield (now closed), lies the rising town of New Ma'rib. Two first-class hotels opened here in 1985, and there are shops, restaurants, a post office and telephones. This is the new capital of a recently developed economic region, where oil has been discovered.

The airfield at Ma'rib has been closed since 1986, so it is no longer possible to make the spectacular arrival by air that visitors once enjoyed.

The town of Ma'rib itself is on the north side of the Wadi as-Sadd, but most of the archaeological sites are on the south side. Normally the tour of the ancient monuments begins with a drive of nearly 10 km to the north sluice of the dam, starting

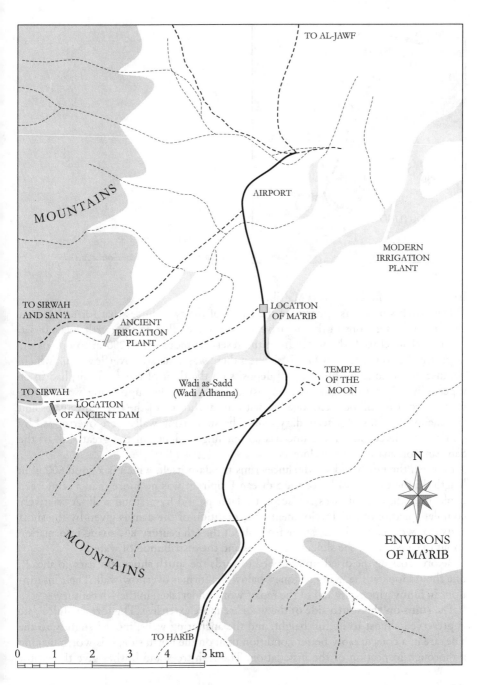

TO AL-JAWF

MOUNTAINS

AIRPORT

MODERN
IRRIGATION
PLANT

TO SIRWAH
AND SAN'A

ANCIENT
IRRIGATION
PLANT

LOCATION
OF MA'RIB

TEMPLE
OF THE
MOON

Wadi as-Sadd
(Wadi Adhanna)

TO SIRWAH

LOCATION
OF ANCIENT DAM

N

MOUNTAINS

ENVIRONS
OF MA'RIB

TO HARIB

0   1   2   3   4   5 km

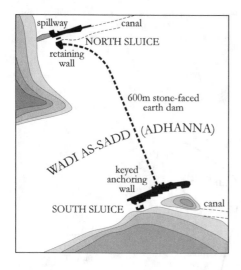

Sketch plan of the ruins of the dam at Ma'rib

from one of the hotels at New Ma'rib.

The **north sluice** was apparently the larger of the two sluices that formed part of the dam. Investigations of the site have so far revealed that on the north side a broad outflow channel took the water from the reservoir more than 1000 m to one of the large distribution cisterns. On this side too there was a massive overflow wall, which, because of the constant build-up of deposits on the floor of the reservoir, had to be repeatedly raised in height. The imposing remains of the supporting walls of the north sluice can still be seen, together with the anchoring of the two sluice gates and the anchoring walls of a secondary dam. The supporting walls were overtopped by part of the sluice gate. Here one has compelling evidence of the great skill of the Sabaean stonemasons and architects.

Between the north and south sluices runs the **dam** itself, which is a good 600 m in length. In the early decades of the Sabaean Empire it was no more than a reinforced bank of earth, but this was replaced at a later period by a stone wall. A relatively complete picture of the development and condition of the dam is given by the short texts that were carved in the stone from about the 6th century BC, giving information about the erection of the sluices, reservoirs and the distribution of water.

Before crossing the dried-up river bed towards the **south sluice** (the cars go ahead), one should look at the 'King's Stones' below the former overflow wall. Their inscriptions in Himyaritic script tell of the repair work undertaken in the 4th century BC.

The **ruins on the south side** of the wadi are more extensive. The former sluice gate is preserved almost to its full height, and the anchoring walls, moved slightly to the side, are in a considerably better condition than on the north side; it is worth making a thorough inspection of the installation. The lush trees and bushes give the visitor

Ma'rib, the new dam (completed in 1986)

some idea - though probably only a faint one - of Wadi as-Sadd at the time of the agricultural heyday. If circumstances permit, you should pause a while at the south sluice.

The next stop is usually the remains of a temple dedicated to the moon god Almaqah. Here five monolithic columns with capitals loom up in a row against the blue sky (colour plate 15). In the last few years a German team of archaeologists has been allowed to excavate the temple. Progress has been severely interrupted by the Gulf crisis and other local difficulties, but by the end of 1995 the excavations should be completed and the temple ruins consolidated.

Here however we come on the dilemma facing all archaeologists, and eloquently described in 1985 by Father Albert Jamme, the famous Belgian expert on South Arabia, who took part in Wendell Phillips's Ma'rib expedition. He wanted nothing more than to see the city excavated; but if the temple, for example, were fully

Sirwah, outer wall of the ancient temple

exposed, who would able to protect it? not just against wind and weather but mainly against destruction by the surrounding tribes, who regard these things as their own property.

As Father Jamme pointed out, our next stop, the half-excavated **Awwam Temple** was seriously plundered in the 1960's when stones were removed to be used for house building. The desert wind has already blown a lot of sand between the remaining columns and walls of this large oval temple (colour plate 16). Here too there are discoveries awaiting the archaeologist but the visitor can get an impression from what is still standing or lying hidden there under the desert sand. It is assumed that the Sabaeans borrowed the design from the South Babylonian method of building in the round. The temple is encircled by a defensive wall, which at some places still stands 9 m high; the blocks are on average 29 cm high and up to 150 cm long, and are slightly curved to fit the curvature of the whole building.

In 1952 the American expedition was only able to uncover the vestibule of the temple. In antiquity the hall was completely surrounded by columns, with a wide doorway leading to the temple interior and a row of three doors, which led out to the forecourt. The outer courtyard in front of the hall ends with a row of eight columns, each 4 m tall. Another 32 piers on the east and west sides each carried a rectangular block supporting the roof timbers.

The **town of New Ma'rib** lies on a solitary hill, which scholars believe to be the citadel of the old capital. Here, as in so many places in Yemen, excavation work could provide interesting information. Excavations have been long in coming, however, although since the Yemen civil war (1962-68) the place has been practically uninhabited. It was bombed several times and ten houses at most remain undamaged. Formerly spolia could be seen built as functional elements into many house walls: stones with Sabaean inscriptions, with the animal symbols of the world of gods, and with ornamental decoration. However, most of these have vanished since the beginning of the 1990's, either removed by the former house-owners to be used elsewhere or else taken to the depot of the National Museum, so it is no longer worth making a tour of the town to look for them. The town mosque, now in poor condition, is built on the site of Sabaean temples and incorporates some of their masonry and marbles.

Sirwah lies about 39 km west of Ma'rib. Once an important town in the Sabaean Empire, Sirwah has since the early 1990's best been reached by a reinforced track which begins at Ma'rib airfield, near New Ma'rib. The track runs northwards past Jabal Balaq and continues beyond Sirwah into the region of the Khawlan tribes with its capital Gihanah (78 km from Sirwah) where the mosque of Asnaf (11th century) contains a fine painted ceiling. In Khawlan the track is already largely asphalted and leads to the main San'a-Ta'izz road. The route can therefore be regarded as an alternative to the main San'a-Ma'rib road (see page 50). However, the Khawlan tribes have preserved strong independence and occasionally attempt to defend their interests by delaying or even altogether stopping tourist traffic through their region.

Sirwah can also be reached from Ma'rib along the north bank of the Wadi Adhanna. About 3 km upstream from the ancient dam a new dam was inaugurated in 1986. Built by a Turkish company and financed by Sheikh Zayed bin Sultan, the ruler of Abu Dhabi and President of the United Arab Emirates (who can trace his ancestry back to the Ma'rib region before the 6th century), it forms part of a large-scale irrigation project which, because of lack of follow-up investment, has remained incomplete. The road runs along the top of the new dam to the south side of the wadi and continues from there to Sirwah.

In Sirwah the visitor will find a fortress-like building with walls that in places are still 9 m high. (The original height was 10.5 m, but Egyptian troops blew up a great deal of the complex before their withdrawal.). It was probably first used as a fortress in the Islamic period - originally it was a temple to the moon god. Some scholars (Fakhry and Doe) suggest that the architect of the moon temple at Ma'rib was also responsible for the Sirwah temple. Much of the masonry dates from antiquity with stone blocks hewn to millimetre accuracy. This is particularly true of the vaulted east side of the building on which there is an almost complete inscription frieze. The upper parts of the rest of the masonry must have been relaid in the Islamic period, as we can see from the ibex friezes and inscribed stones that are now clearly out of the decorative sequence for which they were designed. The interior of the complex shows evidence of extensive rebuilding in Islamic times.

Qarnawu

The kingdom of the Minaeans seems always to have been a landlocked state. It emerged in the region which now forms the province of al-Jawf in the northeastern part of former North Yemen. In its heyday the state stretched still further north and included the oasis of Najran (which since 1934 has been in Saudi Arabia). Ma'in, as the kingdom of the Minaeans was called, was the northernmost outpost of South Arabia on the caravan road to Gaza and Damascus. Of the six South Arabian states of antiquity Ma'in is the one where investigation has been least possible. Only two of the great 19th-century explorers, Joseph Halévy and Eduard Glaser, managed to get to the region. During the civil war in the 1960's al-Jawf was firmly in royalist hands. and even today the tribal inhabitants of the regions claim a good deal of autonomy from the republic. Travelling in al-Jawf is a risky business because misunderstandings will always arise between strangers and inhabitants. Some journalists and aid workers in the 1970's braved the risks, but not even they were able to do more than cast a hurried glance at the ruins of the cities of Ma'in. R. Ruegg, a Swiss doctor who worked in North Yemen in the early 1970's, gave an idea of the frustratingly rich opportunities for exploration in his account of a journey in the east of al-Jawf. 'Our archaeologists ask the people about the location of ancient ruins in the vicinity. These are well known, although the Sabaean (Minaean) names have since given way to Arabic ones. Even today it is impossible not to notice these proud cities, which flourished 3000 years ago: the white walls surrounding Beida, the city gate, the rectangular columns of the temples. Everywhere we found stone blocks covered with Sabaean inscriptions: the ground is scattered with potsherds, fragments of capitals and friezes. Baraqish, which is only a few kilometres away from Beida, situated on low but steep hill, is reminiscent from a distance of Carcassonne, with its well-preserved city wall defended by towers, and in Ma'in too, the former capital of this region, impressive testimonies of the past still survive. Further east, in Wadi Raghwan, we discovered the remains of two ancient cities which had been previously unknown; here too there were walls extending for kilometres, many inscriptions, the ground covered with potsherds.'

In the 1980's, however, a few pioneering tourists began to report back from al-Jawf. Their accounts suggested that there was now more peace and stability in the land 'of the hundred sheikhs and five hundred families', as it was called in one report written in 1976. Nevertheless, the people still feel bound by the traditional law of the numerous tribal groups. Blood feuds between the various groups can still flare up.

Like the independent tourists, the archaeologists began to arrive in al-Jawf in the 1980's. Until then only the Egyptian Ahmed Fakhry had been able to travel in the region, but now French and Italian experts sprang into action. The first thing they did was to make a record of the state of the Minaean city ruins. From this we know that that these ancient cities were surrounded by massive walls between 1200 and 1500 m long, with stabilizing projections that were up to 14 m high. According to the experts the bulwarks were not for defence so much as for prestige and display: the building of massive walls was a way of showing off the riches gained by trade. The numerous inscriptions on the coping of the walls support this theory. The construction would have taken place in the periods when the economy was flourishing. In Ma'in this would have been the period between the 4th and 2nd centuries BC, according to the French archaeologists.

The French also investigated the cult sites on Jabal al-Laus, which rises to 2150 m in the northeast of Wadi al-Jawf. A number of sanctuaries dating from the 5th century BC onwards were discovered. These were roofless walled spaces with stelae, altars, incense-burners and sacrificial stones, and had apparently used for ritual meals

Ma'in, ruins of the Temple of Athtar.

to seal the bond between the individual tribes and the divine powers.

Current knowledge of Minaean history can be summed up as follows. Around 410 BC the mighty Sabaean Empire ran into difficulties. After about ten years of confusion and wars the northern part of the empire under the leadership of the city of Yathill broke away from Saba. Yathill, also known to western archaeologists as Baraqish, soon ceased to be the capital of the now independent north, and a new metropolis was created with the building of Qarnawu. After achieving independence this new Minaean state allied itself with Hadramawt, not only for protection against the Sabaeans, but rather because as trading allies Ma'in and Hadramawt would be able to open a new caravan route that would speed up the transport of goods to the north and so reduce costs. From an inscription found at Yathill it appears that Minaean merchants travelled as far as Egypt and Syria. The trading settlement in the Dedan oasis, now the province of Hejaz in the Kingdom of Saudi Arabia, was founded by Minaeans in the 4th century BC as a base on the way to Aqaba, Gaza and Damascus. Ma'in probably experienced its greatest flowering some 50 to 80 years later, in the first half of the 3rd century BC. The kings ruled from Qarnawu, advised by a committee of men from noble families. The kingdom expanded northwards, but needed all its strength to defend the northern frontier and the caravan routes against attacks from bedouin tribes. At the same time it seems to have been constantly on the defensive against Saba, which indeed managed to retake the initiative, conquering and destroying Ma'in in around 120 BC. For another 50 years or so kings continued to reside at Qarnawu as vassals of their more powerful South Arabian neighbours. The Egyptians, Greeks and Romans still knew of the Minaeans until the middle of the 2nd century AD, although by that time the most important trading partners of the western and northern nations had for a long time once again been the Sabaeans and Himyarites.

Religion and Art

There is no evidence that the religion and art of the Minaeans differed in essentials from those of the Sabaeans. Ma'in was originally the northern part of the Sabaean Empire, and the separation of the Minaeans from Saba was preceded by around 400 years of common Sabaean history. The same gods were prayed to in Ma'rib and Qarnawu - the only difference being that the Minaeans called Ilumquh (the moon god) Wadd. Ilumquh or Wadd was accompanied by a female sun deity and the god of Venus. As in the other South Arabian kingdoms, there was in Ma'in a notable tendency towards nameless gods, which some scholars have regarded as a first step towards monotheism. But in the absence of field work in al-Jawf and the region of Najran our knowledge is severely limited and we just do not know whether in Ma'in such anonymous local gods enjoyed greater veneration than the known South

Arabian gods. However, we do know that the Semitic nomads of the Arabian Peninsula developed the early forms of belief tending towards abstraction and
monotheism, and since the kingdom of the Minaeans was the northernmost outpost
on the edge of the desert they would have had the closest contacts with the nomads,
who may certainly have influenced their religious ideas. As is explained elsewhere
(see pages 65f), long after the fall of Ma'in the Najran oasis, once part of the Minaean
kingdom, was a bastion of monotheism in the form of Christianity, and Christians
were still living at there until shortly after the expansion of Islam.

We can only speculate about the specific characteristics of Minaean art. The
Minaean kingdom was a landlocked state and this must have been a major influence;
certainly Minaean art was slower to open up to eastern impulses than the art of the
South Arabian coastal states. On the other hand the Minaeans must have come into
contact earlier and more forcibly than other South Arabians with the peculiar
Graeco-Roman-Arabian mixed culture of the Nabataeans, who were beginning to
play an increasing role in the Arabian Peninsula from 120 BC onwards. It is also
notable that Ma'in seems for a time to have been the most urbanized land in South
Arabia. Despite the lack of basic research in al-Jawf we know of the ruins of six cities
situated close to each other there, and it would seem therefore that urban culture was
dominant in Ma'in. The excavations by the Italian archaeologists in Baraqish should
provide more information about this.

The features that already appear above ground are in themselves impressive.
Baraqish, although in a badly ruined condition, is still surrounded by enclosing city
wall. Because the town continued to be inhabited in the Islamic period the walls were
not later despoiled for stones. An ancient gatehouse still in situ within the ring of
walls clearly shows how monoliths were used as piers and lintels. The same is true of
the **Banat Ad temple** ruins about 750 m east of the town walls of Qarnawu/Ma'in.
This building (colour plate 17) has been recently described by Piepenburg as 'probably the best preserved pre-Islamic ruin in the whole of Jawf'. An inscription gives the
name of the temple as 'Rasf'. In **Qarnawu/Ma'in** only the foundations of the city
walls remain, but two gates are still in a good state of preservation. As in other
ancient sites there are stones with inscriptions, ibexes and fragments of piers and
capitals. The place is high up and has good views far into the northeastern part of
Wadi al-Jawf.

Travelling in al-Jawf

Since the end of the 1980's a visit to Baraqish has been on the programme of many
travel companies, and individual travellers can also have themselves taken to the
impressive remains of what was once the most important city in the Minaean kingdom. Here too the building of a new road has strengthened the influence of the state

and secured peace in the region. About 86 km from the city centre of San'a, on the main road to Ma'rib (see p. 50), after crossing the al-Fardah Pass, we come to the road to the southern part of Jawf which was completed in 1990. It continues northwards to Baraqish and al-Hazm.

A special permit is no longer necessary to visit Baraqish and Qarnawu/Ma'in. Nevertheless visitors to Jawf are advised to take care. This is probably the most conservative traditional area in Yemen. The inhabitants belong to various tribal sub-groups whose relations with one another are very volatile; sometimes neighbouring groups coexist peacefully, sometimes they are riven by conflicts of interests or infringements of tribal laws. Anyone then crossing the sovereign territories of neighbours who are in conflict will be greeted with great mistrust if not open hostility. As a rule the Yemeni guides will be well informed about such unrest and under some circumstances will refuse to undertake the trip into Jawf. Their assessment of the situation should be accepted as the best guarantee for your own safety. Added to the simple tribal tensions, large parts of al-Jawf are open to the adjacent Kingdom of Saudi Arabia. If (as is often the case) there is political friction between Saudi Arabia and Yemen this may be reflected in heightened tensions in Jawf. Before making a private trip into the region one should therefore be careful to find out about present conditions from people with local knowledge.

At the historic sites in Jawf you will inevitably come into contact with the native population. This is an area where people are accustomed to take note of every strange vehicle and keep an eye on it. If you travel in your own car, or even as a passenger in a car driven by one of the locals, your arrival as a stranger will always be signalled in advance. The best thing the visitor can do is to go to see the local people before visiting the ruins. Making contact in this way means that one has to submit oneself to a particular ritual: as a minimum it requires drinking tea together and may lead to an invitation to a meal. Under some circumstances the ritual can last several hours. At the end the hosts will also expect the stranger to pay with money for the food and drink. Do not be misled, however; this is not simple cupidity. Drinking and eating together sets the seal on a protection pact between the stranger and the natives, and according to ancient tribal custom a fee is demanded for this. It is far better to subject oneself to the ritual from the very beginning than be disturbed in the ruins by armed men asking suspiciously where you have come from and where you are going. Unsatisfactory answers can lead to a lengthy enforced stay.

Those wishing to cross the whole province of al-Jawf from south to north or north to south should entrust themselves to guides who know the region well and are themselves known there.

Zafar

In about 20 BC the rulers of the South Arabian kingdom of Himyar began building a new capital called Zafar. It was the metropolis of a state whose territory mainly comprised the Yemeni highlands. The capital was therefore situated high up, indeed at an altitude of almost 3000 m; its inhabitants were true highlanders, different from, and tougher than, the inhabitants of the plains.

The independent history of this mountain state had begun around 100 years earlier. In a period of great upheavals the Sabaeans had conquered the Minaean state. At the same time civil war had broken out in the kingdom of Qataban: two provinces, Himyar and Radman, had broken away from Qataban and in alliance with the Sabaeans had conquered the western and southern parts of the Qatabanian kingdom. The new state of Himyar/Radman extended to the southern outlet of the Red Sea, and so controlled Bab al-Mandab, the 'Gate of Tears', the straits to the Indian Ocean. At about the same time considerable improvements were made in navigation techniques and the sea route between India and Arabia was opened up. This put Himyar/Radman in a key position commercially and politically, since the shipping to and from Egypt had to pass through Bab al-Mandab and control of the straits brought a high income from duties and tariffs.

By AD 50, about six decades after the founding of Zafar, the Sabaean Empire had exhausted itself in conflicts with the Himyarites and in internal troubles. The once mighty state thus for a time became dependent on Himyar/Radman and was practically ruled from Zafar. The ancient Sabaean dynasty from the heartland around Sirwah and Maryab became extinct and a new ruler from the highlands established himself at Ma'rib, as Maryab is now called. Around AD 190 one of his successors, Sha'rum Autar, once again made Himyar a vassal state of Saba. But towards the end of the 3rd century AD, the Himyarites managed to reconquer Ma'rib together with the Sabaean heartland. The subsequent Himyarite kings were able to extend their power further, as far as the Yemeni coastal plain on the Red Sea. One of them, Shammar Yuharish, supported by the King of Aksum, ended up by controlling a still larger kingdom after his conquests of parts of the kingdom of Hadramawt. He then styled himself 'King of Saba, Dhu Raydan, Hadramawt and Yamnat'- a territory that must have corresponded more or less to what is now the united Republic of Yemen.

Himyarite dam near San'a

Under later rulers Ma'rib again became the capital; that is, the old metropolis of the Sabaeans was now the political centre of a new Sabaean-Himyarite kingdom. One of the Himyarites ruling in Ma'rib, probably Ta'ran Yuhanim, was converted to Christianity in the mid-4th century. His grandson, Abukarib Asad, came into contact with Judaism on a visit to Yatrib, the town later known as Medina. In an act of defiance of the Christian rulers of Aksum he went over to the Jewish faith. This led to the persecution of Christians in several places in the Sabaean-Himyarite kingdom, and Christian Ethiopia reacted by again invading South Arabia. Abukarib Asad's subsequent success in fending off the invaders and expanding the kingdom northwards mean that he is today considered one of the greatest pre-Islamic Arab kings. But his successors allowed the irrigation system of Ma'rib to decay, until eventually the great dam broke forever.

The catastrophe of Ma'rib and the fall of the Sabaean-Himyarite Empire did not, however, mean the end of the history of the Himyarites. At the time the dam broke, probably soon after AD 542, large parts of Yemen were occupied by the Ethiopians. Although these conquerors were the descendants of South Arabian immigrants to East Africa, they were regarded in Yemen as foreign oppressors. The Himyarite nobility and their followers gathered in opposition to the Ethiopians around Saif, a descendant of the Sabaean-Himyarite dynasty, and his son Maeadi-Kareb. Around AD 573 these two Himyarite princes set out to seek foreign aid for the struggle with the Ethiopians. Their journey took them first to Constantinople, but the Byzantine emperor would not consider supporting the Himyarites, who were still committed to Judaism, against the Christian Ethiopians. However, the other great Near Eastern power of the time, the Sasanian Empire of Persia, showed some interest in a Yemeni adventure, but its intervention did not come until some time later. Saif was already dead and his heir, Maeadi-Kareb, had to make another appearance at the Sasanian court before approval was at last given to provide military aid, and in the event the Himyarite prince returned to South Arabia with only a few thousand Persians. Nevertheless the arrival of their prince with an armed force roused the Himyarites to revolt. In decisive battle fought near San'a the Ethiopians were beaten and Maeadi-Kareb assumed the title of viceroy as a tributary prince under the Persians. Supporters of the Ethiopian party eventually exacted their revenge by murdering him, and a long drawn-out war between the Ethiopians and the Persians then ensued in Yemen, which only came to an end in AD 595 with the arrival of a new Persian army. A Persian was now made governor, and thereafter - perhaps up to the present day - the Himyarite tradition lived on only in those tribal princes who if need was defended with arms their independence and individuality against the central power.

Underground Himyarite cistern

1 Youth in Bayt al-Faqih

2 Street in the old Jewish quarter of Sa n'a

3 A welcome in Ma'rib

4 A workmen's café in Zabid

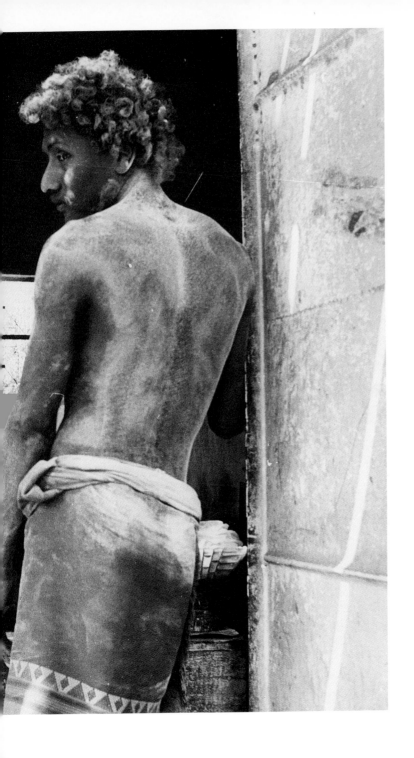

5   Market near San'a

6 In Wadi Duan

7 Suq in Zabid

8   The old town of Ibb

9   Women in the Tihama

Religion

The Himyarites were the dominant people of the late Sabaean Empire, and for the greater part of their history the people in Himyar kept to the faith they had inherited from Saba. The moon, the sun and Venus were worshipped as deities, just as they were throughout the rest of South Arabia and in the kingdom of the Aksumites over on the African coast of the Red Sea. However, when the two great monotheistic religions, Judaism and Christianity, reached the southern edge of the Arabian Peninsula the Himyarites showed great readiness in accepting them. Like their rulers, most townspeople and peasants of Himyar were first Christians, then Jews, then later Christians again. In some periods it is not clear which of the two faiths the Himyarites were following; there is evidence only of their general attachment to monotheism.

Whereas Judaism has survived in South Arabia, at least in some small areas, until our own day, Christianity vanished completely. As late as the 10th century the Yemeni geographer Hassan Ibn Ahmad al-Hamdani, who died in San'a in 945 or 946, reported in his *Description of the Arabian Peninsula* that on the island of Socotra in the Gulf of Aden there were 'approximately 10,000 warriors, who are in fact Christians'. These Arabian Christians, however, would have been converted by the

Yemeni Jew (19th-century engraving)

Christian Ethiopians, or Christians who had been settled there by the Ethiopians. On the mainland Christianity probably came to the Najran oasis - now in Saudi Arabia - through the Himyarites themselves in the first half of the 4th century. This had been preceded by about 140 years of missionary activity in the Himyarite kingdom. Churches were built in the cities of Aden, San'a, Zafar and finally in Najran, where 'a famous building commemorated their martyrs, headed by St Aretha. In this oasis Christianity persisted until 635, when Caliph Omar expelled the community.

Perhaps Christianity could have planted deeper roots in South Arabia if it had not been for the debilitating rivalry with Judaism. Christians were persecuted every time a Himyarite ruler went over to Judaism. While

Stone relief, probably of Christian origin, built into house at Bayt al-Ashwad, near Zafar

political interests certainly had a part in the changing religious orientation of the Himyarite princes, the victory of monotheism over the South Arabian triad of celestial deities was quickly achieved. From around the middle of the 5th century onwards God was called 'Rahmanan' or 'compassionate' by the Himyarite-Sabaean kings; this is also one of the epithets of God in the Koran.

When the prophet Muhammad in 622 left Mecca for the oasis town of Yatrib - later called Medina - there were five tribes living in its vicinity. Three of them followed Judaism. In their origins the tribal people were Semitic Arabs, like most people of Central and South Arabia. Many, though nor all, scholars believe that the Jews of Yemen were also overwhelmingly ethnically Arab, although Hamitic and Negroid influences can be seen. Yemeni Jewry probably has its roots in the Himyarite period (though the Jews themselves claim that their ancestors imigrated to Yemen in the 6th century BC, before the Babylonian captivity) and in the mountains of Yemen the Jews survived the spread of Islam better than the Jewish tribal federation which once had its home in the heartland of the Prophet. The Jewish community in Yemen remained significant until the founding of the state of Israel. According to Ottoman sources there were about 60,000 Jews living in the area ruled by Imam at the end of the 19th century. They had preserved some distinctive features of rabbinical Judaism in their religious practices, but through contact with the Jews in Egypt and Iraq had adopted elements from the Sephardi rite. In 1950-51 nearly all the Yemeni Jews emigrated to Israel, leaving behind only a small group, supposed to number about 6000. This has been reduced very much further in the last few years.

Visiting Zafar

For a visit to the site of the Himyarite capital Zafar we can leave from San'a or Ta'izz. The actual starting point for the journey into the Himyarite heartland is the little town of Kitab at the foot of the Sumarra pass. More or less in the middle of the town is a turning eastwards off the main San'a-Ta'izz road (shared taxis). The road is asphalted for only about a kilometre and then becomes a dust track which can be difficult after rain. After 3 km we reach the village of Ribat al-Qalah, from which several tracks run in various directions. We take the one which leads a short way northwards and then rises in great bends towards Zafar, further to the northeast. The remaining 3 km from Ribat take about 30 minutes (a four-wheel-drive vehicle is not absolutely necessary). The stretch from Kitab to Zafar can also be covered on foot.

The present-day town of Zafar and the remains of the ancient city are situated in extremely attractive country. Near the Sumarra pass, at an altitude of over 2500 m, the road runs round high hills in sweeping curves. In this landscape it is easy to get an idea of the natural environment in which the Himyarites lived. About 2000 years ago the vegetation would not have looked very different, with bushes and shrubs, trees and well-tended fields alternating with steppe-like fallow land. In between are the massive houses that form settlements and villages piled up like castles; their building material and style seem not to have changed over the millennia.

Zafar itself is rather a disappointment. All the villages in this picturesque mountainous country give the impression, as one drives past, of having survived unaltered and unscathed from 100 BC to the present, but Zafar itself looks like a large and not particularly impressive hill. Only in the course of a detailed visit do its distinctive features become apparent.

The great hill itself is covered with boulders, in between which are innumerable worked stones from the period of Himyarite Zafar. The north and west slopes were used for agriculture; the small fields are bordered by dry-stone walls, with stones worked by human hands in pre-Christian times. On the top of the hill, which is an almost perfectly round plateau, a single-storey building has been constructed from stones which may have been used 2000 years ago in the walls of dwellings or religious buildings. The sign over the door reads *Mathaf*, the 'museum'.

It is surprising that anyone has managed to create a collection here, since all the interesting Himyarite stones seem to have important work to do in the modern houses nearby, as door or window supports, cornerstones or as decorative elements in the façades; moreover highland Yemenis are not used to allowing the state to take anything from them. On the contrary, they, like their ancestors, have always expected the state to pay them generously for their good will.

Nevertheless, the little museum has a very informative, albeit limited collection, and it is a good way of rounding off a visit to Zafar. One impressive item is the monumental inscribed stone which records the renovation in AD 447 of the palace on the neighbouring castle hill of Raydan. There are several bronze figures of animals - bulls, leopards, lions - which show Roman influence.

The houses of the present-day village of Zafar are squeezed partly on the north-eastern side of the top of the hill and partly on the eastern slope. A tour of the village to see the buildings with decorated or inscribed stones easily visible will be provided almost automatically; indeed villagers - expecting a tip - will press any visitor to make such a tour. The visitor for his part should also insist on a visit to the natural caves (colour plate 18) in the slopes of the hill. These caves were once used as tombs, dwellings, workshops and storage chambers. About half of them are still used today for food storage. Some of the accessible caves have interesting workmanship: the grottoes are linked by stairways and paths hewn in the rock, which were part of the public road system of the Himyarite capital. The small village of Bayt al-Ashwad not far away was built using stone and marble taken from the ruins of Zafar.

Visiting Baynun and Rada

Hamdani, the Arab chronicler of early Islamic Yemen wrote 'Baynun, a mountain, was bored through; one of the Himyarite kings bored through it so that a water course from the land lying beyond it could be directed to the region of Baynun.'

Baynun was, however, much more than a bored-through mountain and Hamdani acknowledges this fact in another passage, where the royal castle of Baynun - the place was for a time the capital of the Himyarite state - is mentioned by the chronicler as one of the power centres of the ancient Orient, famous for its riches, its pomp and its culture. In any case Baynun was an important place until its complete destruction by the Aksumites, probably in AD 525. The ruins are extensive, but archaeological research entails years of toil, so it is perhaps understandable that the three-man German archaeological team that pioneered exploration here in 1970 concentrated on rediscovering the tunnel through the mountain. This proved to be easy thanks to the cooperation of friendly Yemenis.

Starting from Dhamar, an attractive town with fine architecture, a picturesque market and an old Turkish bath, the trip to Baynun (four-wheel-drive necessary) takes about three hours. The Austrian explorer Eduard Glaser noted at the beginning of the 1880's that Baynun lay 'six hours northwest of Jabal Isbil and eight hours from Dhamar', but these are hours by donkey or on foot. Today the traveller leaves Dhamar - on the San'a-Ta'izz road and easy to reach from either city - on an asphalted road heading eastwards to the provincial capital Rada. About 30 km east of Dhamar one takes a track than runs at first north to the Jabal Isbil, but then turns slightly to the northwest so that Jabal Dhu Rakam can be seen on the left. Driving between the two mountains one reaches Baynun after about an hour's journey.

The visitor will quickly spot the extensive ruins along a broad curve on the slopes around the upper part of the wadi. A walk through them shows how much has still to be done in the way of archaeological field work before even a qualified assessment can be made of the once great city of Baynun and its legendary royal castle. But try if possible not to set foot on the site without the agreement of the inhabitants of the village of an-Numara at the foot of the eastern ridge of the mountain.

Below Baynun's ruins a sharply sunken shaft can be seen. This is the end of a tunnel, no longer passable, which in the heyday of the Himyarite kingdom brought

Baynun, irrigation channel from the Himyarite period

water through the mountain. A second one can be found on the next ridge to the east on the other side of the valley. This tunnel has remained intact for more than 1500 years. If you walk through it you will arrive after about 150 m at the foot of the east side of the mountain. Stone inscriptions record that both tunnels were cut into the rock to irrigate the valley of an-Numara.

The main road from Dhamar in a southeast direction runs through Rada and al-Baydha into the former South Yemen, meeting the main road to Aden (150 km) at Lawdar. The road, fully asphalted since 1993, is now suitable for any vehicle.

On this stretch **Rada** (55 km from Dhamar) is worth a stop. In this town (population 30,000) stands the Amariya Mosque (colour plate 13) built about 490 years ago and restored in 1992-93. The Amariya, like the stylistically related mosques in Ta'izz, has no minaret but is surmounted by six domes. Also of interest is its battlement decoration, a feature which may be of Mesopotamian origin. The ablution hall is held up by ancient Himyarite columns. Besides other mosques Rada has some old houses built in a distinctive manner from hewn stone and fired mud bricks; the style recalls the architecture in San'a. Rising above the town is a still-magnificent fortress, whose foundations supposedly date from pre-Islamic times.

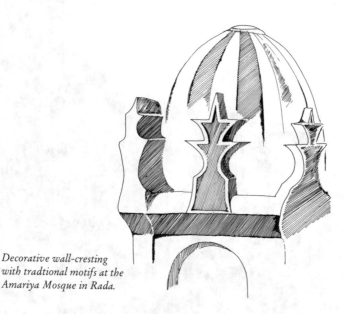

Decorative wall-cresting with tradtional motifs at the Amariya Mosque in Rada.

San'a

San'a must be seen, however long the journey,
Though the hardy camel droops, legworn on the way.
Traditional poem

The finest city I have seen in the Orient ... even Constantinople
would not be excepted if it were not for its mosques.
A German traveller in 1810

As far as we know from the available historical sources, San'a became capital of Yemen for the first time around the middle of the 6th century, when the Christian king of Aksum on the African side of the Red Sea conquered part of the country and appointed a governor named Abraha to rule from San'a. Legend, however, has it that the city was founded by Ham the son of Noah, and scholars assume that the site was important from an early time, and certainly in the Sabaean period. At the midpoint of Yemen's great central plateau, where it narrows to a width of only a few kilometres between the mountain ranges east and west, San'a also controls the major trade routes from Ma'rib, capital of the kingdom of Saba, to the sea. It would be surprising if there had not always been a stronghold here, and indeed the name San'a almost certainly means 'well-fortified' in Sabaic.

More concrete evidence is hard to come by. The leading Yemen experts Carl Rathjens and Hermann von Wissmann wrote in the 1930's that the main mosque in the centre of the city probably had 'foundations dating from pre-Islamic times', and that its ground plan had similarities with that of the Himyarite temple excavated at Huqqa, 23 km north of San'a. But to check this thesis one would have to excavate in the mosque - a difficult undertaking, since only Muslim archaeologists would be considered, and even then the Yemeni clergy would have to be convinced of the relevance of exploring pre-Islamic culture.

Just as unsatisfactory is the state of research regarding the legendary castle of Gumdan in San'a. Historians in antiquity and the early Islamic period relate that a mighty castle stood here during the periods of Sabaean and early Islamic domination; most historians of Yemen assume that Gumdan really existed, although in fact no incontrovertible evidence for it has so far been found. Again, excavation would probably provide some certainty. Rathjens and Wissmann again proposed digging in the immediate vicinity of the main mosque, if the opportunity ever presented itself. Others conjecture that the remains of the castle are in the ground on the outermost eastern edge of the city.

Documentary evidence does exist however for Abraha's construction of a church in San'a. In a letter to the bishop of Aksum, the governor wrote: 'I have built you a temple in San'a, the like of which the Arabs nor non-Arabs have constructed, and I shall not desist until I divert the [Muslim] pilgims of the Arabs to it, and they abandon the pilgrimage to their own temples.' Despite this letter, there has been as yet no sign of the remains of the 6th-century building, which should have been the largest Christian structure south of the Mediterranean. More liberal-minded inhabitants of the Old Town sometimes show visitors a spot on which the Qalis (from the Greek *ekklesia* meaning 'church') is supposed to have stood; and there are columns and capitals in a Christian style built into the main mosque and other mosques, though these are said to come mainly from outside San'a. Otherwise the period of Christian rule, like the period of Jewish dominance that preceded it, left little or no mark in the Yemeni capital. This is probably not just an impression created by the lack of excavation; after all, these two phases were so short that they could only have produced a limited number of durable buildings and works of art. Similarly, nothing has yet been found from San'a's subsequent Persian period, which came to an end with the arrival of Islam in Yemen. In the time of chaos that followed around 635, when fighting broke out between the Arab rulers and the Persians once again seized control, San'a changed hands several times. It would have been at this point that Gumdan castle, together with whole districts of the city, were destroyed.

In fact the present capital has been almost completely destroyed several times. After the centre of Islamic power shifted from the interior of the Arabian Peninsula to Damascus and Baghdad, the Yemenis made repeated attempts to shake off the supremacy of the distant caliphs. San'a was razed in 803 in the course of the suppression of one Yemeni uprising by troops of Haroun ar-Rashid. There was also destruction in 901 when the Zaydi Imam, who had come to power in the north, conquered the capital for the first time. There is again evidence of severe devastation in San'a in 1187, as a consequence of dynastic struggles. The Zaydis gave way at the beginning of the 16th century to the advance of the Mamluks, the slave soldiers who ruled in Egypt, and who for some years had a governor ruling in San'a. In 1546 the Turks, who had meanwhile conquered Egypt, also took over from the Mamluks in the Yemeni capital. They remained there for a period of 72 years before leaving Yemen to rule itself for another two centuries. Ottoman Imperial troops returned in 1849, taking San'a for a short time, and again in 1871, this time more permanently. Nevertheless, the struggle with the forces of the Zaydi Imams was by no means over. San'a continued to be fought over, and in 1905 Imam Yahya entered the city in triumph, though just then a short-lived one. The destruction caused by the fighting was considerable. Not until 1912, after the signing of a peace treaty between the Turkish governor and the Imam, did a period of undisturbed development begin again for San'a. After the assassination of Imam Yahya in 1948 the city was taken by his son, Imam Ahmad, and sacked by his tribal forces; some of this damage is still in evidence.

The city of San'a, as the visitor sees it at the end of the 20th century, dates mainly from the 18th and 19th centuries. The older buildings consist of a few mosques,

A Mamluk

warehouses in the market area and a very few residential buildings. Yet the overall impression of the Old Town is of a city that could date from the 14th or 15th centuries. It was not until the 1960's and 1970's that the traditional style of building in San'a was spoilt by innovations. Concrete construction has since made inroads on the south side of the Old Town at Bab al-Yemen, on the western border of the Old Town and in the old Turkish quarter. However, large parts of San'a still present the image of an Islamic community of the early phase of development, in which urban culture was in complete harmony with its natural surroundings.

Art and Architecture

Apart from a visit to the collection of antiquities in the museum, the main aesthetic experience offered by San'a is its extraordinary architecture. This is a manifestation of an urban culture that had its beginnings centuries ago; already in the 3rd century Ahmad ar-Rada'i was singing the praises of 'San'a of the mansions and towers tall'. Tower houses - which provide security and also prevent unnecessary encroachment on precious arable land - may have been built in Himyaritic times, and the lower stories of a few in San'a today may date back 800 years. Whereas in other Arab cultures religious restrictions meant that artistic expression took shape above all in the field of calligraphy, in Yemen generally and San'a in particular the centuries-old

73

traditions encouraged an emphasis on the rich decoration of the façades of both sacred and secular buildings. On residential houses the façades have various decorative elements picked out in white paint; for instance, there are geometric ornamental bands of projecting bricks in relief (just visible on colour plate 5), where the size of the bricks limits the variety of decoration. Placed horizontally these ornamental strips mark the divisions between storeys.

The oldest houses in San'a are recognizable by their round windows glazed with very thinly cut alabaster panels. In the past alabaster quarried near the capital was always used instead of window glass. In a few older houses the windows play a more important part: usually quadrangular or rectangular, divided into two or three, they take up more of the surface and are hardly distinguishable from old-fashioned European window shapes. But above the ordinary windows there are almost always fanlights, and it is in these the Yemeni sense of decoration is most clearly expressed. Fanlights are either semi-circular, or else part of an elongated oval. Pieces of glass, often of various colours, are fixed in the plaster tracery with its floral or geometric patterns. The older the work, the more delicate and rich the tracery, which often has a different pattern inside and out.

The ornament is generally symmetrical and occasionally also has script twined round it and integrated in a very skilful way. The visitor can see these windows being made in specialised workshops, recognisable by the completed plaster elements laid out in the sun to dry.

Ornamental stonework and plaster tracery from a house in San'a

Decorative floral and geometrical tracery pattern from a window in Yemen. The pattern is first drawn on a slab of plaster and then carefully cut out

As a rule the surrounds of the windows are painted white; usually the paint is drawn up to a point at the top of the window, or the semicircle may be flanked by painted with abstract floral ornaments on either side. Between the windows, extending from one horizontal border to the next, there are sometimes vertical geometrical ornaments in brick with a semi-circular termination. They bear a similarity to the tree of life on carpets and kelims.

The tower houses of San'a - of which there are over 14,000 - are between 20 and 50 m high and built of grey stone (ashlar basalt or tufa) and brown bricks, matching the greys and browns of the mountains near the city. The plaster ornaments make the houses - and the whole city - stand out from the main colours of the landscape (colour plate 2). This plaster is a local speciality, made from a particularly strong limestone called *goss*. On some buildings the ornament runs round the façades in the form of a beautifully worked horizontal frieze. (The plain horizontal strips are often wooden girdles to hold the walls in and absorb shock; they are usually made from apricot wood, which resists decay.) From the first floor upwards the various ornaments increase in number. It is also interesting that five-pointed stars derived from Babylon, and occasionally the six-pointed stars of the Jews are incorporated as decorative elements. The omission of stones in the decoration of a façade creates air holes and light sources, though at the parapet level these gaps are purely decorative.

San'a, family houses in the old town ▷

Round window (left) and carved plaster window (right) from an old house in San'a

Although the architects of recent centuries must have been unaware of the fact, many of their decorative motifs are based on pre-Islamic elements. One of these is the Sabaean script, but you may also spot the horns of an ibex at corners of the roofs of some houses. Ibexes and ibex heads were among the most common pre-Islamic animal symbols. Now, as then, such horns are attached to houses as amulets to frighten away evil spirits. The snake motifs serve the same function.

To make a complete catalogue of these traditional ornaments in San'a would however be a hopeless task, so rich is the material. As Paolo Costa, the archaeologist and adviser to the Yemeni government conceded: 'the details and decorations of Yemeni architecture are so free and spontaneous that they cannot be enumerated in a systematic study. The list of deviant forms would be endless and one would finally be driven to admit that the one rule that governs the creation of Yemeni decoration is the rejection of all rules.'

Structurally, these richly bedecked town houses, from five to nine storeys high, are held together by the strength of the single staircase. They are generally lived in by a single family, which may, however, comprise a very large number of people. Built close together, the houses mostly face onto narrow alleyways, sometimes onto a small square (colour plate 1). At the back there are often vegetable and fruit gardens, which are the property of the city or the nearest mosque. (Market gardens, or

Two sections through a typical Yemeni town house in San'a

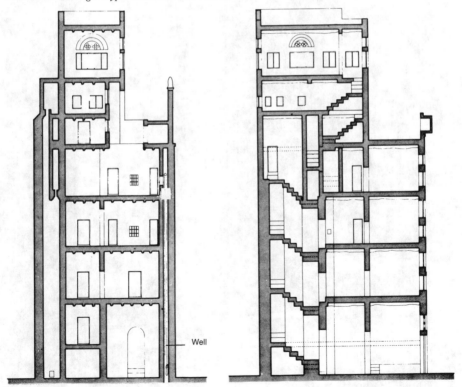

Well

79

bustana, were often part of a mosque's income-producing endowment, *waqf.*) The ground floor generally consists of a hall with adjoining store rooms, and often stables as well. As is usual in Yemeni architecture, the hall is designed to provide defence as well as welcome. One has to remember that the last time San'a was plundered by tribal fighters was as recently as 1948, and that was with the consent of the then ruler, Imam Ahmad, who used the looting of the city as a way of thanking his army of tribesmen for their help in the recovery of the capital from rebel hands. In the 1960's San'a suffered a long siege by royalist tribes and would certainly have been plundered again if it had fallen to them. Consequently many well-to-do citizens continue the tradition of keeping the ground floor of the houses free for any possible fighting. Once the enemy has entered the hall, he can still be shot at from the galleries in the first floor before he tries to storm up the narrow stairs, of which the steps will be up to 30 cm high. These stairs lead up past a mezzanine floor with storage chambers for food (wheat, corn and millet kept in large jars) to the first floor, where the most important rooms are found.

The biggest room on the first floor is used for family gatherings and for the reception of well-intentioned visitors; it is spread with carpets or mats, and one may enter only after removing one's shoes. On the floor along the walls are cushions for sitting on, stuffed with cotton, or increasingly nowadays with foam rubber. Lighter cushions are also provided so that people can rest their backs and heads comfortably against the wall. (Windows are low so that the seated company can look out.) There is very little other furnishing. Clothes are hung from nails in open wall niches. In the houses of rich families these wall niches are closed with wooden doors. Sometimes there are also chests for storing cloths, festive clothes and shawls for cold weather. Bedrooms are furnished in almost exactly the same way as living rooms, except that instead of cushions for sitting on there are mattresses covered with brightly coloured cloths on the floor along the walls. On the second floor above the large living room is the room called the *diwan*, in which the family celebrate weddings, births and religious festivals. Childbirth itself happens here, with elaborate preparation, and it is here that bodies are laid out before the funeral.

On the third floor are smaller rooms for women and children, as well as the kitchen. Traditionally this area is called the *harem* (from *haram* meaning 'forbidden') and men who are not close family members may not enter. Despite the images conjured by the name in the West, it is exceptional for several wives to live together in a harem. Polygamy is practised by only a small percentage of the male population in San'a, in general wealthy men who can afford to accommodate a young wife in another house or in another part of the house. As a rule the harem is lived in by the householder's mother, wife, unmarried sisters and perhaps sisters-in-law, as well as

◁ *A fortress-like rural house on the high plateau of San'a*

81

San'a, view over the roofs of the old town towards Midan at-Tahrir

his children. For all these people there is a single kitchen, its ceiling usually black from soot despite the smoke outlet above the masonry stove. Often a cooker using bottled gas or electricity will be standing next to the traditional apparatus, just as there are almost always western-style pots and pans beside the old stone pots and ceramic vessels. A heavy copper mortar for pounding coffee and spices, a small hand-driven millstone for making coarse flour, oil-lamps made of stone or alabaster, clay or copper charcoal braziers for cold days can also be found, although they are increasingly being ousted by mass-produced utensils from Europe and Japan.

The kitchen is on the third floor because it has to serve both the living rooms below and the main room of the head of the household, called the *mafraj*. This forms part of the upper storey and is built on the flat roof, with windows on three sides to enjoy the often superb views. The name comes from *faraja*, meaning 'freedom from sadness and worry'; the householder retires to the mafraj alone or with friends, to smoke a water pipe and chew *qat*.

The chewing of qat is without doubt the more important part of the daily round. The young leaves of the qat tree (*Catha edulis*) are mildly narcotic. The careful householder buys the daily qat ration in the market if possible himself, and it is important to make sure of the provenance and freshness of the goods. Guests generally bring along their own portions of qat, wrapped in banana leaves to keep them fresh; the host only provides the room and the equipment. Qat sessions play a major social role. Business affairs, political decisions, family matters, the state of the country and society are discussed. It is not all that easy to speak out, however, since to appreciate the stimulating effect of the drug one has to chew it thoroughly and keep the largest possible quantity of leaf in one's mouth. The experienced Yemeni turns it into a lump as big as a tennis ball which he holds in one or both of his cheeks. Water has to be slurped over the chewed lump so that the juice is washed into the stomach. When the leaves are fully chewed they are not swallowed but immediately spat out. So the indispensable equipment of a mafraj includes a vessel of fresh water and a bucket for the chewed leaves. In high-class houses there are also a number of water-pipes, decorated boxes for tobacco and a container for burning charcoal, which is needed to smoke leaf tobacco in water-pipes. Special arm and back rests are provided for comfort.

Lighting is often nothing more than a naked light bulb hanging from the ceiling, which is supported by roughly hewn trunks of palm trees or imported tree trunks. The glass, ceramic or copper candle-holders and the old oil lamps that were once used are still found on the window sills, the lintels of doors and windows, and on the many brackets that the plasterer will have built into the wall. In fact the decoration of the mafraj - which is where a Yemeni will start the decoration of his house - is mainly the work of the plasterer. In particular he is responsible for the tracery set with coloured glass used for the over-windows. The well-to-do householder uses two patterns, set in a single window opening, one facing outwards and the other inwards, so that when they are seen by daylight from inside the two overlap to create a third pattern. A well-appointed mafraj will also have plaster inscriptions of religious verses, with calligraphic skill expressed in the sweep and intertwining of the characters. There may also be pointed plaster arches with script-like ornaments.

The other living rooms in the house will be similar, but plainer. Mirrors, framed documents, perhaps a cheap colour print (often of the creation story showing Adam and Eve, or a scene from the life of the Caliph Ali), are used to decorate the walls.

For the rest, apart from modern technology such as televisions, radios and cassette-players, there is hardly anything to correspond to European ideas of home comfort and furnishings. Cooling is achieved by evaporating water from large jars kept in cooling boxes on the outside of the house. Washrooms and toilets in the traditional town house - as in earlier times in Europe - provide only the bare necessities. The

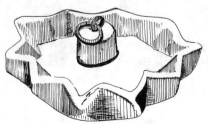

Stone oil-lamp

San'a, town house with its own draw-well (foreground right), in the Old Town

walls of these rooms are usually covered with a water-resistant plaster made of lime mixed with powdered alabaster. (The flat roofs of the houses are covered with a cement that is also made waterproof by the addition of powdered alabaster.) To wash you squat on two stones set into the floor and use a vessel to pour water over yourself. The privy is a hole in the floor through which the excreta fall down a shaft into a pit, which can be emptied from outside the house. Formerly the dried excreta - San'a has a low humidity and the faeces dry very quickly - were used as fuel for the public baths. This was an efficient and ecologically sound system, but the Old Town has now acquired a modern sewage system.

The Mosques

When Muhammad built his own house in exile at Medina, he created an original building type with one section open to the sky and a roofed area. This became the prototype of the courtyard-hypostyle mosque, with a roof resting on columns - on a whole forest of columns in the case of a big mosque. The Prophet also laid importance on making the inner courtyard of a prayer house at least as broad as it is long, for he knew that bedouin are used to sitting side by side in long rows to pray. A traditional mosque consists therefore of a large rectangle along the sides of which are hypostyles (*liwan*), closed to the outside and opening inwards, a fountain in the middle of the courtyard, the liwan on the side facing Mecca emphasized by a greater number of columns and with a decorated prayer niche (*mihrab*) and a pulpit (*minbar*).

Of all the 150 or so mosques in San'a the Great Mosque (Jami al-Kabir) corresponds most closely to the style established by Muhammad. Whether it is also the oldest mosque in Yemen is uncertain. Some Yemenis claim this honour for the al-Ganad mosque near Ta'izz (see page 176ff). In any case, both mosques are among the earliest buildings in the Islamic world. If the Great Mosque of San'a was indeed begun while the Prophet was still alive, this must have been around AD 630 by the Western chronology. There is evidence that the building was extended or rebuilt around 705. The mosque was badly damaged by a flood 170 years later, and it was damaged again in 911 when the Karmatis, a communistic Ismaili sect, conquered and sacked San'a. One of the two minarets - the eastern one - was already in existence at that time; the western minaret was built later. In the 12th century both were thoroughly restored.

The most any non-Muslim visitor may be allowed is a very brief tour of the interior of the Great Mosque. But this will be enough to confirm that a large number of pre-Islamic elements were used in the building: columns, coping stones and roof supports from temples of the old kingdoms and from sanctuaries of the Jewish and Christian periods that came between (colour plate 3). The legendary castle of

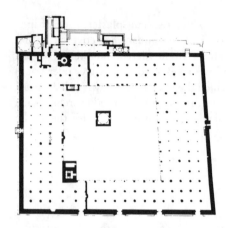

Plan of the Great Mosque of San'a

Gumdan dating from the first Himyarite period is said to have served as a quarry for building the Great Mosque (see page 71). Two stone reliefs built into the exterior of the northwest wall showing pairs of doves or similar birds with rosettes may come from the Christian cathedral built by the Ethiopian governor Abraha. The inner courtyard measures about 80 by 60 m. The columns of the hypostyles on each side are joined by tall round arches and stand in three rows four metres apart. They are made of various sorts of stone and belong to different periods. In the inner courtyard of the Great Mosque - not exactly in the centre, but closer to one of the two minarets - rises a cube-shaped, domed, stone structure, the colour of whose stonework changes in layers. Except for the dome it seems to be modelled on the Ka'ba at Mecca. The building was erected on the orders of the Ottoman governor at the beginning of the 17th century. Its original function is unclear, though it may have been a treasury.

Some of San'a's many mosques are insignificant prayer houses, attached to a partic-ular district of the city. Many were built only after the end of the civil war, that is, since 1970. About 40 of the mosques in San'a are of religious and artistic importance, though many of these are of interest only to specialists. Most of the mosques which will give the visitor an impression of the art, architecture and religion of Yemen today (there are perhaps a dozen of these) are in the eastern part of the Old Town. Three of them are of Turkish origin. The oldest of these, the Mosque of Mahdi Abbas, was built around 1600, in the first period of Ottoman rule in Yemen. It offers a characteristic mixture of two styles: the domed prayer house is typically Ottoman and could just as well have been built in the Balkans, in Ankara, or in Damascus in the time of the Turkish caliphs, but the minaret is Yemeni: its shaft is decorated with plaster ornaments in various vertical and horizontal patterns from the first break at about 15 m right up to the gently rounded top.

This contrast is also the defining characteristic of the other two Turkish mosques.

Stone reliefs on either side of a bricked-up doorway at the back of the Great Mosque of San'a

The Bakiliye Mosque is attached to the eastern city wall. Like the Mahdi Abbas, it was built during the first phase of Yemen's incorporation into the Ottoman Empire (1539-1630), but was also restored during the second period of Turkish rule (1849-1918). The massive dome of the main prayer house and the ten domes over the subsidiary buildings are surely by Ottoman architects, while the minaret of fired bricks is no doubt based on Yemeni designs. The third mosque following this pattern is the Tulha Mosque in the middle of the Old Town.

A text-book example of the purely Yemeni style of architecture is the little Mosque al-Madrasa ('the school'). The main building, the prayer house, is not very lavish - in keeping with the early Islamic style. All the artistic skill developed to the praise of God and his Prophet is concentrated on the minaret, which rises out of the main building. This was built (in the 16th century) despite objections from some Zaydi theologians, and became the pattern for many Yemeni minarets. The square lower section is richly ornamented with religious calligraphy and with patterns which may have their roots in pre-Islamic art; the upper shaft is polygonal at first, then round, and has many decorations like those seen again and again on secular buildings. They are re-whitewashed every year. The same is true of the Abhar Mosque and the Salah ad-Din (Saladin) Mosque in the Old Town. On the rounded tops of the minarets of al-Madrasa and the Saladin is a dove cast in bronze. The bird symbolizes an event during the departure (*hijra*) of the Prophet from Mecca. When Muhammad had hidden in a cave to escape from his pursuers from the ranks of the unbelievers, his pursuers did not think of looking in the cave because the pair of doves nesting above the entrance, which would normally have been scared off by anyone entering.

Also worth mentioning is the Mutawakil Mosque, built by Imam Yahya (1904-48) in the style of the Ottoman rulers he overthrew. From the windows of the National Museum (in its new building) there is a good view from above of this mosque, whose minaret does not rise above the seven domes of the main building.

San'a, a view of a minaret with repainted decoration

San'a, a view over the domes of the al-
Mutawakil Mosque seen from Dar ash-Shukr

The Market

The Prophet was the posthumous son of a merchant. His home city of Mecca was at
the time of his birth (*c.* 570) a city-state of traders who imported much of their
merchandise from Yemen. Before he received the first messages from God at the age
of forty, Muhammad himself had been much involved in trade. It is not surprising
that the market (*as-Suq*) generally had a high status in the early Islamic society of
Arabia - but this was not the case in Yemen. Here a caste system gave the religious
nobility, and the warriors and peasants attached to them, precedence over traders and
craftsmen, a stratification that still obtains today. But even though the social status of
the market in Yemeni society was lower than in other Arab lands, the country still
owed much to this institution. The great urbanization that took place in a society that
was so characterized by tribal associations and tribal laws was due above all to the
markets, which from an early period formed the nuclei from which urban settlements
grew.

San'a became great because its market was - and is - well situated geographically, within easy reach of the tribesmen in the Yemeni highlands. The members of the various tribes, peasants and warriors alike, vied with one another in their demand for high-quality material possessions - especially for weapons. This demand could only be met by full-time craftsmen and their dealers. At the same time the merchandise of the peasants and warriors - agricultural produce, or goods acquired by robbery - had to be sold to raise the necessary money or barter-goods for the craftsmen. In a society where blood feuds were common, such exchanges could only take place at a location controlled by an authority strong enough to enforce the truces between the peasants and warriors. Right from the start San'a, with its strong city walls and its citadel overlooking the marketplace, was a suitable meeting place. The prosperity of the city was shown in its magnificent tall town houses, whose owners also developed a distinctive sense for the decoration of their dwellings.

The most important link between the rural tribal society and the urban centre of the traders and craftsmen was the *samsarah*. This can be translated as 'caravanserai', but at San'a it was rather more than that. Like the caravanserais of the desert and steppes of the Near East and Central Asia, its primary function was to provide accommodation for travelling merchants, their servants, beasts of burden and merchandise. In San'a a samsarah generally belonged to the nearest mosque. The clergy thus had the opportunity to check the standard of faith of the Yemenis arriving from outside. In this way the place gained an almost sacred character, which in turn laid a great obligation on the tribesmen and their partners in the city to keep the peace. This made it possible for members of enemy tribes to visit the market of the capital at the same time. All participants could store the merchandise they had brought for sale or the goods bought in the market, and their animals in the samsarah, which functioned in addition as the state's collection point for taxes, duties and local fees.

The samsarah in San'a has not entirely lost these roles today; visiting traders and buyers still lodge in some of these massive buildings, together with their goods and means of transport. The samsarah remains the storehouse of the suq, the nearest mosque is still generally the owner of the enterprise, and the collector of sales tax and municipal fees still concentrates his activities here. The role that has faded away since the mid-1970's is that of neutral meeting place for deadly enemies. This became less pressing when the government managed to prohibit the bearing of arms in the cities of San'a, Ta'izz and Hudayda by law, thus removing the danger of serious clashes between supporters of rival or enemy tribes. The truces, which had been merely temporary (lasting the length of the visit), have gradually became permanent. They are disturbed today only by political assassinations and occasional shoot-outs in which power rivalries are sorted out against the background of traditional tribal law.

A samsarah has several storeys. On the ground floor are the warehouses and stables. The other storeys are divided between accommodation and storerooms, so that a trader coming from outside the city can sleep next to his merchandise. In most cases each storey is only accessible by its own staircase, so that the movement of goods can be controlled. At each entrance to a staircase there is a room for the guard, whose job is both to prevent theft and to collect any duty owing. Goods are taken to the shops in the market on the backs of bearers or on carts.

The market of San'a, unlike those in Damascus or Jerusalem, or part of the market in Cairo, is not roofed. Its narrow alleys are lined with shops, the great majority of which are windowless huts built of mud open to the street and closed with wooden shutters outside business hours. Most of the wares which used to be made here on the spot have been replaced by industrial products. This means that although the traditional crafts are in serious decline, the old market organization continues as before. Craftsmen and traders are organized in guilds, each of which has an alley, or several alleys, to itself. Just as in the old days, the guilds each elect a leader, and out of the committee of these leaders the *Sheikh as-Suq*, the 'Master of the Market', is appointed at regular intervals.

The finest representatives of traditional craftsmanship in San'a are the silversmiths. For centuries Yemeni silver jewellery was produced principally by Jews, who traditionally preferred crafts that left 'mouth and mind free for discussion of religious topics'; only a few Muslim families competed with them. However, when almost all the Yemeni Jews emigrated to Israel between 1948 and 1950, this old and highly developed craft was faced with extinction. The reigning Imam ordered that before they left the leading Jewish silversmiths had to train Muslim craftsmen. So while the departure of the Jews meant that the number of silversmiths shrank considerably, it did not mean that this, the most interesting form of Yemeni applied art, vanished altogether. In San'a market one can find half a dozen silversmiths who continue the tradition, though with limited means in poorly equipped workshops (see page 277ff.). In the same guild district are the traders offering silver jewellery in old or new styles. These traders specialize increasingly on business with foreigners. The rise in prices seems to have eased off since the 1980's because many Yemenis now prefer gold to silver jewellery.

Another traditional craft is practised by the makers of the Yemeni curved dagger, called the *jambiya* (pl. *janaabiya*). Since the dagger is still a status symbol for men in North Yemen, to the extent that the majority of male Yemenis between the ages of twelve and eighty want to own one, demand is always very great and the prices high. In fact the production of the blade and the hilt falls into two different processes, performed by two distinct groups of craftsmen. In the past iron ore was extracted and smelted in the north of Yemen, in and around Sa'da; but this home production has now almost ceased, and today imported steel, usually of poor quality, such as recycled leaf springs, is used to make the blades. In any case the most important parts of the jambiya are the hilt and sheath, which show the social status of the owner. A simple, 'popular' jambiya has a hilt and sheath made by the same craftsman, who also fits the hilt to the blade, but the finer pieces - those carried by tribal princes, the *sada*

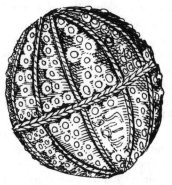

Yemeni silversmiths' work: a hollow ball for a decorative chain, and a finger ring

(religious aristocracy) and by rich merchants - are usually made by three craftsmen. The hilt of elaborately worked silver or carved horn, and the sheath, also made of worked silver, are each made by specialist craftsmen, and the third craftsman involved is the smith, who makes the blade, which even for these expensive pieces is still of inferior steel. For a really first-class jambiya there is also a fourth craftsman, the maker of the belt for strapping the dagger to. A good belt has a brocade cover and is decorated with ornaments, suggestive of calligraphy or a symmetrical pattern similar to those seen on the houses of San'a.

Yemeni craftsmanship also lives on in pottery, which is for sale in the market at San'a. It is not made in the capital, but produced in various parts of the country and conveyed there via the samsarah. There is a range of rustic utilitarian objects, which today are still much in demand among the Yemenis and may be of interest to foreign visitors. A number of different sorts of small vessels for burning frankincense and other fragrances on charcoal can be seen. These are either fired at high temperature and glazed, when they sometimes decorated with three-dimensional hens or cocks, or else fired at low temperature and then brightly painted. The ceramic parts of hookahs can also be bought in the pottery market. Beaked cups for tea and Yemen's national drink, *qishr* (a strongly spiced infusion made from the the husks of coffee beans), ashtrays and small bowls can be found mainly in pale green or light brown glazed pottery. Wherever there are potters offering their wares, the sellers of stone vessels and pans are not far away. These heavy cooking vessels are only used rarely today in Yemeni households; they used to be seen on food stalls in the country. Nevertheless there are still a few manufacturers of the vessels, each of which is hewn from a single piece of stone, mainly from the region around Sa'da in the north of the country.

Like all markets in the Near East, the suq at San'a offers an array of unusual basketwork. Reeds, palm fibres, cane and strong grasses are woven especially in the coastal plain, though they are for sale almost everywhere. Baskets and mats are much used in the spice market of San'a as containers and packing material. A comprehensive range of spices can be found in all the best suqs of the Near East, such as Damascus or Cairo, but San'a's market is richer still in some specialities. Husks of coffee beans (for qishr) from many sources are available, as is raw coffee. Qat, delivered fresh every day, is also bought by men, seldom by women. Out of the range of spices the following are worth mentioning for the visitor: fennel (*shumar*), thyme (*zatar*), cinnamon (*qirfah*), tamarind (*tamar hindi*), ginger (*zinjabil*), turmeric (*hurud*), pepper (*filfil*), cumin (*kamun*), cardamon (*heyl*), cloves (*zirr*) and fenugreek (*hilbah*). Also available is henna and frankincense (*buhur*) as well as many fragrances, essences of flowers and perfumes from India. Near the spice market are the streets where cereals, pulses, dried fruit, nuts and almonds are sold.

For most locals the central market with the alleys running off it is the most important place for shopping. All necessary food is available there, as well as clothes, utensils, weapons, household goods, raw materials and jewellery. The few modern shops in the New Town are aimed more at resident foreigners and well-to-do Yemenis who have acquired different lifestyles and consumer demands from living abroad.

The range of merchandise for sale in the traditional market is today dominated by Asian and European mass-produced goods. It sometimes worth looking out for products from China: some of the smaller items are sturdily made, and the beautiful and hard-wearing plain porcelain from the People's Republic is very good value.

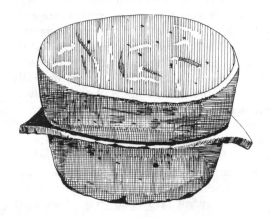

Stone cooking pot

Interior of a house in the Jewish Quarter, showing the different levels

Walks in San'a

Like many early travellers, Carl Rathjens and Hermann von Wissmann in the early 1930's compared the plan of San'a to a 'figure of eight stretching from west to east, with the ends five kilometres apart'. In the earliest aerial photographs, taken about 50 years ago, San'a is clearly recognizable as a slightly misshapen figure of eight. The eastern oval, its walls still complete, enclosed the whole of the Old Town, while the western oval, also walled, consisted of the former Turkish quarter, the Jewish quarter and other suburbs. The two parts of the figure of eight were held together by the palace area.

Since then - and particularly from the mid-1970's onwards - the appearance of the city has changed a good deal. The walls around the western oval have completely vanished, and only some sections of the wall of the Old Town are still standing. Of the four city gates of the Old Town noted by visitors in the 1930's, only one, the Bab al-Yemen, survives. The New Town, built partly of concrete, has fitted in at the narrow point where the two halves of the figure of eight meet. Around the two ovals new suburbs are springing up, but in these the traditional building methods still predominate.

At the approximate centre of today's city is the former palace district of al-Mutawakil, where the National Museum is located, from which there is an excellent view of the city. The former parade ground on the western edge of the palace district is now called Midan at-Tahrir, 'Liberation Square'. This is the departure point for city buses and shared taxis, and most hotels are not far away. Midan at-Tahrir will also be the starting point for our walks in San'a. The first of these takes us into the Old Town.

From Midan at-Tahrir through the Old Town to Bab al-Yemen
(about 4 hours)

From the square we cross the Sharia Abdul Moghni and taking one of the larger alleys running southwards we come first to the Vegetable Market (the Bab as-Sebah market named after a gate that stood here until its destruction earlier this century). After about 15 minutes we reach the Mahdi Abbas Mosque, built by Turkish architects around the turn of the 16th-17th century. At the mosque we reach the *saila*, a wide ditch that runs though the whole western side of the old town from south to north (colour plate 7). The saila only fills with water after heavy rain (*sail* means 'flood') and so hardly any bridges have been built across it; indeed it is even used as a thoroughfare for cars and carts. The only extant bridge was built, presumably for military purposes, by the Turkish governor after severe flooding in 1887, and was restored in 1968. It can be seen from the Mahdi Abbas Mosque, and we will cross it

Bab al-Yemen, rebuilt by the Turks in the 19th century

when we make our way eastwards further into the Old Town, but not before taking a walk up and down the bed of the saila, since here one has a clearer view of the façades of the houses than in the narrow alleys of the Old Town.

Continuing eastwards we come after about ten minutes to the Tulha Mosque. Through the narrow passages a few metres to the north of it one of the larger gardens of the city can be seen; San'a was once rich in gardens, but many were neglected during the drought of the mid-1980's. Returning to the Tulha Mosque, we continue in an easterly direction, and after a few minutes are in the middle of the Suq (Market). An hour or two should be allowed for a first exploration of the maze of cramped and narrow alleys. To find one's way out of the labyrinth of shops head directly southwards. The route passes the east side of San'a's main mosque, the Jami al-Kabir (Great Mosque). Like all the mosques in San'a (and throughout northern Yemen) this is not open to non-Muslims, except through the mediation of an influential local contact. Continuing straight on in a southerly direction we reach the Bab al-Yemen. Taxis can be found in the square in front of the gate, embellished with a fountain in the mid-1980's, and there is a tea house, near which, in Zubairi Street, is the bus station for Ta'izz and Aden. Those not yet exhausted by the walk, can take a stroll westwards along the city walls. After about ten minutes this route arrives at the south entrance of the saila, where there is another beautiful view of the Old Town.

San'a, cattle in a street in the old town

A fountain in Abdul-Moghni Street

A very similar tour can be made, again beginning at Midan at-Tahrir but this time turning south along the saila at the Mahdi Abbas Mosque. Once in sight of the walls, we turn east. As we enter the Old Town the Barum Mosque is on the left; after about five minutes there is a beautiful view through to the Abhar Mosque on the right of the street. Still continuing eastwards, we pass several magnificent town houses and finally reach Bab al-Yemen. With a bit of luck it should be possible to find, in the square on the inside of the gate, a working oil mill, where in a gloomy basement a blindfolded camel walks round and round a massive stone tub in which a heavy mill-stone on a wooden axle crushes oil-seed.

From Midan at-Tahrir to Bab Shaub and via al-Qasr to Bab al-Yemen
(about 4 hours)

Crossing the Sharia Abdul Moghni we leave the square and take the street heading directly eastwards to the Old Town. North of the Mahdi Abbas Mosque we come to the saila, which we follow northwards for about ten minutes before bearing to the northeast. We now pass through the northern part of the Old Town, which is mainly

Bab Shaub at the beginning of the century; the gate has since been destroyed (photograph by H. Burchardt)

a residential district, but still has many interesting houses and corners. After about 20 minutes we reach the Bab Shaub, a gate of which only the name remains. This is the departure point for shared taxis northwards, to Amran, Huss (also spelt Huth) and Saʿda. On reaching the site of the gate we can either follow the remains of the city walls in an arc southwards to the Qasr (Castle); or take the direct route to the south in the direction of Bab al-Yemen, turning off to the east half way to get to the Qasr. Either route will give a good idea of the oldest part of Sanʿa. This part of the city rises by about 15 m to the east at the foot of Nuqum (3000 m), the mountain that dominates Sanʿa. The Qasr is a few metres higher than its surroundings; some archaeologists conjecture that it was built on the heap of rubble from the Sabaeo-Himyarite castle of Gumdan. Extensively rebuilt by the Turks, the Qasr remains an obvious strategic strongpoint; it is still used by the military and is out of bounds for visitors. But this should not deter you from following the street that leads to it, since it passes the interesting Bakiliye Mosque and a well-preserved portion of the city walls. From the Qasr Bab al-Yemen is only a 15 minute walk to the southwest along the walls, but you can also go westwards through the residential district to the main market street, which runs directly southwards to Bab al-Yemen.

Visit to the Market

Anyone staying in San'a for any length of time will be able to get a good taste of the social structure of a traditional society and its arts and crafts by making one or more visits to the market. The best starting point for such a visit is the Bab al-Yemen, rebuilt by the Turks in the 1870's, and again after the damaging siege of 1911. For centuries, strangers could only enter San'a through the Bab al-Yemen, which was said to have protective powers: any ill-intentioned visitor would be instantly struck down as if by lightning. The present gate itself is in a Late Ottoman style that bears no relation to traditional Yemeni architecture, and is of no particular interest, but it is a good orientation point.

Women's window in the Ottoman style

From the square within the gate we first head directly northwards, before bearing right along an alley at the first fork. This alley also continues northwards; along its sides there are often hawkers selling pottery or basketwork. After about ten minutes we reach an outlying part of the spice market, and turn left to arrive at the square in front of the Ali Mosque. This is named after the Prophet's son-in-law, who is said to have stayed in a house on this site when he came to convert Yemen 'by both force and argument'. Daggers, watches, clothes and other merchandise are for sale here. We turn east at a right angle and take the narrow alley through the clothes market. After about five minutes we come to the silversmiths, whose work and wares form the most interesting part of the market.

If we turn left (i.e. west) at the Ali Mosque we arrive at the part of the market above the Great Mosque. We can then explore this area heading southwards, passing spice merchants, coppersmiths and ropemakers, until we reach the Great Mosque itself. The observant visitor will also spot the Samsarah al-Mizan, the 'Storehouse of the Scales', a massive brick building looming over the huddled market booths.

San'a, a bookseller with his son

San'a, market scene with containers for live chickens

From Midan at-Tahrir through the Turkish Quarter to Midan as-Solbi

The former Turkish Quarter of San'a forms the western oval of the 'figure of eight' described by Rathjens and Wissmann (page 94). The western town is in fact a conglomeration of several suburbs and in the last hundred years has become increasingly important. During this period it has seen three decisive changes. First the Turks began to develop the suburb of Bir al-Azab (Spring of the Sweet Waters) as a residential and administrative district for their civil servants and officers. (One interpretation of the name is 'Well of the Bachelors', appropriate since the Turkish soldiers stationed here were unmarried.) Then some sixty years later, around 1950, around 7,000 Jews left the Jewish Quarter of the western town for a new life in Israel. Lastly, since 1970 almost all the government buildings have been located here, and there are many new offices and business premises, including the first concrete high-rise buildings.

However, a walk from Midan at-Tahrir to Solbi (also known as Gorge) is worth making to see the houses built by the Turks around the turn of the century, in which their own architecture was happily combined with that of the Yemenis. From this there developed the modern architectural style that tradition-conscious Yemenis still choose today for their houses. It is a style that does not reject modern comforts, yet avoids faceless standardization. The Bir al-Azab quarter fell into decay at the end of the 1960's, until new prosperity in San'a made conservation and restoration possible.

The General Organization for Tourism used to have its headquarters in one of these beautiful houses of the Turkish period, a few minutes away from Midan at-Tahrir. Standing in the middle of the square, choose the middle one of the three streets running westwards. The house, which has a front garden, is on the western side of a small square which we pass on the left. On the solid substructure rise three storeys built in the modern San'a style, richly decorated with symmetrical ornaments above the windows. The garden is symptomatic of the Turkish taste - their houses in San'a often had a second mafraj overlooking a garden and fountains, and they planted many cypresses and other trees in the town (most now sadly gone). Another showpiece of the western town is the building known as the 'House of the Army Commander', built shortly after the turn of the century, which stands where Republican Palace Street turns into Gamal Abdul Nasser Street. Now the British Embassy, it is a wonderful mixture of Turkish and Yemeni architecture. From the Turks comes the strong substructure and the oriel windows in stone and wood, which were intended, in the tradition of the Ottoman harem, to allow the women to look out without themselves being seen. The brick upper part of the building is Yemeni. The over-windows on four storeys show almost the whole range of indigenous ornament dating back over millennia. If there is time, it is worth halting a while in front of this building to look at the details of the decoration through binoculars.

We now return to the alley through which we came to the former Tourist Corporation house. It continues westwards to Solbi. About halfway along, set back a little from the street front, stands a Turkish-Yemeni house once in royal ownership and now the offices of the local authority. This house too repays close inspection. Finally - if we are not staying there - we should visit the Dar al-Hamd Hotel. Once a prince's palace, this is located in the northern part of the western town and its exterior is a successful example of the further development of the Turkish-Yemeni style in the 20th century. The interior gives a good idea of how such rich Yemeni houses were organized.

Those interested in the recent history of Yemen and San'a should not miss a visit to the Military Museum on the south side of Gamal Abdul Nasser Street where it enters Midan at-Tahrir.

The former Jewish Quarter

West of Solbi is the **Ga al-Yahud**, the quarter where until the beginning of the 1950's between six and seven thousand Jews lived. Before the founding of the state of Israel North Yemen counted around fifty to sixty thousand Jews among its inhabitants

Jews in a San'a synagogue at the beginning of this century (photograph by H. Burchardt)

who, 'more than anyone else,' it has been written, 'preserved rabbinical Judaism familiar, to a certain extent, to the Christian reader from the New Testament'. Their services 'gave an impression of utmost antiquity, recalling Talmudic times'. 'This is a world centering round the synagogue, where simple people, craftsmen and labourers, are versed in religious lore and are able to follow arguments based on the Scriptures.' Yemeni Jews were also passionately interested in the ritual slaughter of animals and the reading and interpretation of their carcases. Their music was famous and remains an important heritage for Israel. This was a male society, however, and the women lived a secular life in Arabic alongside the men.

Several thousand Jews from Yemen settled in Palestine at the beginning of the century, and after Israel was established the remainder petitioned the Imam for permission to emigrate. Great difficulties had to be overcome before this section of the population, which was so important for the economy (an importance that had in the past kept the community in relative safety), was allowed to leave the country and head for Aden, then under British control, to fly on from there to Israel, in what was known as 'Operation Flying Carpet'. Their integration in Israel was not always easy. There was, for instance, the bizarre episode of the baby kidnaps, where Ashkenazi Jews bought Yemeni babies, famous for their beauty, having them spirited out of

101

hospitals. A little over a hundred Jewish families remained behind in Yemen; they live in a village near the town of Sa'da and in other small villages on the plateau. In 1985 the unofficial estimate for the Jewish population in North Yemen was 6,300, but in San'a there are now no Jews at all. The district where they lived, which was granted to them in 1680 on their return after their temporary expulsion from San'a (before then they lived among the Muslims in the Old Town) stood neglected for a few years. But now it is again fully populated, by Yemenis and foreigners.

A short perambulation through the very narrow maze of alleys of the former Jewish Quarter is worthwhile only if you happen to be in the vicinity, since the exteriors of the low houses of this district, built close together and hidden by the outer walls, are not particularly rewarding. An excursion to 'Ga', as they say in San'a, is of interest, however, if one of the inhabitants will show you inside his house. The Jews' houses, which appear so inconspicuous from the outside - a tyrannical imam in 1761 destroyed all the synagogues and houses over 9 m high and ordered that henceforth no Jewish house could be any taller- conceal in their interiors a high level of architecture and interior design. A well-built house in the Jewish Quarter will as a rule be arranged around an inner courtyard (see illustration page 93). Since they could not build upwards, the Jews went downwards, that is, the Jewish house, unlike the Arab one, has a basement, which is often very deep. This basement, which usually has emergency exits connecting with neighbouring land, was a place of refuge in time of danger. It was also used as a storeroom for wine and brandy, which the Jews were permitted to make - for their own consumption only of course. Often the master's workshop, if he was, for instance, a silversmith, was also located in the basement. The living rooms and bedrooms on the three upper floors are - in comparison with the usual San'a house - strikingly low, because of the restrictions placed on Jewish building. The height of each room was calculated individually depending on its purpose, so that in houses in 'Ga' each storey will have rooms at various different levels. Often the interiors have plasterwork decoration and upper windows, with ornaments made with more care and variety than in the Arab houses. Outwardly, however, the Jewish house shows no decorations at all; the splendour of the Jewish houses is supposed to have been the reason for the expulsion of the Jews from the Old Town in 1679 and their year-long exile in the unhealthy climate of the lowland town of Muza.

The narrow alleys of the former Jewish Quarter are very lively even today, but the life has changed since the departure of the Jews. What it used to be like can be guessed from this description by Rathjens and Wissmann, writing in the early 1930's:

'The Jewish Town is only the quarter where the Jews live, though they are otherwise able to move freely anywhere in the city and have property, workshops and shops everywhere. The Jews are immediately recognizable by their dress. The men wear a small black cap and hanging from their temples to their shoulders are curled sidelocks; for the rest they wear a dark blue or black kaftan-like shirt reaching down to the feet. Over their shoulder or on their head they carry a black cloth folded together in which they can carry burdens as in a sack. The women and girls are quite unveiled. Their faces are framed with a hood decorated with silver embroidery and beads, their dress is dark blue and over it they wear a cloth patterned with white dots and stripes. Regular, indeed beautiful, facial features are frequent with a relatively light complexion. They are are very full of the joys of life and enjoy celebrating festivals, in which their very good wine and raki-like spirits play an important part. They are the most skilful craftsmen and live in prosperity and the greatest cleanliness. A dense swarm of people prevails in the narrow alleys all day, particularly in front of the synagogues, called *kanissa*, which are immediately recognizable by their bright whitewashed walls. Economically and culturally they do not suffer under the present imam, but for religious reasons they have a lower social standing.'

San'a - towards the year 2000

In the early 1980's it seemed as if the architectural gem that is old San'a was beyond saving. The city was then experiencing a building boom, to cope with the sudden four-fold increase in population. Anyone who had made any money built a new house on the far edge of the city. The sons of rich citizens no longer necessarily wanted to start a family of their own in the ancestral house of the extended family. The prosperous increasingly turned their backs on the Old Town. Often only the elderly and those without enough money to move stayed behind in the outwardly magnificent but uncomfortable traditional houses. Impoverishment seemed inevitable. But then the prices of building land and building work increased enormously, and the prospect of returning to old San'a began to seem attractive as people began to invest in traditional architecture again.

In the 1990's the Old Town will not only be restored in the proper sense of the word; that is to say people are not content simply with improving the sanitation system introduced in the last decade, paving more streets, consolidating the old buildings, and restoring individual houses and warehouses (samsarah). More ambitious schemes to beautify old San'a can also be seen. Whether the outcome will be entirely happy remains to be seen.

On the southern edge of the Old Town, from the saila to Bab al-Yemen, the historic defensive walls of mud and stone are being restored, and a paved road has been created in the saila in front of the walls. But there is a danger that the open space made here will remain as a rubbish heap. The overall appearance of the city has suffered a number of intrusions, such as the gigantic new building of the Ministry of Telecommunications and Post, northwest of Midan at-Tahrir, which is now complete. It overshadows the 'Turkish Town', which previously was only sparsely built over on the edge of the historic city, but at least the principle has been established of placing all large-scale buildings only at the periphery of the city. One slight

San'a, restoration work on the old city wall in 1992

comfort is that the telecommunications tower uses elements of the traditional architectural style.

Weak points in the city's infrastructure remain the reserves of drinking water and the sewage system, rubbish disposal and traffic control. But energetic measures have a prospect of success. Although at present San'a has almost a million inhabitants, twenty times the population at the beginning of the revolution in 1962, it must be remembered that it is not the only attractive urban centre in the country. Of Yemen's population 78% still live in farming settlements, 12% in other cities and towns, and only 10% in San'a itself.

The National Museum

In September 1987 the National Museum was moved from Dar ash-Shukr (House of Thanks) to the larger Dar as-Saad (House of Happiness) in the palace district of al-Mutawakil. Its new home is a thoroughly renovated palace erected in the 1930's in the traditional style, situated only a few hundred metres north of the old one and is approached through a stone gateway from Abdul Moghni Street. A number of exhibits have been added, but the most important thing is that the collection of antiquities, which is still modest in size, has recently been rearranged in a much larger space. The history of Yemen, from the early period around 3000 years ago, through Islamicization in the 7th century and up to the present day, is fully documented; photographs are shown where there are no suitable exhibits in the collection.

In the entrance hall the visitor is greeted by the over-life-size bronze statues of Himyarite tribal kings, reconstructed from many fragments during five years' restoration work in Mainz. These figures of kings dating from the end of the 3rd century BC are considered classic examples of the mixed Graeco-Romano and South Arabian culture in the period around the birth of Christ. They are exhibited with documentation which includes photographs of Greek and Roman statues virtually indistinguishable from the South Arabian figures; indeed the only identifying characteristic is the inscription in Sabaeo-Himyarite characters. Thanks to this we know that King Damar alay Yuhabir and his son Tharan donated these figure to three men of the family of Daranih for the entrance hall of their palace.

Statue of a Hellenistic ruler

These royal Himyarite figures are evidence not only of the range of cultural migrations and the strength of reciprocal cultural interpenetration, but also of the extraordinary scope of modern restoration techniques. Instead of simply reassembling the fragments of the figures, the Mainz restorers made casts of the individual pieces, which were used to make new moulds, from which the present figures were made. The original fragments are displayed next to the reconstructed figures of the kings.

Old South Arabian art, predominantly from the five centuries before Christ, is to be seen on the first floor. One of the oldest pieces must be the weathered image of a goddess found at Jawf al-Baydah, dated to around the 5th century BC. Its rarity lies partly in the fact that it is made of wood; very few wooden pieces have survived the millennia.

Another piece worthy of particular attention, because of its good state of preservation and fine detailing, is the bronze statue of a walking man (see illustration on page 46). According to the inscription he is Ma'adkarib, who

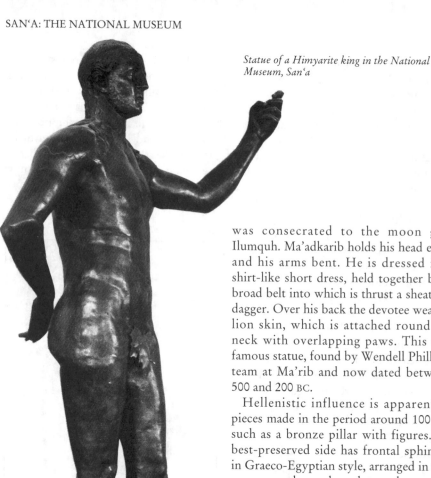

Statue of a Himyarite king in the National Museum, San'a

was consecrated to the moon god Ilumquh. Ma'adkarib holds his head erect and his arms bent. He is dressed in a shirt-like short dress, held together by a broad belt into which is thrust a sheathed dagger. Over his back the devotee wears a lion skin, which is attached round his neck with overlapping paws. This is a famous statue, found by Wendell Phillip's team at Ma'rib and now dated between 500 and 200 BC.

Hellenistic influence is apparent in pieces made in the period around 100 BC, such as a bronze pillar with figures. Its best-preserved side has frontal sphinxes in Graeco-Egyptian style, arranged in five rows one above the other and sporting necklaces or pectoral jewellery. At the corner is a vertical pictorial strip with recumbent ibexes, the truly Arabian animal. Also attributable to the mixed culture is the fragment of a revetment panel with a Hellenistic meander strip below which is a fabulous beast, half-horse and half-dragon. More genuinely Yemeni, again, are the friezes with ibex heads. These are architectural elements, probably cresting for walls.

Thousands of inscriptions engraved in stone, set on cliff walls or cast in bronze, bear witness to the culture of pre-Islamic Yemen. Some of the stone and bronze inscriptions are to be found in the National Museum.

The first floor also houses a sub-section with finds from the region of the kingdom of Ma'in (al-Jawf), which includes a collection of coins covering the Himyarite period.

The second floor now contains the Islamic department, which given more investment could soon realize its potential. For the moment it contains only historic weapons, copper and bronze vessels with chased decoration, and a collection of coins. An interesting photographic display documents the restoration of the 16th-century Amariya Mosque at Rada (colour plate 13), but this might remain on display only for as long as the restoration work continues.

Dar as-Saad ('House of Happiness'), formerly a prince's palace, now the National Museum

Fragment of wall revetment, in Dar as-Saad

107

Around San'a

Yemen's capital stands on a plateau about 80 km long and in places 20 km wide. Seasonal rainfall and artificial irrigation using wells make the region very fertile. In the sheltered valleys there is high-quality fruit production; grapes, apricots, quinces, peaches, lemons, oranges, almonds, figs and walnuts are only a few of the crops grown here, together, of course, with qat.

This densely populated plateau is an example of an integrated landscape of cultivation and settlement. The towns and villages can be either surrounded by walls or else open land settlements with a gradual transition from the village centre to the open fields, interrupted by a few houses. Most of the old houses rise up like towers and are variously rectangular or round. They have four or five storeys and their outer walls are not as articulated as in San'a. It is a typical feature of the houses in the countryside that they almost always have just one door and a few loophole-like windows. The building material used in the countryside was stone or - depending on the local conditions - unfired mud bricks. Bricks are also used for houses in a few villages.

Although San'a and the villages of the plateau belong to the same cultivated landscape, there are considerable differences between the inhabitants of the capital and those of the country towns and villages. From the second period of Turkish rule (1871-1919) San'a developed such a strong economy and high level of culture that the tribal ties of its permanent inhabitants began to loosen and in many cases to dissolve completely. In the countryside such ties have remained to a considerable extent, and the further away one gets from San'a the more strongly they can be felt. In practice this means that in the countryside one has to observe the rules and customs of Islamic society. Although a stranger cannot of course possess a comprehensive knowledge of such social rules, a modicum of attention paid to local manners will make travelling safer and one's presence more welcome.

It is advisable in meetings with local people in villages or in the open countryside to show polite reserve; before reaching for your camera you should exchange greetings. You should not disregard the division of the sexes that is usual in many eating places in the countryside; often in restaurants foreign women are directed to the room provided for female travellers. If you can show that you are able to eat your meal using only your right hand (the left hand is considered unclean) your skill will

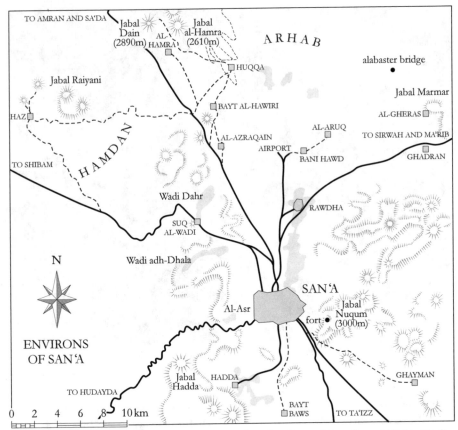

Sketch plan of the immediate environs of San'a, including the villages of Rawdha and Hadda, Wadi Dahr and the ruins of Huqqa

be much appreciated. The dress code does not require that strangers dress as if they were Muslims, but to gain the respect of the local people and for your own safety it is advisable to be more decent and covered-up than is customary in the West.

Suggested Excursions

In the immediate vicinity of San'a there are several interesting destinations which should be visited by the independent traveller: these trips are a good way of getting accustomed to travelling in Yemen. If you have enough time you should use a shared taxi; it is the customary mode of travel in the country and the cheapest.

Rawdha, street trader with parasol

Rawdha, melons from Wadi Dahr

For Rawdha and Hadda half-day excursions are sufficient. Rawdha (departure from Midan at-Tahrir) is 10 km north of San'a, about halfway to the airport; in a few years the town will have become an outer suburb of the capital. Hadda (departure from Bab al-Yemen) is about 10 km southwest of San'a and with its garden restaurants and orchards as well as a nearby grand hotel it has developed into a popular destination for the more westernized locals.

At **Rawdha** the traveller alights in front of the Mosque of Ahmad Ibn al-Qasim, which is built in the Arab style and dates from the 17th century. Its almost square courtyard is surrounded by porticos with pillars, and the outer walls are richly decorated with plaster ornaments. With a little luck you can get permission to look round (though not on Fridays and festivals). But even if you only see the outside the mosque is worth visiting for a close look at the minaret, which is built of fired bricks and adorned partly with inscriptions but mainly with geometric ornaments.

Just 50 m or so to the right of the mosque stands the Rawdha Palace Hotel. This was one of the summer palaces of the royal family. Like the Dar al-Hamd Hotel in San'a the princely residence had been converted to provide tourist accommodation,

Bakery in Rawdha

and is a good opportunity to observe Yemeni tastes in the arrangement of rooms and interior decoration. It is also worth going out on the hotel's flat roof to take in the view over the village and across the plateau.

A tour of Rawdha provides the opportunity to discover a few beautiful residential castles in the old rural style. As well as these the village also has a public steam bath (*hammam*) dating from the Turkish period. It is sunk into the earth so that only the domes - typical of Turkish baths - protrude.

Hadda offers tempting walks on lanes running between the mud walls of its orchards. The terrain slopes up in the direction of the Jabal Hadda and a brook springs from the foothills of the mountain. Its water is fed through a network of little canals to the orchards. The paths are shaded by great walnut trees. The attractive hilltop village of **Bayt Baws**, 7 km from Hadda, is also a popular destination for excursions from San'a.

A visit to **Wadi Dahr**, about 16 km northwest of San'a (departure from Midan at-Tahrir) is worth a whole day, since the valley and the adjoining wadis are suitable for longish walks. You should arrange to be dropped off above the wadi, which is buried

View of the valley bottom from the southern edge of Wadi Dahr

deep between sandstone cliffs, for a view across from the western or southern edge of the valley. The varied red and brown hues of the sandstone form a remarkable contrast with the green of the orchards, especially in spring, when there is also the white, red and yellow of the blossoms.

The descent is made by a road that winds down to the very bottom of the valley, where the former summer residence of Imam Yahya (1904-48), built in the 1930's, dominates the village of Suq al-Wadi. The hero of the struggle against the Ottoman Turks, Yahya consolidated the hold of Zaydi Islam over the Yemen, ruling the country with a firmness befitting a medieval autocrat. The house itself is impressive and made more so by being built on top of a steep rock formation; today it is used frequently as a guest house or conference venue by the government, but for a gratuity it may be visited when not in use. There are richly traceried windows and a magnificent view. From the summer residence you can take a long walk along the eastern cliff wall northwards, following the course of the riverbed, which usually contains only a little water. The way back passes along lanes between orchards.

Above the summer residence on the western cliff stand the ruins of a fort from the

Hajja, provincial capital in the High Yemen northwest of San'a

Turkish period, which seems to have incorporated the remains of an important Himyarite castle. Caves can also be seen, at a considerable height along the narrow cleft in the valley. These have been used - possibly from prehistoric times - as dwellings, and also as tombs. Nearby there are rock engravings of ibexes, leopards and dogs, dominated by the figure of a deity over 2 m high. The engravings have not yet been properly analysed by scholars, but it has been suggested that are the work of people who were living in Wadi Dahr about 6000 years BC. From the rock engravings it is not far to the remains of a sacrificial site, with steps hewn in the rock and ritual basins.

It is also worth setting aside a whole day for an excursion to the market town of **Amran** (departure from Bab Shaub), about 50 km north of San'a, west of the main road to Sa'da. This is an Islamic Yemeni town still completely surrounded by its defensive ramparts. A tour outside as well as inside the walls is recommended. The

Rawdha, view over gardens and houses ▷

113

big inner gate to the town has stelae and architraves with Himyarite inscriptions and symbols built into it. Some of the older houses in Amran also shelter such stones; with patience and luck - and perhaps the help of someone with local knowledge - you should be able to find them.

Amran has a market on Friday; in other words the main commercial event of the week coincides with the Islamic weekly holiday, and the town then has a particularly large number of visitors. Although the goods for sale are hardly any different from those found at other highland markets, a visit to Amran should be timed to fall on a market day for the experience of seeing a small Yemeni town fulfil its original function as a meeting place and commercial nexus for all the traditional elements of what is essentially still a tribal society. Peasant farmers and merchants, with their customers, the tribal politicians and warriors will all be here, as well as the craftsmen themselves. Craftsmen, however, are tied to their locality and have a low social status.

Shortly before Amran the new road forks off to the left towards Huqqa. The town is a 65 km drive from here, but the journey is worth making because it takes you - in comfort - through a model Yemeni landscape: rich cultivated terraces, defensive towers, mountain lairs to the right and left of the road, as well as many magnificent distant views.

Whichever route to **Huqqa** is taken, however, travellers should find out in San'a beforehand about the advisability of visiting the town, since for a time in the 1980's its inhabitants began to show some resentment at the tourist invasion.

The village of Bayt al-Huqqa, where the houses are built up of volcanic rock, is only about 23 km from San'a, but lies beyond the San'a-Sa'da road and so on this route can only be reached by four-wheel-drive vehicles. Setting off from the city centre you first head for 18 km in the direction of Amran before turning off on a track to the northeast. After the road junction you make straight for a mountain shaped like a bedouin tent. Before the eastern foothills of the mountain lies a village with striking blue and green houses. Leaving the village on your left-hand side you take one of the tracks heading eastwards. It leads to a flat elevation from which you can see Huqqa on a distant plateau, recognizable by a white dome at its southern end.

In Huqqa the two German scholars, Rathjens and Wissmann, were able in 1928 to carry out one of the archaeological excavations that have been so rare in Yemen, during which they found a temple and uncovered its remains. The best individual finds went to the collection of the National Museum in San'a, while the temple foundations were partly reconstructed. This reconstruction, however, was short-lived: scarcely had the two Germans left than the royal family ordered further digging in the same area, presumably in search of treasure. In the course of this enterprise the building stones of the temple were scattered and gradually disappeared. Rathjens and Wissmann left us a reconstruction drawing (see page 19), which shows that the temple was a complex of buildings grouped around a rectangular courtyard lined with colonnades on three sides. Beneath the foundations of the temple lies a great cistern, which you can look into today through cracks in the roof.

Today a visit to Huqqa is worthwhile only because of the many spolia built into the houses, which include some good examples. Several of the small boys in the village, with whom one should get on good terms from the start, are in the habit of showing strangers the ancient architectural elements: inscriptions, sacrificial stones, column bases or capitals.

Another rewarding day excursion from San'a (departure from Bab al-Yemen) takes us to the towns of **Shibam/ Kawkaban** and Thula. The first two are 36 km northwest of the capital. Shibam (there are several places with this name in South Arabia) stands at the foot of a steep cliff wall; Kawkaban is on the peak of the mountain above the cliff, some 350 m further up (colour plates 41 and 42). Recently it has been possible to reach Kawkaban by car on a paved road; those on foot

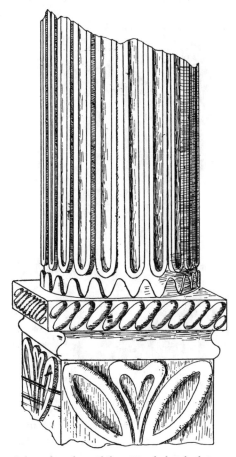

Column base from Shibam/Kawkaban built into a shop in the market

and camel or donkey caravans will need about an hour to climb the not excessively steep, but narrow and very winding path between the two towns. With its bushes, flowers and narrow shady passes this attractive walk provides many beautiful views of Shibam and the plain of San'a below. (Some of the most interesting birds in Yemen can be spotted here; see page 273.) Kawkaban itself is a half-deserted town (like Ma'rib, it was exposed to heavy air attacks during the civil war) but it demonstrates how no peak is too high and no site too inaccessible for a Yemeni village. Kawkaban was the refuge of the people of Shibam and still has the feel of a fortress.

The mosque in Shibam is one of earliest in Yemen. It was built about 1000 years ago on the foundations of a Himyarite temple and contains numerous columns and

Na'it, remains of the Temple of Talab

other architectural elements from the ancient religious building.

From Shibam and Kawkaban to **Thula** (colour plate 26) is about 10 km and you will easily find someone to give you a lift. However, since the landscape and climate are very suitable for walking, you should go at least part of the way on foot (the track ends at Thula).

Whereas Sa'da in the north is the ideal of a traditional Islamic city of mud construction, Thula is an example of early Islamic town building in hewn stone. The little town has a complete system of defences with parapet walls, towers, cisterns and underground passages. Just as Shibam has Kawkaban, so Thula also has a fortress hill. The ascent is shorter (about 30 minutes), though in places steeper than the one up to Kawkaban. But it is worth the effort for the Himyarite defence system that has survived on the summit. There is also a bird's-eye view of Thula with its cisterns (also dating from the Himyarite period), and views over the country to distant horizons (see illustration page 123)

The village of **Hababa** 2 km beyond Thula also has interesting stone architecture. A unique feature is the beautiful water basin in the main square, which gives the village centre a special charm. A 10 minute drive (half-hour walk) from Hababa brings us to **Zakati**. This village takes its name from the *zakat*, an annual tax paid to the Imam; it is famous for its fortified samsarah (caravanserai).

After another 30 minute drive (or 3 hours on foot) we come to the beautiful tiny village of **Bukur**, which has spectacular views.

Na'it lies about 40 km north of San'a, east of the road to Sa'da. It can be reached from Rayda or by the extension of the San'a airport road, but both these routes are suitable for four-wheel-drive vehicles only. The village should only be visited in small groups and with a guide who knows the area.

The landscape of High Yemen northwest of San'a, near Kawkaban

119

Manakha, view of the town centre

Na'it has great archaeological importance. On the edge of the volcanic landscape of Arhab it stands partly on the remains of the ancient city of the same name. From the field of debris rise two monolithic pillars like those in the Ma'rib region. These are part of a temple area recently identified (by Professor Walter W. Müller) as sacred to the moon god Ta'lab. All around are the foundations of religious buildings, carved marble and alabaster fragments, cisterns, and potsherds in great quantities; you can wander over hills that clearly consist of the debris of up to two and a half millennia. A comprehensive excavation would certainly produce results, but hitherto the watchful inhabitants - whose company you will certainly have - have blocked any systematic field research. A few small excavations are however undertaken by the owners of pieces of land. What happens to the finds is not known, though many spolia can be seen in the walls of the houses.

Somewhat below Na'it and to the west is a famous ancient cistern often illustrated on postcards. It is about 65 m long, has a basin for ablutions, and is still used occasionally to supply water to the village. From here it is an hour's walk to the hilltop village of **Zafar** (not to be confused with Zafar near Yarim) with ruined fortifications

Hajarah, fortified house fronts

and palaces covering a vast area. This was an important town in the 13th century.

Manakha (departure from Bab al-Yemen by bus or taxi) can also be visited from San'a by following the 'Turkish Road', consolidated in the 1960's by Chinese aid , for 70 km. At the village of Magraba on the road a turning on the left leads south to Manakha. Shared taxis and motorcycle-taxis wait at the junction to provide a shuttle service. The drive takes about 10 minutes, the walk about an hour.

Manakha is a mountain town at an altitude of 2200 m and is the urban centre of the 'Fertile Mountains', the Haraz Mountains, the highest point of which is Jabal Shibam (3000 m). Agriculture is practised here more intensively than in other places in North Yemen. The produce is sold at Manakha which in turn supplies the surrounding villages with services and luxury goods.

The town is also the starting point for some beautiful walks in the Haraz Mountains. About 7 km from the provincial capital are a number of villages whose inhabitants - around 7000 people - are Ismailis. The Tayyibi branch of this Shi'ite sect, to which most Yemeni Ismailis belong, is not connected with the Eastern

121

Dhi Bin: view of the ancient cistern

Ismailis who are followers of the Aga Khan. (Most Ismailis in Haraz belong to the Sulaymani sub-sect, whose *da'i, or* leader, is based at Najran; the rest are Dawudis, led by a da'i in Gujarat in India.) Their separation from the mainstream of Islam has made the Yemeni Ismailis an industrious community who define their place in Yemeni society through hard work. Nowhere else in Yemen are the terraced fields so carefully built and the house façades so lovingly decorated as in these villages.

A footpath runs from Manakha to **Hajarah**. This fortified village lies to the west of Manakha at about 2300 m, and can be reached in about an hour by a dusty track. Just before reaching Hajarah the track turns off southwards where the fertile Wadi Houzan begins.

A trip to **Dhi Bin**, a town about 40 km northeast of Rayda, is strongly recommended. From Rayda (San'a-Sa'da road, 82 km) a four-wheel-drive vehicle is necessary. To see the ancient and beautiful mosque of al-Mansur near Dhi Bin, you will probably have to consider staying the night (tent or simple inn).

From Rayda you are on the track that runs to the upper course of the Wadi al-Jawf. West of the track there are various little villages in which Yemeni Jews still live. The journey through this region is very impressive and makes clear how arduous agriculture can be in Yemen: all the fields have been scratched out from beneath a covering of dark brown or black lava scree. The stones have been used either in the walls supporting the terraces as windbreaks, or for pillars to support the vines. It seems that the topsoil is often brought from far away and tipped onto the field framed by stones. It is hardly surprising that grapes cost about $5 a kilo in Amran market.

Dhi Bin is an interesting village with fortress-like houses built of multicoloured lava. In front of its small mosque is an enormous cistern dating from the Himyarite period. It is still used today to supply water to houses here. The principle tourist sight in the region is the mosque, dating from the 13th century AD, which stands on a high mountain. To get to it continue a little further on the track towards Wadi al-Jawf and then turn north. This brings you to the back of the hill and the minaret will

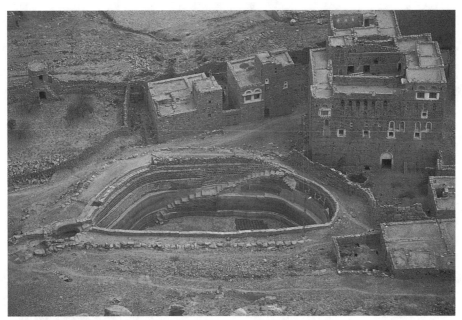

View of an ancient cistern (Thula)

already be visible. A lone farmstead is the starting point for an ascent (500 m) up a scree-covered slope. The walk to the top of the mountain takes about an hour.

Awaiting you at the top are the remains of a castle supposed to have been built in the Rassulid period. The first Rassulid ruler, Umar Ibn Rassul, came to Yemen in about 1210 as the vizier and army commander of the sultan Saladin (Salah ad-Din), then ruling in Cairo and Damascus. In 1229 he assumed the title 'al-Mansur' ('the victorious' or 'aided by God') and made himself independent. Zaydi authority was at that time restricted to the high north, with its centre at Sa'da. From Ta'izz the dynasty founded by Umar Ibn Rassul ruled the greater part of mountainous Yemen, including San'a and Dhi Bin, where Sultan al-Mansur left a funerary mosque remarkable for its carved and painted coffered ceiling and its walls richly decorated with ornaments. Part of the ceiling has fallen in, but UNESCO has promised to restore it and as a first step has built a corrugated-iron protective structure over what is still there The guardian lets tourists in for a fee. As well as the ceiling and wall decoration, there is the grand stone sarcophagus of Umar Ibn Rassul with its rich ornament. The mosque's brick minaret is also finely decorated with lozenges and bands of bricks with coloured glazes.

Zabid

Though it was once the capital of the first independent Islamic Yemen, Zabid today is not even a provincial capital, but only the administrative centre of a district. A little town, it lies about halfway on the well-constructed road from Ta'izz to the provincial capital Hudayda. Apart from its historical importance, it is an ideal centre for visiting the coastal plain, which has a character entirely distinct from the rest of Yemen.

This coastal plain - called the Tihama, which means 'hot earth' - stretches for more than 450 km between the sea and the mountains, from Bab al-Mandab northwards to the frontier with Saudi Arabia. It is 30 to 45 km wide, and very important as an agricultural region. During the rainy season clouds driven here from Africa deposit most of their rain over the western foothills of the Yemeni central massif. The annual rainfall in the hot coastal lowlands correspondingly increases as one approaches the mountains, from about 50 to 500 mm. Rain falls mostly as heavy storms, however, so that precipitation varies considerably from place to place and year to year; rain-irrigated cultivation is possible only in good years. After heavy rainfalls millet is sown even in what appear to be unpromising sandy soils, and the harvest can be gathered after only one or two months. In years with low rainfall cultivation is restricted to the margins of the wadis running down from the mountains. Here river-basin irrigation, as practised in ancient Egypt, is used. After heavy downpours, when the wadis carry water for a short time, it is diverted by banks of earth into a system of canals and fields. A single thorough drenching of the soil is usually enough for a whole harvest of millet. Just at the edge of the mountain range the wadis carry water for longer, so date palms, subtropical fruit and vegetables can also be grown.

In the western flat land there are now increasing numbers of grand projects involving pump-fed irrigation. Cotton, lucerne, tobacco, tomatoes and vegetables are the most important products of such industrial agriculture in the Tihama. With the area available many more such projects could be launched here, but there is the danger that the water table will drop too far and salt water from the sea will seep in.

Two million of Yemen's approximately 14 million inhabitants live in the Tihama. The peculiarities of the region have left their mark on its people, making them clearly different from the highlanders. The flat coastal strip was always much more difficult to defend against intruders than the mountain massif, so it is hardly surprising that

African influences are discernible almost everywhere in the Tihama - in the outward appearance, in the dress, attitude and customs (such as public circumcision) of the people as well as in their tools and houses. The marked mingling with African ethnic groups can in part be traced back to the slave trade, which continued in Yemen into the present century. In the early millennia whole tribes certainly crossed the Red Sea between Africa and Arabia. It has therefore been assumed that the dark-skinned people of the Saranik tribes, the largest tribal federation of the Tihama, were the earliest inhabitants of the region, but in fact it is not clear whether they first lived on the Arabian or African side of the Red Sea.

The inhabitants of the coastal strip were under foreign rule more frequently and for longer periods than the mountain people. The Ottoman Empire, which twice ruled Yemen, first established its authority in the coastal plain and only much later in the highlands; Mamluks, Arab sects, the Egyptians, and even the Portuguese and Italians all sought the Tihama. When from the 16th century onwards Yemen became a trading partner again as the supplier of coffee to Europe and Asia, the Tihama port of Mokha (also spelt Mocha, Mucha and Mokka) became a meeting place for foreign traders and the local inhabitants. It was partly through these contacts in the Tihama that the interest of the West in the exploration of Yemen was aroused.

The influence of Mecca and Medina, which had been at work in the Tihama since the early period of Islam, in combination with the equally important influence of the authorities in Cairo, resulted in a religious split from highland Yemen. While the people of the mountains followed their distinctive Zaydi brand of Islam (see page 291), the inhabitants of the Tihama continued to adhere to the mainstream Sunni branch of the faith. Of the schools of this branch the one that predominates among Sunnis of Yemen is the Shafi'ite; it has been estimated that 30-35% of the inhabitants

Aga (commander of a large unit of troops) in the Ottoman army

125

Landscape in the foothills towards the Tihama

of Yemen are Shafi'ites (so called after the Islamic legal scholar ash-Shafi'i, AD 767-820). Together with Ta'izz province the Tihama is a stronghold of this Sunni school. Since its understanding of the law includes absolute acknowledgement of the established state power, rulers have always found the coastal strip easy to govern. Religious disputes, in particular theological interpretations of the law, are still decided by the Islamic al-Azhar University in Cairo.

There was once a famous Islamic university in the Tihama itself, located in Zabid and drawing students from many Arab lands; it has been claimed as the birthplace of algebra. The town of Zabid is supposed to have been founded in 819 by Muhammad Ibn Ziyad, who was also the founder of a dynasty. From 821 Ibn Ziyad ruled large parts of Yemen from Zabid. He should be regarded as the first Islamic Yemeni national ruler since he obtained a large degree of independence, and even some formal recognition from the caliph (Muhammad's successor as leader of the faithful) in Baghdad, which was then the centre of Islamic power. For around 200 years the Ziyad princes steered the destiny of the coastal strip. During this period Zabid became a centre of Shafi'ite learning, and even after the Ziyad dynasty came to an end in 1012, the city still remained authoritative for Shafi'ites in other countries. For almost 500 years princes of various houses followed one another, many ruling from other places - but the reputation of the Islamic university of Zabid continued to grow. The last Sunni ruler, Ahmad at-Tahir, was at first able to extend his influence over the greater part of present-day Yemen, but he then came into conflict with the Mamluks operating from Egypt, who finally overthrew him and occupied several towns. Zabid was one of the places which the Mamluks chose to hold, until towards the end of 1538 the Ottoman commander Süleyman Pasha landed at Mokha. Zabid was taken a few days later after short-lived resistance. Soon afterwards the whole of the Tihama was in the hands of the Turks and their auxiliaries.

Incorporation into the Ottoman Empire put a stop to the attempts of the Portuguese to establish themselves in the Tihama (though in 1551 Aden came for a short time under Portuguese rule). The highlands, on the other hand, caused the Turks much greater problems. It was to be eight years before they managed to capture San'a. The Ottoman governor split his territory into two administrative units: the mountain region, ruled from San'a, and the coastal region, ruled from Zabid. Within 20 years Zabid alone remained a centre of Ottoman power, the Imam having seized back the mountain region. From 1569 to 1607 the Turks -

Coastal Arabs with a Wahhabi (left) (19th-century engraving)

using the Tihama as their base - won back parts of the mountain region. But the series of uprisings left their forces so exhausted that they withdrew in 1625 and Yemen became the first Arab state to achieve independence from the Ottoman Empire.

In the 19th century the Tihama again became the scene of conflict between foreign powers. First came the Wahhabis, supporters of a puritanical Islamic teaching which had emerged at the end of the 18th century from central Asia and created an empire. They advanced first to Mecca, Medina and Jeddah, then south as far as the port of Mokha. The Imam of Yemen called on the Egyptians for help against these intruders. The leader in Cairo at that time was the former Turkish officer Muhammad Ali, who was himself dreaming of creating an empire. In 1819 he sent troops to Yemen and they occupied several ports as well as Zabid. Muhammad Ali's soldiers remained in the Tihama for more than twenty years before British pressure forced their withdrawal. The Turks tried again only a few years later: in 1849 a small expeditionary force arrived overland and was able to conquer Hudayda and later San'a. Yemeni resistance forced the Turks to vacate San'a again, but they left a small contingent of troops in the Tihama. It stayed there until in 1872 a whole army arrived and was able to conquer North Yemen again for the Ottoman Empire. Nevertheless Turkish rule over the next 47 years was relatively secure only in the coastal plain; in the mountains there was continuous resistance which from time to time flared up into open rebellion. On several occasions the Turks had to withdraw from San'a and other towns.

Loheya, Egyptian-influenced plasterwork above the entrance to a Koranic school

Together with Zabid, **Mokha** is the city in the Tihama that has played the most important part in Yemen's history. It apparently owes its existence to a sheikh called Ali Ibn Omar ash-Shadhili, who settled there around 1430. Soon other people moved to the place to be near the pious man. Sheikh Shadili was a lover of coffee (which the Arabs had discovered a few decades earlier on the opposite side of the Red Sea, in

1 SAN'A Town house in the Old Town. The later conversion of the ground floor into shops has deprived
the lower storey of its defensive character

2 SAN'A View across the roofs of the Old Town towards the northwest
4 SAN'A Two members of the religious aristocracy (*sada*) in the market
3 SAN'A In the main mosque. Some of the columns date from antiquity

 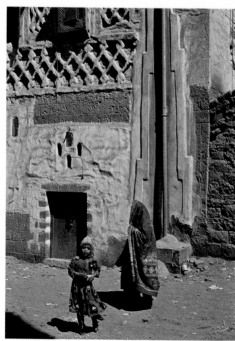

5 SAN'A Ornamental brickwork on a mosque   6 SAN'A In the Old Town

7 SAN'A The southern end of the *sa'ila*, the broad ditch running through the whole of the west side of the city

8 WADI DAR The summer residence of Imam Yahya, built around 1930

9 JIBLA A thousand-year-old town to the west of the Ta'izz-San'a road ▷

10 TA'IZZ Ashrafiya mosque

11 ADEN A lone minaret near the main post office

12 IBB View of the medieval city

Mokha, geometric ornament on a house façade

Ethiopia), which he found helped to keep him awake in his devotions. It is said that some Indian seamen who came to him by chance were given some of the invigorating brew. The Indians then spread the fame of Mokha and coffee. Or so the legend relates. In any case the town increasingly became a centre for exporting coffee, which was grown not around Mokha itself, which is too low, but in the Yemeni mountains at altitudes of between 1000 and 2000 m, from which it was brought down by beasts of burden. Thus from the 16th century onwards camel caravans again made their way through parts of Yemen to the coast - just as they had 2000 years before when carrying frankincense. The Dutch trader Pieter van den Broek reached Mokha in 1616 and reported that in the market he had seen goods from Hungary, Venice and Nuremberg being exchanged for coffee and goods from the Far East.

Mokha is no longer an international mart, since coffee production nowadays is not of high quality. Yemenis themselves often prefer the drink made from the husk - *qishr* - of the coffee beans, which is removed after the fruit has been dried. This drink, flavoured with sugar and sometimes ginger and cinnamon, was popular in the harems of Ottoman Turkey, where it was called Sultan's Coffee.

As van den Broek's observations suggest, coffee had become an important commodity by the first half of the 17th century. Both the English and Dutch founded trading stations in Mokha; the French came about a hundred years later, and bombarded the town, lightly, in 1738 in pursuit of unpaid debts. Niebuhr met men who remembered with amusement how 'fiery cooking pots chased the Governor about the town'. In 1803 for the first time a ship flying the flag of the United States of America anchored outside Mokha. By this time, however, trade was dominated by the British, who were also looking for bases. Already in 1799 they had occupied the island of Perim in the Bab al-Mandab straits, which however they abandoned owing to the lack of drinking water. It is probable that they also had their sights on Mokha as a British base. A Royal Navy warship bombarded the town and it was occupied by Marines. Officially the attack was a punitive measure to end hindrances which the British trading station in Mokha had experienced. The advantage was not pursued, however, since imperial interest turned to Aden, which was captured in 1839. This meant that the fate of Mokha as a port was sealed; Aden under British rule soon reduced the status of the old trading centre irremediably. The turmoil of wars during the 19th century was an additional factor hastening Mokha's decline.

Hudayda is mentioned for the first time in 1515, about twenty years before the Turks appeared on the scene, when an Egyptian sultan occupied the port. For the following 300 years Hudayda was overshadowed by Mokha, which in this period had better mooring and anchorage. At the beginning of the 19th century Hudayda, like the other towns of the Tihama, suffered during the Wahhabi invasions, as well as under the Egyptians, who had been called in to drive out the intruders from the north. From 1849 the little port was again in Turkish hands. The town and harbour of Hudayda were systematically modernized by the Turks, probably to counterbalance British-ruled Aden.

Loheya, another port in the Tihama, is said to owe its existence to a sheikh who moved there in the 15th century, and whose tomb attracted increasing numbers of settlers. The houses of early Loheya would have been built only of reeds, straw and brushwood. More solid houses appeared as the settlement increased in importance - again because of the coffee trade. Merchants built stone huts for themselves and their wares, importing the stone from considerable distances, though they also used large pieces of coral from the Red Sea (and often decorated their graves with the snouts of sawfish). Loheya was the port at which the famous Royal Danish Yemen Expedition with Carsten Niebuhr arrived in 1762. After the second Ottoman invasion of Yemen, Loheya

Bayt al-Faqih, decoration over a doorway

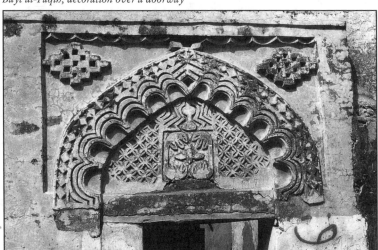

Bayt al-Faqih, brick decoration on a town house

became for half a century an important link of a chain of bases with which the Turks sought to secure the shores of the Arabian Peninsula under their rule.

Bayt al-Faqih began as a settlement of coffee merchants. Its origins go back to the beginning of the 18th century and, once again, to the intervention of a famously pious man, Sheikh Ahmed Ibn Musa. Sheikh Ahmed was a great *faqih* - hence the name of the town, which can be translated as 'house of the learned man'. The coffee trade soon transformed the village into a commercial centre, however. Niebuhr describes it in his *Travels*: 'This city is in a fortunate situation for trade, being only half a day's journey from the harbours of Loheya, Hudayda and Mokha, from which this commodity is exported... This trade brings to the town merchants from Hejaz, Egypt, Syria, Constantinople, Fez, Morocco, Habbesh, the eastern coast of Arabia, Persia, India and sometimes even Europe.'

In the middle of the town the Turks later built a stone fortress, Husn Osman, to strengthen their presence in Yemen.

Art and Religion

Early South Arabian culture has left no trace in the Tihama; there are no temple ruins, remains of dams, statues or reliefs. Yet the coastal strip along the Red Sea and the zone southeast of Bab al-Mandab was of course fully integrated into the various dominant states at different times. The Sabaeans set off from the coast on the Red Sea to acquire new land on the African shore; Ausan was destroyed by its neighbours, not least because they envied the early South Yemeni state its control of Bab al-Mandab; and later the Himyarite-Sabaean empire used its strong sea power to control - for a time - the whole coast of the Yemen.

One of the very few sites of interest is the Qatabanian port of Okelis, the remains of which were found as early as 1857 by Captain R. L. Playfair, an officer of the Indian Army and the first Political Resident at Aden. Though he prided himself on his discovery, there was little, even by his own account, that was worth a visit: 'The ruins are situated about a mile from the sea, inside the Straits, at a place called by the natives, *Dakooäa*: little remains save a few foundations of houses built of madrepore

Zabid, typical Tihama decoration on a house

[a type of coral], which barely appear above the ground; but these suffice to show that the construction is very ancient, and quite dissimilar to any work constructed by the races now inhabiting the country.' Perhaps more would have come to light if systematic investigation had been carried out. Although the site was firmly in British hands for about 120 years, no archaeologist ever seems to have pressed for an excavation: it probably did not seem promising enough.

Besides Okelis, early accounts mention Muza as an anchorage on the Red Sea. Certainly in both towns solid buildings would have been constructed and works of art produced or imported. There may be several reasons why practically nothing has survived. For climatic and geological reasons construction in the Tihama was lighter and airier than in the highlands, with wood, straw, skins and mud the preferred materials for secular buildings. Temples and fortresses, however, were built with heavy stones brought in from the mountains, and the former would have contained devotional objects of alabaster, marble and stone. When the first cultural flowering was past, the mud-built secular buildings quickly fell into unrecognizable ruin, and the religious buildings were easily plundered for their stone, thanks to the proximity of the sea. Interesting finds might be made if the fortifications from the Turkish period - some of which are massive - were completely dismantled.

In any case old architecture in the Tihama is restricted to the Islamic period. In this respect the coastal strip has a life of its own, which includes some important monuments. The religious buildings in Zabid, Bayt al-Faqih, Loheya and Hudayda are distinctly different from those in the highlands: Egyptian and Turkish influences have combined with Yemeni tradition and produced a distinctive Tihama style. One striking feature - particularly apparent in Zabid - is that most houses are not rendered and the brick façades are often left in their natural colour. The Zabid façades also sport ornamental motifs not seen elsewhere in Yemen. Indian influence is apparent in food, music and crafts.

Folk art in the Tihama is very lively. Straw, leather, wood, textiles, coral, shells and meerschaum are the materials used. The craft products are on sale in the markets and are intended primarily for local customers, but the woven baskets, ceramic and clay pots, incense-burners, leather belts and sandals, mats and cotton material also make excellent souvenirs. The characteristic conical straw hats are sometimes so finely woven that they can hold water. It is worth taking into account the market days (usually weekly) in the various towns of the Tihama when planning an itinerary.

Tour of Zabid

Zabid needs at least a day for a thorough visit, but anyone who has time and an eye for details should certainly stay longer: there is enough to discover in the narrow alleys of the market, on the façades of the houses, in the mosques and fortifications to

Zabid, view of the citadel and the Iskanderiya Mosque

Zabid, town gate and defensive buildings from the Ottoman period

keep one occupied for several days. The stay can be broken by an excursion to Bayt al-Faqih nearby.

The town is a small one: you can walk around the outside in a few hours, and also inspect the remains of the walls and defensive towers. You can plunge into the maze of alleys between the houses without fear of losing your bearings - you will probably end up back at the town's main square in front of the **Citadel** which occupies a part of the east side of the town walls. A massive gateway opens outwards from the town, another one faces inwards. The fortress, built of fired bricks, is reinforced by several sturdy defensive towers with blunt tops. Between two of these towers rises the minaret of the **Iskanderiya Mosque** (Alexandria Mosque); part of the base of the minaret also forms the corner pier of the bastion. Both citadel and mosque incorporate Egyptian and Ottoman work, meaning that they were constantly added to and repaired between the 16th and 19th centuries. Beneath the foundations there may be remains of other buildings from the early Islamic period.

The **city walls**, stretches of which have fallen into ruin, were already substantially decayed when Niebuhr saw them in 1763: 'the very ruins are sold by poor people who gather out the stones and sell them for building new houses'. Most of what can be seen today dates in fact from the rebuilding undertaken by the Turks from about 1850 onwards. According to Niebuhr, the Turks had also provided an aqueduct; this brought water from the mountains to the town and has now vanished.

The **Government Palace** in the main square, is interesting though 19th-century. The main building is constructed of fired bricks; the brick ornaments of the upper windows stand out particularly clearly on an otherwise flat façade. Curving round the pointed archway that leads to the white-plastered subsidiary building are three bands of luxuriant ornament.

During the tour of the narrow alleys you should try to discover as many as possible of the 80 or so **religious schools** that remain. These buildings from the heyday of Shafi'ite erudition, erected and maintained by donations from various countries in the Arab world, are usually distinguished by their magnificent construction and clear lines. Some display, besides the standard decorations, inscriptions in various styles, also executed in brick. Many still contain considerable libraries. The focus of all the religious schools was the **Great Mosque**, also called al-Asha'ir Mosque, which today is still the spiritual and intellectual centre of the town. Its main entrance is reached down several steps, since the street level has risen by about a metre since the portals and the surrounding wall were built - an indication of the mosque's great age (15th century). The inner courtyard is surrounded by pointed arcades resting on masonry columns, with only a light wooden roof. The minaret, built of brick and rendered, is short and sturdy; it has what is known as a beehive roof, which was probably adopted from the Syrian-Mesopotamian region. The beauty of this mosque lies not in its decorations but in its uncluttered lines.

A stroll through the area around the town is also recommended. Doum-palms,

Khokha, typical Tihama decoration on a merchant's house

camel-thorn and other trees give it the character of a garden suburb. Lovingly decorated houses and thatched huts line the ways. There is another mosque within sight
of the town, the **Mustafa Pasha**. With its sturdy, defensive-looking minaret, a dozen
domes and a high surrounding wall it looks more like a fortress than a house of
prayer. It was named after the first Ottoman governor in the Tihama following the
conquest of 1539-40.

From Zabid via Hays to Mokha and Khokha

Heading southwards by bus or shared taxi on the well-made Tihama highway for 35
km between fields of cotton and cereals, you reach the town of Hays which is famous
for its pottery. Leaving Hays by a metalled track, it is nearly two hours to the fishing
village of Khokha on the Red Sea (28 km), where there is a very pleasant beach and
the locals are used to foreigners bathing. Grilled fish is available very cheaply. Spending the night on the beach is usual here, and particularly in groups it is not considered

dangerous. But there are sharks beyond the reef.

Continuing southwards from Hays a 75 km journey brings you to the crossroads with the Mokha-Ta'izz road. To get to Mokha turn west and continue along the asphalt road for about 40 km, less than 30 minutes. Because of its decayed state the town of **Mokha** (see page 128) may be a disappointment, but the old lighthouse and the Great Mosque are still worth a look. The latter is about 500 years old and has a richly decorated minaret which becomes noticeably more slender as it rises through five sections. In character it is entirely different from its counterparts in Zabid. The Mokha mosque is rendered, whitewashed, and above all bedecked with plasterwork ornament, where in Zabid bare bricks and geometric brick predominated.

It is also worth looking out for the ruins of the old merchants' houses of Mokha, with their richly ornamented façades.

Mokha has now become an industrial centre, with a new harbour, built next to the old one, that currently takes second place on the Yemen coast after Hudayda.

The return to Khokha can be made along the coast, using an unfrequented track (about 60 km or 3 hours; four-wheel-drive vehicles only).

Hudayda, remains of the old Governor's Palace in the dilapidated Old Town

The Red Sea can still yield a rich harvest

From Zabid via Hudayda to Loheya

Bayt al-Faqih is 35 km north of Zabid along the Tihama highroad, travelling through agricultural country. The trip is particularly worthwhile for the Friday market, which is one of the biggest in the whole of Yemen. Its strong points are pottery, basketwork and leather goods as well as local textiles, including famous scarves. The Turkish citadel in the town centre and the funerary mosque of Ahmad Ibn Musa (see page 131) are also worth visiting.

Hudayda (65 km from Zabid), the gateway to North Yemen from the Red Sea, is a modern town with a population of more than 100,000 (colour plates 46 and 53). Its high temperatures combined with high humidity, very heavy traffic and the predominantly concrete architectural style all make the town close to unbearable. So if at all possible you should use it only as a pit-stop, since the hotels have baths where you can wash away the dust and sweat of the journey, the hospitals and pharmacies are relatively well stocked, and the postal and telephone service show a pleasing level of

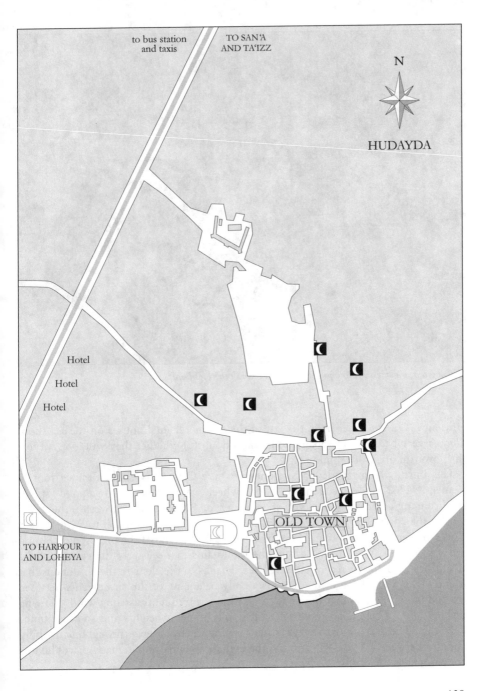

Veiled women are less common in the Tihama than in the highlands

efficiency. On the other hand the last of the old merchants' houses on the sea shore are in a very bad state of repair and it seems doubtful whether they will long survive the powerful urge for rebuilding.

The journey from Hudayda to Loheya, where Carsten Niebuhr first set foot in Yemen in 1762, no longer requires a four-wheel drive. There is now a good asphalt road running north, on which you should stay for 109 km, turning west in the direction of the coast. The road to Loheya, remade in 1986, runs parallel to Wadi Mawr. This river region, with a population of about 60,000, is one of the biggest agricultural areas in Yemen. Wadi Mawr drains the mountains in a westerly direction, but the river dries up before it reaches the Red Sea. Thanks to the clefts in the mountains that it and other wadis have made, there is a daily balancing of the air currents between sea and mountains, so that in the daytime there are frequently strong winds blowing up the valley. These can carry moist air rapidly to great heights and so cause thundery rain. There is almost always water flowing in the valleys throughout the hilly country between the coastal plain and the high mountains, and in many places luxuriant oases have formed.

Loheya, view from the Ottoman fortress to the main mosque and harbour

The road between Hudayda and Jizan (in Saudi Arabia) is the main route for traffic. Those driving to Yemen from Europe via Saudi Arabia by car have a journey of 265 km from Jizan to Hudayda. The road goes through **al-Zaydiya**, a town which specializes in the production of curved daggers for the sada.

This journey is a good introduction to a little of the northern Tihama. Here Arabian and African elements have reached a better balance than in the southern Tihama where African features tend to predominate. In the north too there is intensive cultivation, and irrigation by means of the rattling motor-pumps can achieve considerable results. In many places, however, water is drawn manually out of wells 10 or 15 m deep to water the livestock and perhaps irrigate a tiny vegetable garden. In spite of their hard life the people of the northern Tihama are friendly and open. The women are seldom veiled, and they tend to dress in lightweight, brightly coloured shawls.

The straw-thatched houses of the region are built with higher domes than in the south. The roof is supported by a central post whose carved tip will be seen protruding beyond the thatch. The dome is tied together with strong ropes and the whole

141

African influence is evident in the houses of the northern Tihama

roof rests on a round substructure made of mashed mud, sometimes also of unfired mud bricks. Inside, the huts are painted with great verve and an astonishing variety of subjects. Decorative plates are also hung up, as many as an owner can afford.

A few kilometres outside **Loheya** the soil becomes almost completely barren. This is a scarcely perceptible depression which is sometimes flooded with seawater. The salt crusts left by the sea appear rock hard, but are in fact nothing more than a fragile crust covering a treacherous ooze. So take care. Loheya is built on a slight rise and consequently becomes an island when the sea penetrates inland. The highest point in the town is occupied by the Ottoman fortress, which in its present form is a defensive work of the 19th century. You can scale the fortress hill and get into the fort by climbing over a partly collapsed section of wall on the western side. The walls offer a fine view of the main mosque with its fourteen domes, overtopped by the vaulted dome of the tomb of of Sheikh Salih, the town's founder. Beyond the mosque you can see many thatched houses, not circular this time, but tent-like rectangular huts with pitched roofs. The stone buildings, former merchants' dwellings or warehouses grouped around harbour, were long ago abandoned by their original owners, after the harbour silted up and lost its importance. Street traders occasionally set up business in the ruins.

The harbour at Loheya is still used by fishing boats, and some of the high-sided Arab sailing boats, or dhows (colour plate 23), are still sometimes built there. Tasty snacks can be found in the market on the shore of the shallow bay, such as hard white cheese, which goes well with the flat bread baked in oil. The tea houses are good for watching the water fowl: cormorants, pelicans, herons and many others.

There is no hotel in Loheya. However, if you want to, or have to, stay the night, accommodation is available, possibly in the school or hospital.

The return to Hudayda can be made along the coast. There are two tracks running

Bajil, Tihama decoration on the wall of a house

south between one and five kilometres apart for most of the way; eventually they meet the overland road between Hudayda and Saudi Arabia. There are plenty of opportunities for bathing in the Red Sea on the way.

From Hudayda to San'a

The stretch from Hudayda to San'a (226 km) can be covered in four or five hours, but since it is along one of the most beautiful mountain roads in Yemen, it is worth leaving enough time to enjoy it properly. Rebuilt with financial and practical assistance from the People's Republic of China, the road was started in 1960 but took nearly ten years, mainly because of the mountainous terrain, but also because of the civil war. Before the Chinese the Turks had built and maintained a metalled road to

Terraced fields are found in Yemen up to an altitude of 3000 m above sea level ▷

the capital following approximately the same course, and this in turn probably followed a path which ran from the San'a region to the sea in Sabaean and Himyarite times.

In the Turkish period the climb up to the plateau of San'a took at least three days. Natural obstacles or Yemeni attacks could make it take many times longer. For thousands, perhaps tens of thousands, of soldiers in the Ottoman army this route was a march to their deaths from the strain of the journey or the bullets of the Arabs. Today the Hudayda-San'a road is safer than the stretch from Ta'izz to the capital. The 'Chinese Road' is very well built but has so many tight bends that progress is slow; the long, straight stretches of the road from Ta'izz, by contrast, tempt drivers to excessive speeds, so there are frequent accidents.

From Hudayda we reach the foothills at **Bajil**, famous for its livestock market. A metalled side road (120 km) runs north from here, making an alternative route to Loheya via al-Mihlaf and al-Qanawis. Just beyond al-Qanawis a track forks off to the east towards Hajja. Here the lower slopes of the massifs are often no longer terraced. People live by keeping small livestock and selling wood: there are collection places at intervals along the road for wood supplied from the side valleys. Intensive wood-gathering and clearance are hastening soil erosion, but the lack of other fuel seems to make this inevitable.

A different area of agriculture is marked by the deep wadis in this region, some of which carry water all year round. The water is used to irrigate every square metre in the narrow valleys. Here several harvests are gathered each year: millet, maize, beans, lucerne, bananas, papaya and qat grow very well here. Above 1000 m we find ourselves increasingly in the region of terraced farming. Since the mid-1980's there has been a fine road which turns off about 7 km north of Bajil and runs southeast to Madinat ash-Sharq (formerly Madinat al-Abid) and on to **Ma'bar** (on the San'a-Ta'izz road). This route offers magnificent scenery of the middle part of mountainous Yemen and very beautiful views of the subtropical landscape of the Wadi Siham, though nervous travellers may be worried by the sometimes abrupt bends in the road and the serious danger of falling rocks.

During the climb up from the foothills there is a slow transition in the appearance of the settlements as the Tihama type of straw-thatched hut gives way to stone houses with flat roofs. The higher you get the taller houses become, and many villages stand in extreme positions on mountain tops and ridges.

From Madinat ash-Sharq a track almost 50 km long (four-wheel drive required) leads to **Hammam Ali,** a traditional bathing place on the upper course of the Wadi Rima. Here Yemenis enjoy hot springs with sulphurous water (men and women on alternate days) as medicinal baths.

The main stretch of road between Bajil and San'a (140 km) runs between the Jabal Dahnah and the Jabal Izzan into the mountain region proper. At first it follows the course of the Wadi Surdad, whose constant water allows intensive cultivation at its

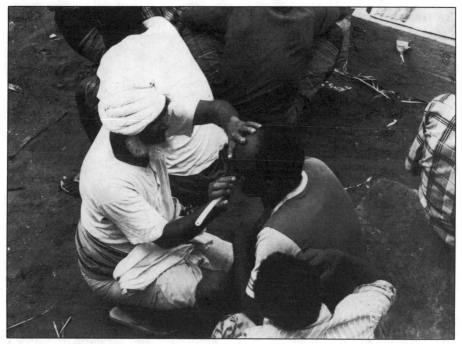

One of the services available at the markets of the Tihama: barber at work

margins. The road frequently leaves the river valley to hug the mountain sides, surmounting rocky outcrops and passing through cliffs.

Hans Helfritz travelled along this road several times in the 1930's. Of the section near Manakha he wrote: 'At Suq al-Khamis the mountain wall suddenly drops sheer away for many hundreds of metres. And whereas up above an air of almost northern freshness prevails, the deep valley immediately at one's feet is full of hot steamy air and covered with rank tropical vegetation, like a jungle. But on its far side the mountain wall rises just as sheer to a height of almost 3000 m and, high above on the narrow ridge, Manakha can be seen.'

The road reaches its highest point at 2750 m in the pass beyond Manakha near the village of Suq al-Khamis mentioned by Helfritz. From the pass, if the weather is good, you can see the highest peak in the country, Jabal an-Nabi Shu'ayb, an extinct volcano. Beyond here the road descends more than 2000 m to the plain on which the capital stands.

Sa'da

The early history of Sa'da and its environs are chronicled in the extensive writings of the Yemeni geographer al-Hamdani (*c.* AD 900). According to him, Sa'da was 'already a region of tanning in the time of the great ignorance', that is, in the period before Islam. The city was located in 'the middle of the great *qaraz* region', qaraz being a sort of acacia whose sap is used to make gum arabic; and in its wider environs were to be found the best wadis of the Khawlan, with 'the finest wine, the most horses, good seedfruits, grapes and livestock'.

Hamdani's information is one the earliest pieces of written evidence we have about Sa'da, but the site on which the city stands must already have been of great strategic, commercial and political importance at the time of the kingdom of Ma'in. Nearby is the beginning of Wadi Najran, which forms a natural road northwards. The city, which is at an altitude of about 2000 m, is almost at the centre of a broad basin 35 km in length: it is the ideal place for caravans to assemble as they came from the central highlands and from the southeast (in other words from the heartland of Ma'in and Ma'rib) before continuing to the important trading outpost of Najran. Moreover, in

*Turks in Yemen
(19th century)*

148

antiquity there were already goldmines about 30 km to the west of the present city. It can therefore be assumed that the region has been settled for over 1000 years. However, the vicissitudes of history, as well as the simple fact that the principal building material was impermanent mud, meant that nothing has been found from the early period.

In the 5th century AD, however, there is written evidence of the massacre of a Christian tribe here by one of the Jewish Himyarite kings, Dhu Nurwas, 'he of the flowing hair'. Twenty thousand are said to have died; the Emperor Justinian wrote letters of protest. At his behest the Ethiopians intervened twice, eventually to conquer the Himyarite Empire.

In the history of Islamic Yemen Sa'da first appears in 897, when an immigrant, al-Hadi Yahya Ibn Hussain, declared himself Imam and made Sa'da his capital. Imam al-Hadi had come to northern Yemen from Basra on the Persian Gulf, and had brought with him a new interpretation of the relationships of loyalty in the 'House of Islam' following the death of the Prophet Muhammad. This interpretation was based on the teaching of Zayd Ibn Ali of Medina, the great-grandson of Ali, the Prophet's son-in-law, so al-Hadi and his followers became known as Zaydis. When the Zaydis arrived in Sa'da region and organized a federation of tribes, whose secular and spiritual leadership lay with the Imam (literally: 'prayer-leader') al-Hadi, the Zaydi state in Yemen was born. It was to last until the revolution of 1962.

Imam al-Hadi ruled from Sa'da until 911. He controlled only a small part of the north, and indeed in the early stage of the Zaydi state the Imam was scarcely more than a tribal chief, whose following increased or decreased depending on shifts in loyalties among the tribes.

The next three Zaydi Imams all resided in Sa'da. They were able to expand the area of their power, though still mainly in the highlands. Later rulers preferred other small towns, such as Hajja, for their capital. It was not until 1261 that Imam Yahya Ibn Muhammad as-Seraji made Sa'da the metropolis of the Zaydi Islamic state. The coastal plain (the Tihama) was never more than sporadically incorporated into the area controlled by the Zaydis. The people on the shores of the Red Sea followed a different branch of Islam (see page 125); and besides they were - even if sometimes only nominally - subjects (through his local representative, the governor) of the Caliph, the earthly successor of Muhammad, who resided in Damascus or Baghdad.

In 1564 the soldiers of the Ottoman Empire came up from Tihama, where they had been established since 1539, and fought their way through to San'a. Imam Sharaf ad-Din withdrew to the mountain fastnesses of Kawkaban, about 25 km northwest of San'a. From this time onwards the capital and the whole of the highlands were constantly fought over. In 1597 Sa'da again became the capital of High Yemen when al-Mansur al-Qasim Ibn Muhammad established himself here as Imam of Zaydi tribes. Imam al-Qasim travelled around the country preaching the struggle against economic exploitation by the Turks, and he was finally successful in his efforts to coordinate the revolt of the Yemenis into an organized rebellion. A Cairo chronicler of the Ottoman Empire wrote around this time: 'Nowhere have we lost as many soldiers as in Yemen. Our soldiers vanished there like salt in water. If we checked our lists of soldiers, we confirmed that from the time of Ibrahim Pasha [1524] up to today we have sent 80,000 soldiers to Yemen, of whom only 7000 have survived the expeditions.'

Yet another 39 years were to elapse before the Ottoman Empire recognized that it could not sustain these high losses and pulled out of Yemen. In 1635 after the complete withdrawal of the Turkish troops the Zaydi state was again independent and free. Thereafter the capital was to remain in San'a - until the return of the Turks to the highlands in 1872. Sa'da, the cradle of the imamate, was still a special, holy city. In 1962, when the last Imam, al-Badr al-Mansur, was overthrown, he took refuge in the caves in the mountains northwest of Sa'da, where he continued what proved to be a vain struggle to return to the throne.

Religion and Culture

In the first two centuries following the lifetime of the Prophet numerous Islamic sects appeared. After the death in 661 of the Caliph Ali, son-in-law of the Prophet, and that of Ali's son Hussain at the battle of Kerbela in Iraq in 680, the struggle to decide which of the successors of Muhammad should be leader of the faithful grew into a religious schism. The party of Ali and Hussain - the Shi'ites - was still strong in Iraq and neighbouring Persia. Its influence reached the religious centre of Basra, where Zayd Ibn Ali, born in 697 and a great-grandson of Ali and the Prophet's daughter Fatima, founded a sect based on Shi'ite principles. In 740 Zayd fell in battle against the Sunni Caliph Walid II, who was based in Damascus. Zayd's resistance of the Damascene Caliphs who had seized the caliphate from the family of Ali was seen as a struggle against injustice, and Zayd's followers, the Zaydis, travelled all over the Arabian Peninsula in search of more supporters. At last in the north of Yemen they

Sa'da, view of the district where the religious aristocracy live

found fertile ground for their teachings.

In the Sa'da region the Zaydis came across tribes who recognized no secular authority except their own tribal leaders. These independent Yemenis, only loosely integrated into a primitive social structure, gave a sympathetic hearing to the Zaydi message. According to the Islamic scholar J.A. Williams, 'the Zaydis... believe that God has no eternal and uncreative attributes, and that the Koran is created. They also, for the most part, do not accept predestination.' By contrast, for the Sunnis the Koran is 'sent from God', and everything that happens is preordained by God. The Zaydis also drew a political teaching from their resistance to fatalism: they denied that one had to accept a ruler who had been found to be unjust, while the Sunnis felt obliged to do so on the grounds of the Tradition of the Prophet (*hadith*).

The Egyptian expert on Yemen, Muhammad al-Azzazi, has also analysed the political content of Zaydi teaching: 'They believe that every Zaydi with the qualifications for the Imamate has the right to rise in revolt against an "unjust" ruling Imam and claim the Imamate for himself. This principle is the cause of the rivalry within the Zaydi leadership in Yemen... Since the Zaydi teachings reject total obedience to the ruling Imam, they allow - unlike all other branches of Islam - the simultaneous existence of several Imams in various regions.'

Most of the qualifications for the Imamate - they number fourteen in all - are undemanding. A candidate must be male, free-born, tax-paying and healthy in mind, senses and limbs; he should be just, pious and magnanimous and have administrative capabilities. Points eleven and twelve require that the candidate be a descendant of Ali and Fatima. He has to show bravery; and he should have a comprehensive knowledge of the Koran and the exposition of the Holy Scripture and of religious regulations.

The demand that the candidate be a descendant of the Prophet may come only eleventh and twelfth in the list, but it is in fact the main requirement. Unless it is met the other virtues are of no avail. The importance attached to this privilege of birth soon brought about the development in the Zaydi state of an aristocracy, the *sada* (singular: *sayyid*) (colour plate 4). In theory the Imam was chosen by the members of this aristocratic class. In practise, however, the Imamate became hereditary within a few families. Nevertheless the ruler had to pay attention to the interests of the sada. He accommodated the religious aristocrats by providing them with government posts. The sada were not rich landowners by birth; the land belonged mainly to the tribes, so the aristocracy could only achieve prosperity by being functionaries of the Imam. In the thousand years or so of the Zaydi Imamate in Yemen the number of members of the religious nobility rose to around 50,000. The dissatisfaction of the population, which intensified greatly in the 19th and 20th centuries, was mostly caused by abuse of office by the sada. On the other hand, right up to the end of the Zaydi state there was many a sayyid whose work as a peacemaker in tribal conflicts meant that he was venerated as a saint. As Carl Rathjens wrote: 'The sada are the expositors of Islamic law and ritual regulations, the *ibadat*. In all tribal hostilities they are called on as arbiters or peacemakers. Usually they live away from the village... and such places are then privileged, just like a number of larger towns in the highlands... Like various saints' graves, in wartime they are inviolable places of refuge or asylums, called *hijrah*. Also inviolable and under unconditional truce are the markets, which are places with stone huts set apart between the tribal territories and populated on only one day a week, market day.'

In many respects religious law was in competition with traditional tribal law. This conflict has not been completely resolved even in our own day. It is true that some points of tribal law could be evened out; in other cases, however, the religious law had to adapt to it. So the population of the Yemen highlands remained tied to their rigid code of honour, which laid down the limits for warfare between enemy tribes. In the same way the means of breaking a cycle of blood vengeance was taken over from pre-Islamic times. Of these traditions Rathjens writes: 'The primeval law of blood vengeance would have brought after it an endless sequence of reciprocal murders, if it had not been possible to redeem the blood guilt of the murderer with a

`Sa'da, the crumbling city wall

blood price, *ad-diyah*, which was paid to the family of the person killed.'

Tribal law also regulated the protection of such persons who were socially too weak to be incorporated into the system of blood vengeance, or who were not Muslims. In the past if a stranger wanted to pass through the territory of a tribe, he had to make contact with a tribesman, who for a fee became an escort with full responsibility - including the duty of blood vengeance - for the life and property of the traveller in his care. If the escort himself turned against the person he was protecting, this atrocious crime could not be paid for with any blood price - the perpetrator was driven out of his own tribe and became an outlaw. Among older Yemenis at least the role of escort, even if without remuneration, can be seen in a moderated form if they find themselves travelling with strangers.

Religious law and tribal law, together with the customs attached to them, led to a strict division into castes and classes within the population of the Zaydi state. After its fall this division has become looser, but it varies in strength between different regions. In the larger towns and in the Tihama these differences have clearly levelled out, but in the Saʿda region on the other hand the barriers of caste and class have continued almost without a break. The head of the tribe is always the sheikh, but the sada are a privileged estate outside the tribal association, from which any travelling craftsmen or seasonal workers temporarily in the tribal territory are also excluded.

Saʿda, a building under construction showing the zabur *technique.*

The few remaining Jews, in both town and country, have scant social privileges. Members of despised professions suffer greater discrimination: these include smiths, potters, butchers, vegetable sellers (particularly sellers of garlic and onions), fountain workers, bath attendants, bleeders, barbers, coffee-house keepers, musicians and executioners. The town-dwellers look down on the tribesmen, and *vice versa*, though the more recently settled retain links with their tribes.

Architecture

Houses in Sa'da look as if they have grown naturally out of the soil, whose colour they exactly match. Appearances are deceptive, since the houses do have definite foundations, built up in layers in shallow excavations up to floor level; and it is the earth spoil from the excavations that is used in the construction of the exterior walls, mixed with mud and chopped straw. Unlike the buildings in southern Yemen, for example, there are no mud bricks, either air-dried or fired. Instead the earth and mud mixture is worked into layers about 60 cm thick, and the mass is beaten with boards and clubs until it is solid. Layer is laid on layer, with each ring taking about a day's work and having to be left several days to dry. As each new layer is added it is turned

Adding another layer of mud and chopped straw

up at the corner, so that at roof level the corners protrude like battlements. This technique serves both to stabilize the building and to allow each coil to project one or two centimetres beyond the one below it, while the whole wall is made to lean inwards as its height increases.

This method of building houses of four and five storeys using layers of mud is known in the Sa'da region as *zabur*. Some houses are rendered on the outside with another coating of mud so that instead of the layers a smooth brown wall is created, though it is soon covered with cracks and fissures like an elephant hide. Apart from the two main mosques and the sides of the city gates all the buildings in Sa'da are constructed using the zabur technique. As elsewhere in Yemen the rooms at ground level are used for defence and for storage and therefore have no windows. The first row of windows is in the middle of a house or even higher up and the openings are smaller than is usual in other parts of the country. Above an up-ended rectangular and unglazed window there is often a semicircular fanlight the same size filled with a sheet of alabaster. The wall around these combined windows is painted white with a mixture of lime and plaster.

Apart from these window surrounds the houses have very few decorative elements. Some have battlements at roof level, such as are often found in southern Yemen. The tops of the walls are secured and whitened with alabaster plaster and lime. Older houses - zabur houses may be one or two hundred years old - feature little boxes built outwards from the walls, but these are privies (from which the excreta fall directly into the street), rather than decorative elements *per se*.

On the other hand much care is lavished on the design of doors. Many door-frames

Sa'da, fortress in the town centre, built on a slag heap from a former iron works

sport beautiful carved bands with verses from the Koran, and there will often also be floral and geometric patterns on the panels. Door knockers also have very original decoration. The heavy round bolts that are sometimes seen serve both for security and as decoration.

Tour of Sa'da

Paolo Costa, whose book on the architecture of Yemen was published in 1977, enthused about Sa'da, which was then, as he wrote, the only major city in Yemen untouched by modern development. 'The mud walls surround Sa'da like a giant hoop, which holds together the separate houses and leaves the surrounding plain empty.' Any tour of Sa'da should begin with a walk on the mud walls encircling the city (2 to 3 hours). The visitor will soon realize that the enthusiasm of 1977 is no longer fully justified, for in recent years the old Zaydi capital has certainly been

Town plan of Sa'da. The encircling wall is no longer complete

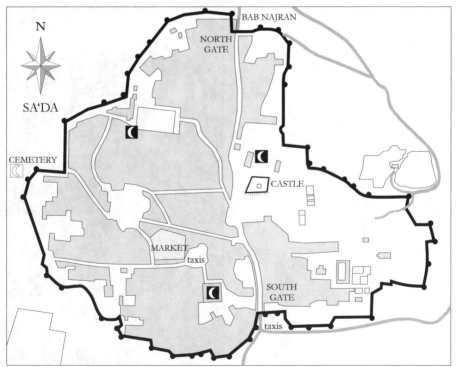

touched by modern development, thanks
to a building boom in the 1980's that also
brought in a great deal of freight traffic.

The heavy lorries and their drivers have
left their mark in the city. Outside the
south gate a whole satellite town has
become established, with garages, workshops, hotels and restaurants. At two
points exit roads have been arbitrarily cut
through the walls, and in the city itself
some houses in a dubious architectural
style have sprung up. Also in many places
crudely decorated iron doors have
replaced ones that had been lovingly carved
in wood.

You can easily climb up on top of the
city walls at the **South Gate** (the road to
San'a). From there you can walk round to
the North Gate (Bab Najran) and thus
cover a good half of the walls. The view
from the top of the wall is often into
private gardens, onto rooftops and into
the open windows of houses. The greatest
discretion is needed, since more members
of the religious aristocracy live in Sa'da
than in other towns. You should therefore be very cautious when it comes to
taking photographs.

From the city walls the two main
mosques and other prominent buildings
can easily be found amongst the houses
and gardens. The city is dominated by the
fortress built on a hill of slag and refuse in
the centre. Its function was probably
more to keep the population under
control than to defend the city against
outside aggressors (illustration page 156).
Between the fortress and the city walls
(north side) is another, black hill, also of
the slag that was produced in large quantities for several centuries, when iron ore

was mined near the city and smelted within its walls.

Bab Najran deserves special attention. It has a massive defensive tower built of mud strengthened by an inlay of rocks and walling of baked bricks. Here the walls are laid out in several bold curves, so that the defensive passages extend up to the forward tower and follow the road into the city for some way beyond the actual entrance. At the beginning of the 1990's one expert, U. Dambleff-Uelner, wrote: 'The walls must be regarded as one of the outstanding architectural monuments in the Arab world because their 16th-century layout has survived complete (though in need of repair). It may still be possible to preserve them for posterity.'

The **Great Mosque** (it is *not* possible to view the interior) was built in the 12th century. It is the funerary mosque of the first Zaydi Imam, al-Hadi Yahya, and of eleven other Imams (colour plate 14). On the south side of the mosque twelve domes, each one of a different design, rise over their graves. Also of interest is the **an-Nizari Mosque**. Although not as high, it still rises clearly above the surrounding buildings, distinctive thanks to a basement of massive hewn stones and a superstructure built of baked bricks.

A walk through the narrow alleys of Sa'da almost inevitably ends or begins at the **main square**. Here there are a few tea houses which also offer food. The departure point for shared taxis to San'a, formerly in the square, is now outside the

Sa'da, view of the Imam al-Hadi Mosque from the town walls

159

Sa'da, the market is frequented by men only

city walls.

Branching off from the main square are the alleys of the **permanent market**, consisting mainly of one-storey booths. Some of the merchandise is made in the market itself. Among the most interesting examples of traditional production are the cooking pots made of hard stone. Sa'da pottery is also worthy of attention. Daggers, are mostly offered at very high price; the blades are no longer forged in the city itself but in surrounding villages. The small silver market, mainly run by Jewish tradesmen, is full of interest.

But as elsewhere the market in Sa'da has been flooded with imported goods: brocades from Damascus, cotton textiles from Asia, Indian flower oils, cigarettes from Saudi Arabia, Japanese cassette players, and, oddly, coffee cups from China, although hardly any coffee is drunk in Sa'da, tea and *qishr* (the infusion made with dried coffee husks and flavoured with ginger) being preferred.

The **weekly market** in Sa'da is held on Sundays and is mainly for agricultural produce. Very few housewives will be seen in the market, since shopping is left to the men. Many heads of families even buy their wives' clothes for them. The tradition of the harem has continued here almost unchanged, as described, not all that long ago, by a German ethnologist in her journal: 'The women of particularly strict religious

13 RADA Amariya mosque
14 SA'DA The mosque containing the tomb of the founder of the Imamate, al-Hadi Yahya, and eleven other imams

15 MA'RIB Monolithic piers from the partly uncovered temple to the moon god

16 MA'RIB Drifting sand is slowly covering the temples uncovered in 1952

17 MA'IN Temple ruins east of the city walls

19 TIHAMA Permanent market in the foothills ▷

18 ZAFAR Cave tombs in the region of the Himyarite capital, some of them inhabited today

20 DHALA Country women fetching water

21 TIHAMA Market woman with a painted face

22 SA'DA Two of the last of the remaining Yemeni Jews

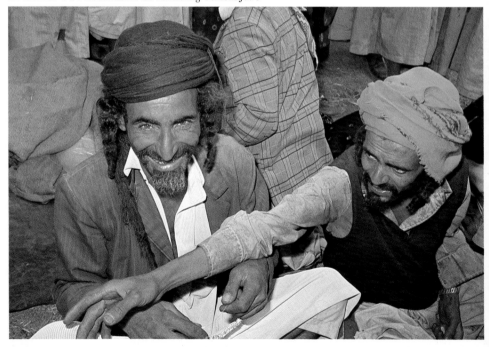

23 ADEN A dhow under repair

24 SHIBAM Mud bricks are made at the edge of the building site

25 SUMARRA PASS Landscape west of the top of the pass on the Taʻizz-Sanʻa road

26 THULA View from the castle hill over a mosque and houses in the town

families may not even visit neighbouring harems. In other districts of the city - outside the actual sada quarters - "Friday parties" are especially enjoyed. On the Islamic holy day whole swarms of women pay visits on each other. They are then dressed in gold and silver brocade. All of them are fragrant with Indian essences; many have decorations painted on their faces in the form of little branches or blossoms. In the harem where a "Friday party" takes place - without any males present - the hubbub of voices is drowned by Arab songs from a battery-powered cassette player, mixed in with the gurgle of water-pipes. Innumerable cups of tea, flavoured with fresh mint, as well as many glasses of qishr are drunk. Qat is a vice of women as well as men. Mingling with the smoke of the water-pipes is the heavy fragrance of burning incense; in Sa'da one is still reminded of the incense trade that once made the prosperity of South Arabia. Every household has its own incense mixture which it believes is absolutely the best.'

Around Sa'da

The plain around Sa'da is good walking country. Walks lasting 1 to 4 hours stay within sight of the city, indeed one can plan out the various routes by eye from the city walls beforehand. Wadi Sa'da itself is ideal for walking. To the southeast of the South Gate is Jabal Abbelle, which can be reached on foot in an hour and a half. From Bab Najran a 3 hour walk in a northeast direction will bring one to the lower course of the Wadi Agnam.

A prehistoric rock engraving near Sa'da

About 6 km west of Sa'da is the village of **Ruras (Ghuras)** which should be visited for its particularly impressive mud buildings. There are still a few Jewish families living here, but difficulties have arisen for tourists since the mid-1980's and the police now try to prevent photographs being taken. Some Jewish silversmiths from Ruras (colour plate 22) visit the market at Sa'da fairly regularly. You can buy from them there and usually take some photographs. (The Jews may not be here much longer, as some 300 were secretly flown to Israel in 1993 and most of the remaining 2000 are said to be keen to follow suit.)

A two-hour car journey northwestwards (four-wheel-drive required) takes one to the rocks of **Umm-Layla** (Mother of Night), a bizarrely eroded sandstone region with chasms, grottoes, tall overhanging precipices and watercourses. Inscriptions and drawings on some rocks suggest that in early times a branch of the caravan route from Aden to San'a, Sa'da, Mecca and Gaza ran along here.

Only 7 km from the gates of Sa'da, also to the north, are early - possibly prehistoric - **rock engravings**, including a large figure of a god and a bull. In the same place there is an old cistern. At present, however, no permits to visit areas north of Sa'da are being issued.

From San'a to Sa'da

San'a and Sa'da were linked in the late 1970's by an asphalt road built with Chinese help. The distance of 232 km can be covered by shared taxi or bus in about 4 hours. (Shared taxis in San'a depart from Bab Shaub; two buses a day leave Sa'da from the South Gate.)

The journey northwards first passes the towns of Amran and Rayda. Beyond Rayda the road begins to climb once again by several hundred metres; and the last of the San'a plateau is seen at a pass about 2450 m high. Peasant farmers live on either side of the road; they are members of tribes and although sedentary and citizens of a state, will be armed. San'a lies in the region of the tribal federation of the Hashid. The road to Sa'da crosses part of the territory of the Bakil tribal federation, and then reaches Hashid land again. The province of Sa'da is in Bakil territory. The Swedish Yemen scholar Tomas Gerholm wrote that the outsider possibly finds Yemeni tribes such a difficult quantity to grasp because he starts from the wrong assumptions, particularly western notions of 'primitive tribes'. Seen at close quarters, each tribe breaks down into a number of individuals who are not particularly concerned about belonging to it. The tribe can be regarded as a latent organization that only manifests itself when conflicts break out with another tribe or with the state. Such 'latent structures' are not found everywhere in Yemen, but they are particularly common in the Zaydi area, and especially in the territories of the Hashid and Bakil where the traditional pattern

Tribal warrior from the Arhab region

has more or less survived.

The attractive stone-built town of **Huss** (called **Huth** on many maps) on the San'a road (124 km from San'a) is a good starting point for an excursion into one of the most important Zaydi traditional regions. Almost 50 km west of Huss lies **Shahara**, a village built at an altitude of 2600 m. It has repeatedly served the Zaydi rulers as a refuge, its inaccessibility and the obduracy of its inhabitants making it an impregnable stronghold.

The trip from Huss to al-Qabai, the starting point for a visit to Shahara, can only be made in a four-wheel-drive vehicle or on foot. The track drops well over 900 m to take us to an altitude of about 1000 m above sea-level and so

In Huss camels are still used as beasts of burden just as they were in the days of the incense caravans

into the subtropical zone of Yemen. Since the valley has a plentiful supply of water, the vegetation is luxuriant, and the whole region is known for its intensive agriculture. Besides cereals, bananas, papaya and coffee are also grown. There are thickets of palms and reeds with papyrus in which tropical birds live. To get to know this region in more detail it is worth exploring it on foot and camping out under canvas.

Al-Qabai is an unassuming town with no overnight accommodation. However, tour operators do maintain a rest area for camping. Car-owners in al-Qabai offer their services for trips to Shahara (with prices now reckoned in dollars, and a $10 minimum.) An early morning is advisable, and one should drive perhaps two thirds of the way. Some 45 minutes out of al-Qabai the road comes to one of the old footpaths,

Tribal warrior from the Khawlan region

from which the climb up to the South Gate of Shahara can be done in just under an hour.

The way leads past a spring with a beautiful setting, then zigzags steeply upwards, often by steps hewn in the rock. The views over mountains and terraces are consistently spectacular. Just after the South Gate we come across one of the more than 20 cisterns, which ensure a water supply up here. A further 30 minutes' walk brings us to the village itself.

Shahara is still a very impressive place, despite Egyptian aerial bombardment during the civil war. There are now several good funduqs, some in imposing houses near the former palace. The famous stone bridge (colour plate 27) is outside the East Gate. It dates from the 17th century and crosses a chasm several hundred metres deep to the neighbouring mountain. The descent to al-Qabai is also possible from here, but it is hard to find.

The main stretch of the Huss-Sa'da road (another 108 km) skirts outlying parts of the great Arabian desert. The soil becomes more sandy and mud increasingly replaces stone as a building material. Vineyards can also be seen, surrounded by high walls, the corners of which have towers with crenellated parapets.

Sa 'da, the Great Mosque: cupola over the grave of al Hadi Yahya

165

Ta'izz

The Yemeni geographer al-Hamdani (c. 900 AD), who is usually thorough, does not mention the city of Ta'izz in his *Description of the Arabian Peninsula*; Hamdani is so reliable that one can assume that the city did not exist in his time. However, there is definite evidence that Turanshah, a brother of the great Saladin, moved his residence from Zabid to Ta'izz after his conquest of Yemen around 1175. So it must have been around the year 1000 - at a very rough estimate - that the city was founded or at least given the name it bears today. Jabal Sabir, the mountain at whose northern foot Ta'izz stands, was known even before this because of its pre-Islamic (that is, Himyarite) castles. In 1509 Ludovico di Varthema of Bologna became the first European to visit Ta'izz. In 1546 the city fell to Ottoman imperial forces.

Ta'izz has been Yemen's capital on more than one occasion. When Turanshah's descendants gained their independence their territory was ruled from Ta'izz. The governors appointed by the Ottoman Sultans also resided in Ta'izz for as long as they were unable to conquer or hold San'a. Even in our own century Ta'izz was for a time the royal residence, this time for the whole of North Yemen. After the 'Free Yemeni' reformists murdered the old Imam Yahya in the spring of 1948 and proclaimed Abdullah al-Wazir as Imam, Crown Prince Ahmad had great difficulty suppressing their revolt. When he had finally succeeded, he gave his tribal fighters permission to plunder San'a, and made Ta'izz his residence, refusing to return to the rebellious city. Ta'izz remained the capital until his death in 1962. After the fall of the monarchy in the same year San'a again became the metropolis of North Yemen - but throughout the civil war it was threatened by royalist tribal fighters, so most foreign embassies and some of the new republican government apparatus remained at Ta'izz, the 'second capital', until the end of the 1960's.

Situated at an altitude of 1400 m, halfway between that of the coastal plain and the San'a plateau, Ta'izz was for hundreds of years the gateway to the High Yemen for visitors and intruders alike. Mokha, the port that lies about 100 km west of Ta'izz on the Red Sea, served from the 16th century onwards as a sort of ghetto for foreign traders. Numerous restrictions were imposed on the growing foreign settlement at the port, so that the import of new goods would not bring with it the import of new ideas. On the occasions when a foreign delegation was allowed entry to the interior -

Ta'izz at the beginning of the century. The Ashrafiya Mosque is now completely built up (Photograph by H. Burchardt)

to conclude a trade treaty, for instance - the first place the foreigners came to was Ta'izz. Often the Imam, or a prince appointed by him for the task, would receive the delegation here in the 'second capital', and then send it back home again. Other visitors had to wait for weeks in Ta'izz before they were invited to continue their journey to San'a - or were forced to return to Mokha empty-handed.

Later, from the middle of the last century, the proximity of British-occupied Aden was felt in Ta'izz. Mokha sank back into obscurity once Aden had been modernized, and Ta'izz, situated about 200 km north of Aden, now directed its trade towards the British colony. In this period too thousands of Yemenis emigrated to Aden from Ta'izz and its environs to learn previously unknown trades and earn money. New ideas could no longer be kept out of the High Yemen. It was in Aden that the federation of Free Yemenis was formed that removed Imam Yahya in 1948 and sowed the seeds of the republican revolution in 1962.

For early visitors to Yemen, finally receiving permission to travel from the Tihama to Ta'izz after a long wait at the coast, the move to the highlands came as a release. The effect of the difference of 1400 m in altitude can still be experienced by today's traveller. The Tihama was once a hotbed of fever, and for many foreigners (including

167

nearly all the members of the 1762 Danish Expedition) any prolonged stay there meant death.

The convenient location and the proximity of the coastal plain were not always to the advantage of Ta'izz; once intruders had subjugated the Tihama, they soon came to attack the city at the foot of Jabal Sabir. Before the first Ottoman invasion, and in the 200 years or so after the Turkish withdrawal, Ta'izz experienced much fighting and devastation, and was never again completely rebuilt. The remains of the old town are therefore relatively modest. In the 1950's Günther Pawelke, the first West German envoy to North Yemen, wrote: 'How many inhabitants does Ta'izz have? As many as you want, one could answer. It depends on whom you ask or which book you consult. The printed figure may be 272,000, but I go along with the travellers who have seen the town as it is and estimate the population at 3,000 to 4,000.'

Since then the population of Ta'izz, and of much of Yemen, has been officially measured. According to a census taken in the second half of the 1970's, Ta'izz had 91,000 inhabitants; by 1992 this figure has already risen to 250,000. Far fewer than half these people live in the historic part of the city, which used to be completely surrounded by a wall, and an extensive new Ta'izz has spread out over the surrounding hills. Unfortunately the concrete mixers have been at work in Ta'izz more than in the towns of the highlands. But the site remains beautiful, the weary traveller will be revived by the town's climate and the civilized hotels, and there are also enough traces of historic Ta'izz to be worth hunting out in what is now the commercial metropolis of southwest Yemen.

A young man from Ta'izz province

Tour of Ta'izz

The interesting old buildings of Ta'izz lie to the southwest of the modern part of the city (where most of the hotels are). Some of them can be seen across the valley from the Ma'rib and Ikhwa hotels, which are built on a hill opposite. Particularly prominent are the two minarets of the Ashrafiya mosque, which stands just at the foot of the mountain. In the same direction, west of the Ashrafiya, is a part of the city walls that is built up the mountain. Two sturdy ruined towers form part of this section of wall intended to protect the old city of Ta'izz against enemies who might make their way down by following the dry bed of a stream on Jabal Sabir. In front of the Ashrafiya Mosque and city walls stands the Mudhaffar Mosque. It was given a minaret for the first time in 1985, and from a stylistic point of view the addition is disruptive. The rest of the old town and the permanent market (suq) extend north of the Ashrafiya.

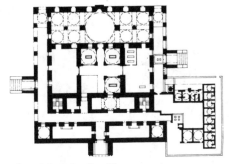

Plan of the Ashrafiya Mosque

The **Ashrafiya Mosque** (colour plate 10) can be reached on foot from the hotel quarter in about 30 minutes; several streets run down the valley and then up a slight incline to the mosque. To get a general view of the mosque you should continue up the hill. Footpaths to right and left lead past the mosque and then climb in gentle zigzags. The level of the minaret domes can be reached without difficulty and you will then have a very fine view over the Ashrafiya and the Mudhaffar mosques below, as well over part of the Ta'izz.

According to the latest research the Ashrafiya Mosque was built in two phases in the 13th and 14th centuries. It was commissioned by the two successors of Turan-shah, al-Ashraf I and al-Ashraf II. The oldest part is the rectangular prayer hall on the north side, with a main dome flanked by eight smaller ones. The rectangular courtyard was probably also created during the first phase of construction, followed by the south side of the building with the two minarets. This addition made the plan of the mosque into an almost perfect square. Later still came an annexe on the east side for the accommodation and instruction of students, for the Ashrafiya was (and still is) a place of religious teaching.

The ceiling and domes of the prayer hall itself have rich plaster ornaments. Three corners of the courtyard are occupied by the tombs of Yemeni sultans. To judge by the style, the domed tombs were designed in the 15th century by architects from Cairo. Indeed the architectural style of the Ashrafiya can be described as a combination of Yemeni art with Egyptian influences, which were already strong in the 13th and 14th centuries. The Ashrafiya underwent a thorough renovation in 1987-88.

From one of the two minarets of the Ashrafiya the architectural importance of this part of the city can be clearly seen. Below to the north are the domes of the Mudhaffar Mosque, founded about a hundred years before the Ashrafiya and considered the finest surviving mosque from the Rassulid period (c.1210 to 1370), despite the addition of the new, San'a style, minaret.

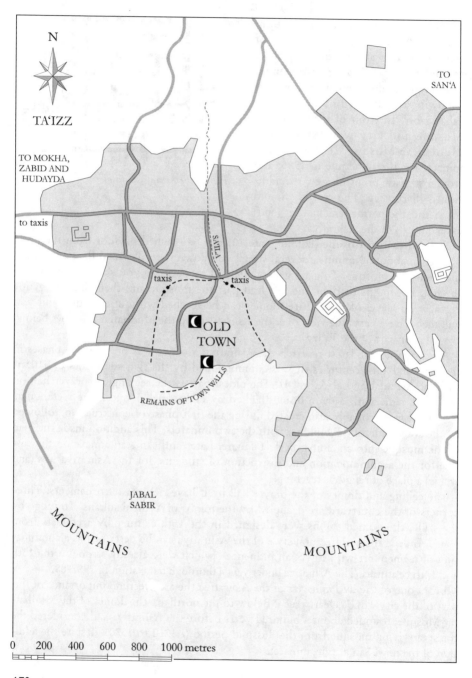

N

TA'IZZ

TO SAN'A

TO MOKHA, ZABID AND HUDAYDA

to taxis

SAYLA

taxis   taxis

OLD TOWN

REMAINS OF TOWN WALLS

JABAL SABIR

MOUNTAINS   MOUNTAINS

0   200   400   600   800   1000 metres

Ta'izz, Mudhaffar Mosque built in the 16th century showing Egyptian influence

The **Mu'tabiya Mosque** to the west was probably planned by the same architect as the Ashrafiya. Its proportions are even more harmonious and balanced than those of the madrasa of the lattero. Visible further to the west, below the old city walls built over a hill, are the gleaming domes of the **Abdel Hadi Mosque**, which manages without a minaret. It is situated in the oldest part of the city and could be five or six hundred years old.

The fourth historic mosque in this district is the **Taqwiyah**, recognizable by its short, stubby minaret. Built in the 14th century, the mosque now stands below ground level. It is surrounded by a wall and is difficult to see.

As a rule only male visitors travelling as individuals are allowed to visit the inside of the mosques. But it is a good idea to contact the Koranic school on the east side of the Ashrafiya, where it is often possible to find English-speakers, who may perhaps also be able to arrange a visit to the mosque for mixed groups or couples.

The **Palace of Imam Ahmad** stands to the east of the old town, on another hill. It

Sketch plan of the city of Ta'izz, from an aerial photograph

is a half-hour walk from the Ashrafiya and is well worth a visit. Most of the exhibits are commonplace household items or gaudy diplomatic gewgaws, typical of the gifts commonly traded by oriental potentates in the first half of the 20th century. But there are also some beautiful carpets and old weapons, as well as costumes which show what the Yemeni woman of the harem and her husband wore for various occasions. Also of interest is the exhibition of historical photographs. But the main attaction is the opportunity to look inside one of the larger houses of the Yemeni rulers. It is noticeable that the penultimate Imam did not deviate from the traditional architectural style for the sake of personal comfort.

Another museum is the **Salah Palace**, about 30 minutes' walk beyond the southeast edge of the city. This palace was also the property of the family of the Imam and surpasses the town palace in size and furnishings. It houses a collection of Sabaean and Himyarite stone inscriptions, pre-Islamic statues from Ma'rib and Yarim, and oil lamps and bronze elements from the Himyarite period. There are also examples of Islamic art, an ethnographical department and a section for modern art with works by the Ta'izz-based painter Hassem Ali Abdullah. Unfortunately none of the collections is adequately displayed. Less than 20 years ago, Claudie Fayein found nothing in the Salah Palace except 'a score of lions in cages - descendants of those that once escorted the Imam in procession, collared and held by chains carried by slaves'.

The Market

From the hotel hill a 20 minute walk southwestwards brings us to the the Great Gate (Bab al-Kabir), once part of a wall encircling Ta'izz, and now the entrance to the permanent market. This is smaller than the market in San'a, but Ta'izz has something more to offer both as an experience and in terms of the merchandise. The dominant impression here is of the greater part played by women, both as vendors and as customers. In the villages on Jabal Sabir from which they come, these women have a very different role from that of their sisters in the highlands. Like the 'market mammies' in West Africa they regulate the sales of almost all the products of the agriculture and small industries in the region. Their economic power is so great that most are also able to take the profits in the form of jewellery. They dress very much to their own taste and are emancipated enough not to be veiled in the conservative Islamic manner. Naturally this permissiveness has its limits: they wear headcloths - usually red - because a Moslem woman ought to cover her hair. They also wear trousers tied at the ankles, and skirts over these trousers. But having done enough in the interests of seemliness, they can look their male customers freely in the face - and

Ta'izz, domes of the Ashrafiya Mosque and the Mudhaffar Mosque with its new minaret

even call call out to attract custom.

The geographical location of Ta'izz means that there is a bigger range of foodstuffs available than in San'a; the region is rich in subtropical fruit, and there are freshly-caught fish from the Red Sea.

As a market for silver jewellery Ta'izz is the equal of San'a. Since the unification of Yemen characteristic South Yemeni pieces are now appearing again in Ta'izz market. The region south of the city, the Hujjariya, has in recent centuries been occupied not by nomads, but by prosperous farmers, traders and merchants. Consequently the silver jewellery from this region is somewhat more lavish, one could perhaps say a little more baroque, than the jewellery of the highlands, which is tailored to the taste of the bedouin. In Ta'izz silver jewellery is mainly for sale in enclosed shops, not at open booths. Several of these shops are situated near the Bab al-Kabir.

Excursions around Ta'izz

In 1763 the Swedish botanist Per Forskål, a member of the Danish Expedition found it impossible to obtain permission to climb **Jabal Sabir** (3000 m), and even in the early 1950's it was still forbidden by order of the Imam for any foreigner to climb the mountain. According to Günther Pawelke this was to prevent foreigners from reconnoitring Ta'izz and its environs from above for military purposes. It is true that from the mountain you have a view over nearly the whole of Ta'izz and the region stretching out north, east and west as far as the eye can see. However, the Yemeni government has accepted that it is now possible to take accurate high-altitude aerial and satellite photographs, and so the mountain has now been opened to foreigners.

A four-wheel-drive vehicle is no longer absolutely necessary for the drive up Jabal Sabir, but before paying an inflated price for a taxi for yourself alone, it is worth going to Bab al-Kabir (the eastern gate) to see if a seat is available in a shared taxi. The drive, first on an asphalt road, then on a track, takes almost half an hour (6 km) and ascends 1600 m. At the top the visitor is greeted not only by a magnificent view, but also by a fine example of a Yemeni high-altitude landscape under cultivation. Because of its geological composition the mountain acts as a reservoir of water; its little valleys are full of gushing springs and flowing streams. In many places the water is diverted so that terraces can be used to maximum agricultural advantage, yet this irrigation system does not destroy the harmony of the landscape. Qat plantations predominate on the terraces, but coffee is also grown, and in the valleys subtropical fruits are cultivated. There are footpaths suitable for walks, and the descent (along the road) can also be made in a few hours under your own steam.

The trip to **at-Turba** (75 km southeast of Ta'izz, a two-hour drive in a shared taxi) will show more magnificent Yemeni landscapes. At-Turba lies on a plateau at an altitude of 1800 m; immediately beyond the southern end of the village the terrain suddenly

Yafrus, Mosque of Ahmad Ibn Alwan

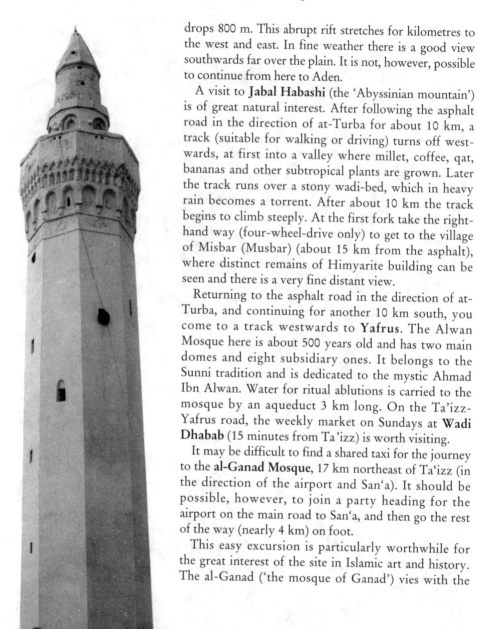

drops 800 m. This abrupt rift stretches for kilometres to the west and east. In fine weather there is a good view southwards far over the plain. It is not, however, possible to continue from here to Aden.

A visit to **Jabal Habashi** (the 'Abyssinian mountain') is of great natural interest. After following the asphalt road in the direction of at-Turba for about 10 km, a track (suitable for walking or driving) turns off westwards, at first into a valley where millet, coffee, qat, bananas and other subtropical plants are grown. Later the track runs over a stony wadi-bed, which in heavy rain becomes a torrent. After about 10 km the track begins to climb steeply. At the first fork take the right-hand way (four-wheel-drive only) to get to the village of Misbar (Musbar) (about 15 km from the asphalt), where distinct remains of Himyarite building can be seen and there is a very fine distant view.

Returning to the asphalt road in the direction of at-Turba, and continuing for another 10 km south, you come to a track westwards to **Yafrus**. The Alwan Mosque here is about 500 years old and has two main domes and eight subsidiary ones. It belongs to the Sunni tradition and is dedicated to the mystic Ahmad Ibn Alwan. Water for ritual ablutions is carried to the mosque by an aqueduct 3 km long. On the Ta'izz-Yafrus road, the weekly market on Sundays at **Wadi Dhabab** (15 minutes from Ta'izz) is worth visiting.

It may be difficult to find a shared taxi for the journey to the **al-Ganad Mosque**, 17 km northeast of Ta'izz (in the direction of the airport and San'a). It should be possible, however, to join a party heading for the airport on the main road to San'a, and then go the rest of the way (nearly 4 km) on foot.

This easy excursion is particularly worthwhile for the great interest of the site in Islamic art and history. The al-Ganad ('the mosque of Ganad') vies with the

al-Ganad, minaret of what is perhaps the oldest mosque in Yemen

al-Ganad, facilities for ritual ablutions

Great Mosque in San'a for the honour of being the first Islamic place of worship in Yemen. It is unlikely that scholars will ever resolve the dispute over their relative antiquity. Both mosques may - as is claimed - have been founded in the lifetime of the Prophet (who died in 632), since the Persian governor of Yemen accepted the burgeoning new faith very early on. Which came first would depend on which route from Medina was chosen by Muhammad's envoys: the highland road (via Najran and Sa'da) to San'a, or the coastal road (via Loheya and Zabid) to Ta'izz.

Although the mosque has been restored, enlarged and restored again over the centuries, it has retained its basic plain structure. It is almost square, with open porticos, cells for students and a prayer-hall arranged around a courtyard. Rows of piers and columns support simple ceilings composed of tree-trunks, planks and straw, above both round and pointed arches. The outer wall, built of fired bricks, is battlemented with 200 merlons. A single, pointed minaret, more than 70 m high, rises from one of the porticos. The interior of the prayer-hall has almost no decoration, yet its purely architectural expressiveness makes the mosque unmistakably a sacred place. Note the washrooms and toilets in front of the mosque - they are a model of beautiful design, using the simplest materials from the area.

The present ground level around the al-Ganad is several metres above the base of the walls where they rest on the foundations - an indication of the deposits that have built up here over thirteen centuries.

From Ta'izz to San'a

Almost all the early explorers followed this very well-known route in western Yemen (now 256 km), whether they landed in Loheya, Hudayda, Mokha or Aden (which is now only a two-hour drive from Ta'izz). The travellers in the 1920's and 1930's were also nearly always sent on the road from Ta'izz to San'a (or made to return in the other direction). By contrast the road from Hudayda to San'a could only be used in certain exceptional circumstances and with a special permit from the Imam. Consequently the literature is full of descriptions of the road between Ta'izz and San'a and of the regions and towns along it. Familiarity did not breed contempt, however; even in the 1950's a trip by car along this road could still be described as a highly dangerous adventure.

Most alarming to earlier travellers was the ancient pass at Jabal Sumarra, though it had been improved in the second Turkish period. It is still today the busiest route between the two main towns of the Yemen but now runs along a new road, built initially with financial and technical assistance from the United States, and then upgraded from gravel to asphalt with aid from West Germany.

Turkish troops on the march

Leaving Ta'izz on the main road to San'a in a shared taxi or bus, we pass Ta'izz airport and al-Ganad. Then a gentle ascent begins, slowly leading from the still subtropical Ta'izz district up to the high mountainous region. Before reaching this we pass through a very fertile plateau, about 40 km long and up to 10 km wide. This is one of the main grain-producing regions of Yemen. The biggest crop is durrah (sorghum), the principal cereal grown in the country.

About 50 km from Ta'izz the road ascends to a height of 2200 m (fine panoramic view). Just 3 km beyond this pass, shortly before a track turns off to the west to the town of Jibla (see page 181ff), a massive group of trees stands on the right of the road; near them is as surviving piece of the roughly paved Turkish road. On the other (western) side of the road is the beginning of a footpath to Jibla (following the wadi, 40 minutes).

Ibb, 60 km north of Ta'izz, is one of the important medium-sized towns of North Yemen (colour plate 12, b&w plate 8). The outer district along the road is not of any interest, but in old Ibb, which has a history going back several hundred years, the traveller will find a dozen mosques, remains of city walls more than 10 m high and an ancient aqueduct, as well as narrow alleys with houses five or six storeys high.

'Here, among tall, whitewashed houses that seemed to be tossed upon the dark and tumbled sea of the mountains like stiff, white foam, I glimpsed a world still buried in the middle ages,' wrote David Holden only 30 years ago. The Imam's rule here was absolute and effective: 'my arrogant young guides pointed out a mummified hand nailed to a post inside the town's main gate.'

The old town of Ibb, built on a hill at the foot of Jabal Badan, is still worth visiting today, especially since it is slightly off the main tourist tracks. A walk round the town gives the chance to see some fine examples of old doors and gateways. The new town has some simple inns. The traditional market is in the old town.

Ibb is a provincial capital and the centre of an important agricultural region. On the nearby plateau cereals, vegetables, sugar cane and fruit are grown.

Beyond Ibb the road climbs another 600 m in the next 50 km. At 2700 m we reach the highest point on the road through the **Sumarra Pass** (fine panoramic view). Günther Pawelke and thousands of travellers before him struggled over another pass about 10 km west of here.

From the Sumarra Pass via Kitab (starting point for Zafar, see page 62f) the road goes to **Yarim**, which is on the edge of a volcanic region. It was at Yarim in 1763 that Forskål, one of the most brillant members of the Danish Expedition, died of malaria contracted at the coast. From Yarim an asphalt road runs southeast via Hammam Damt to Qataban. **Hammam Damt**, about 55 km from Yarim, is worth a detour. The weird volcanic landscape reaches a climax at the spa resort of Damt ('hammam' means 'bath') where there are hot springs and conical volcanic rocks. The tallest of these is the volcano known locally as the 'Throne of Bilqis' (see page 37f), which can be climbed up a flight of metal steps. From Hammam Damt to the south the road, built after unification in 1990, leads into the former South Yemen and towards Aden (209 km).

After returning to Yarim, we go on to Dhamar, descending about 500 m. Continuing the journey to San'a, there is another climb of 400 m up to the **Jislah Pass** at a height of more than 2600 m (fine panoramic view). After this we cross the highlands, parts of which are used for intensive agriculture with artificial irrigation. Four or five hours after leaving Ta'izz we arrive at San'a (Bab al-Yemen).

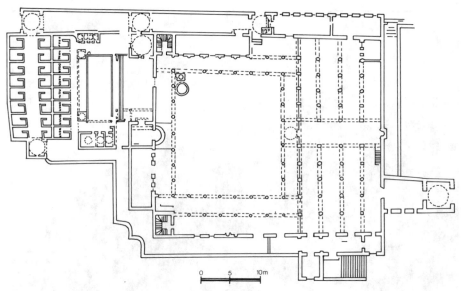

Plan of the main mosque at Jibla

Other Excursions

Both the road that runs westwards about 2 km south of Ibb, and the footpath 3 km south of the town link **Jibla** with the main road (about 3 km). Jibla (colour plate 51), a medium-sized town, is well worth a visit - the pace of change in Yemen can be felt by noting that in the late 1950's David Holden was, so the Jiblites claimed, the first European to visit the town. It has spread out on a conical basalt hill, around which flow two little rivers which join at the east side of the hill. The lower town has three bridges dating from the 14th and 15th centuries. A good half hour is needed for the ascent the highest point of the upper town. There is an historic mosque (perhaps 9th century), as well as imposing town houses and fortifications on the highest point of the hill. The construction of the upper town on the steep slope shows the architects' confident mastery of statics.

The **main mosque**, also called the Sayyida Arwa Bint Ahmad Mosque 'the mosque of the Lady Arwa, daughter of Ahmad' (colour plate 40), is a reminder of an interesting piece of Yemeni religious history. It was founded, according to documentary evidence, in 1088/9 AD, when the territory of the Zaydi Imam did not yet extend as far as Jibla. The town, founded about 20 years before the mosque, was in the hands of

Jibla, minaret and domes of the Najd al-Jum Mosque

181

Coffee cultivation in the highlands (19th-century view)

Ismailis. The ruling Fatimid Ismaili family, the Sulayhid dynasty, controlled a large area of Yemen. Ruling some of the time from San'a, and some of the time from Jibla, it survived from 1064 until 1138.

These Ismailis were the Tayyibiya branch of Fatimid Ismailism (or 'Sevener' Shia). Ali as-Sulayhi, founder of the Sulayhid dynasty, preached Fatimid Ismailism; his daughter-in-law, Arwa, recognized at-Tayyib as the rightful successor to the Fatimid line in Yemen and as the 'disappeared' Imam, whose incarnation she herself represented. A learned man was appointed to lead the sect after her death (but not as Imam); the Tayyibiya sect made many converts in India, so the spiritual head moved to Gujerat in the 16th century.

Sayyida Arwa Bint Ahmad became the leader of the Sulayhid dynasty after her husband, al-Mukarram Ahmad, abdicated because of ill health in 1086. She recognized at-Tayyib as the rightful successor to the Fatimid line, thus starting the Tayyibi tradition in Yemen's Ismaili community (there are still said to be around 80,000 Ismailis in North Yemen). The sultana (or malika - queen - as she is usually called today) expanded Jibla further. On her death in 1138 the Sulayhi dynasty became extinct.

Two minarets dominate the main mosque in Jibla. Scholars believe the minaret at the south corner of the mosque to be the older one and date it to the period of the

mosque's foundation; the lower part is rectangular and built of masonry, on which is set a cylinder also of masonry. The second minaret occupies the eastern corner of the mosque; it is a little taller and has an octagonal shaft, which becomes cylindrical just below the muezzin's balcony. The eastern minaret has been dated to the 12th century.

On the northwest side stands the prayer hall proper, built on a difficult sloping site. To the southeast it opens into the great courtyard surrounded by porticos. The mihrab (prayer niche) in the hall shows Persian influences. In the western corner is the tomb of Sayyida Arwa. Its decoration is modest, as befits an Islamic burial place, but the beautiful inscriptions in early kufic and naskhi scripts deserve attention.

Shared taxis are available for the drive to **al-Udayn,** about 15 km west of Ibb, and a lovely spot. About halfway begins the descent to the bottom of Wadi Ana, 800 m below, following a dirt road that winds round 69 bends to reach the bottom. Many of these bends are so narrow that the car has to stop and reverse to take the corner. On the opposite slope terrace agriculture in the best Yemeni tradition can be seen: qat, coffee and fruit are grown in tiny carefully terraced fields.

On the valley bottom the sheltered situation results in an almost tropical climate. The wadi carries water for most of the year, and tall trees line the course of the river. Coffee, bananas, papaya and

Minaret of the Saiyyani Mosque near Jibla

bamboo are grown beneath the trees.

Al-Udayn has a mosque that is picturesque, but of no great historical interest. The return from al-Udayn to Ibb makes an attractive walk.

For those who want to see more of the magnificence of Yemeni scenery and to get a sense of what earlier travellers experienced, the journey over the old Sumarra Pass road to Yarim (colour plate 25) is recommended. There is no through traffic with shared taxis on this route, but a four-wheel-drive car can be rented at the village of al-Makhadir halfway between Ibb and Yarim.

To cover the distance of nearly 40 km takes four or five hours. The drive, mostly at walking pace, goes up and down hill in sharp bends, stops for a time at a water-filled wadi and finally climbs up to a point 20 m higher than the modern motor road. This old route, known as the Turkish road, has also been affected by progress (it was widened in the late 1950's) so the journey along it is not the adventure it was. Nevertheless one can still imagine the columns of camels, donkeys and people making their way through the unspoiled landscape: in antiquity this was probably a major caravan route.

The Imam Ahmad

From 1948 to 1962 North Yemen was ruled by the 66th Zaydi Imam, Ahmad. 'Priest-King of the Zaydi Muslims, he had inherited and perfected a complete autocracy,' wrote David Holden in 1966. 'Possessed of the authority of a descendant of the Prophet and of a royal line that began in the 9th century, he ruled with minute command and brusque brutality.' He extended the rule of the Zaydis over the rest of the population, a rule that was severe and detailed in the extreme but which imposed peace and stability on the country. Like a medieval monarch, his court followed him around, often from his capital at Ta'izz - he distrusted San'a- and the seaside village of Sukhne. There he gave an unprecedented press-conference, attended by Holden:

When the Imam's word came through at last to Ta'izz we were flown to Sukhne in one of the Yemeni Airlines' DC3's. These were modern conveniences that the Imam had embraced of necessity, along with a group of Swedish pilots to fly them. They did treble duty, flying unscheduled passenger services to Aden and elsewhere, carrying the Imam and his officials between their various palaces and captitals, and distributing elements of the tribal army in emergencies. Ours dropped us at noon on the Tihama desert, with the mountains inland hidden in a yellow dust haze and the little white palace alone at the head of a shallow wadi seeming far too small and insignificant to contain the Imam's almost legendary power.

The Imam himself, however, was as legendary as they come. He was a short but immensely burly figure running to fat in old age, for he was 68 when he held this, the first and only press conference of his turbulent life. His dress was that of any Yememi sayyid - a black, gold-edged cloak, white gown, and white turban bound round a brightly-embroidered, cylindrical hat. He wore a gold-handled dagger and sat hunched over a table in a white-washed room surrounded by his bodyguard, with two small sons at his feet and another small adopted son at his right hand. The Director General of the Foreign Ministry, Sayyid Hassan Ibrahim, a courteous, soft-spoken, small-boned man who had once been Ambassador to the Court of St James and had the feline inscrutability of a born diplomatist, stood by his chair to interpret for us.

The way he spoke revealed a remarkable man. His voice came in rapid, hoarse gasps, as if he was in pain - as indeed he might have been, for he spent his days at Sukhne only in order to treat his chronic rheumatism in the water from the local hot springs. He was popularly reputed to be suffering also from half-a-dozen other less mentionable diseases; and although blood analyses performed by American doctors some years later scotched one old canard by proving that syphilis was not among the old man's afflictions he certainly looked as if his frame and his mind alike had been taxed beyond the strength of most men. His face worked uncontrollably with every utterance, his hands tugged at his black-dyed beard, and his eyes - starting from his head with goitre and the effort of speech - rolled like white marbles only tenuously anchored to his sallow flesh. (It is worth noting perhaps that the story that Ahmad regularly tied a cord round his neck in his youth to make his eyes pop and increase the general fearsomeness of his appearance, is almost certainly untrue - although it has been repeated in several respectable places.) At a glance one might have thought him literally staring mad. But if he was he remained uncannily alert. Nothing in the room escaped him: his eyes could be riveted in the instant upon the slightest move-ment, and he listened to every questioner with an intensity so fierce and so impatient that he seemed at times about to leap up, crying 'Off with his head!' like the Queen of Hearts in *Alice in Wonderland.* He answered everything without a note or a consultation, pausing only to allow Hassan Ibrahim to translate his replies, with the gratuitous aid of the Imam's adopted son, who evidently fancied that his command of English was as good as any old Ambassador's, and who followed the whole bizarre scene with sharp attention. The boy was, we learned, the offspring of the Imam's former chauffeur who had died protecting the old man in the last attempt on his life; and the Imam seemed to favour him even beyond his own sons, patting him indul-gently at his interventions and sharing a fearful, mocking smile with us as he did so.

These flashes of grim, ingratiating humour, when the full lips were drawn back over broken teeth and the dark brows were lowered over popping eyes, gave an extraordinary humanity to what might otherwise have seemed a mere broken monster. One grasped not only the power, cruelty and suspicion of a total despot, not only the weaknesses of pain, sickness and age with which his will seemed to be in open, tigerish conflict, but also the sense of a man fearfully alone. Beyond the boy - or perhaps, the boys, for his own young sons were no doubt objects of his affection, too - there was probably no-one in the room whom he trusted. Like all absolute rulers, he was doomed to be absolutely solitary; and he derived such human warmth as he could only from those who were not yet in a position to betray him. Yet even this he seemd to feel was a weakness, and he sought to cover it with sardonic humour - distancing himself from his own indulgence towards the boys by sharing a joke at his own expense with us. He was, I think, an intensely self-aware man who knew that if he ceased to calculate and observe his own actions for an instant he opened the door to betrayal. By no stretch of the imagination could he ever have been described as attractive, physically or temperamentally. On the contrary, he was fearsome and ugly. But he had the same sneaking, human appeal, the same capacity to compel reluctant admiration, as Shakespeare's Richard III. And here I recall that it was not Lewis Carroll's Queen of Hearts who first cried 'Off with his head!' in such a peremptory fashion, but that same Richard.

> *Talks't thou to me of 'ifs'? Thou art a traitor:*
> *Off with his head!*

Imam Ahmad

At the time, the resemblance between the two men did not occur to me; but in memory, it is compelling. They share to my mind the same ferocity, quickness and suspicion, the same grim quality of laughter. They share an obvious physical weakness - at least in the Imam's later years - and a compensating sense of immense and steely will-power. They share their inevitable solitude, and even, I believe, the same pride in their powers of sexual conquest. Years after my only meeting with the Imam I heard from sources who, although impeccable, shall remain nameless, of his preoccupation with his failing sexual powers in the last year or two of his life. He weighed by then nearly 300 lb., for he had given up walking anywhere and generally had to be lifted into his car on a specially powered seat that swivelled out to one side. But he still enjoyed the company of women and sought to impress them, with all the vanity of an old man; and great was the rejoicing in his palace one day when, after a long course of hormone drugs supplied by an American doctor, he called in his household to observe that he had achieved an erection for the first time in eighteen months.

Essentially, and above all, however, Richard III and the Imam Ahmad shared a medieval background. Often coarse, cruel and sombre, their worlds were each full of enmity and conflict, dominated by dynastic rivalries and family treachery. Nine of Ahmad's brothers died violent deaths, often at his instigation; and when Ahmad's father, Yahya, was machine-gunned to death in 1948, and a rival briefly seized the throne, Ahmad, preparing for his own successful *coup*, might well have echoed Richard's speech:

> *Why, I can smile, and murder while I smile...*
> *Can I do this, and cannot get a crown?*
> *Tut! Were it farther off, I'll pluck it down.*

For two weeks in 1955 Ahmad was overthrown by a half-brother and imprisoned in his palace at Ta'izz. Then again, more than ever, we might have heard another echo of Richard in the field at Bosworth as the Imam one day snatched a Bren gun from a careless guard and mowed down his captors single-handed.

> *Slave! I have set my life upon a cast,*
> *And I will stand the hazard of the die!*

For Ahmad the dice rolled well. Where Richard died, he lived for a few more years to end his life, against all the odds, in bed. But in preserving his life and kingdom with all his force and all his skill he had, willy-nilly, opened windows upon a new world that nobody could close again. When we left him in his little room at Sukhne, his eyes rolling, his lips drawn back in a farewell grin, we were taken to a long cool chamber elsewhere in the palace where a meal had been laid on trestle tables. The first course was Russian salad from a Heinz tin. With facetious thoughts of the Crown Prince in Moscow and Soviet rifles on the Aden frontier, I turned to one of the Yemeni officials and asked what significance we should attach to this strange coincidence. 'None,' said he, 'except that it is the Imam's favourite dish. He just likes mayonnaise.' Within three days this curious intelligence from an unknown dateline in the Yemen was published in several of the chief newspapers of Britain and America. The kingdom of silence had been breached at last.

Timna

No other ancient site in the six kingdoms of ancient South Arabia has been as thoroughly investigated as Timna, the capital of Qataban. In 1950-51 a team of archaeologists led by Wendell Phillips was able to work undisturbed at Timna for almost twelve months, in striking contrast with their time at Ma'rib where every move was hindered during the nine months they managed to stay (see page 25ff). Moreover it proved possible for most of the pieces found in Timna and the inscriptions copied there to be taken to Aden, or to the United States and Europe, for scientific analysis. Scholars were thus able to continue building on their discoveries after the end of the 1950-51 campaign, even though the later political situation prevented their own return to Timna.

For all that we do not even know exactly how the name of Qataban's capital was pronounced. The writers of antiquity give the name as Tamna, Thumna or Thomna, and it could also be written as Temna - the spelling that Wissmann preferred. Like other Semitic scripts, such as those still used for Arabic and Hebrew, the South Arabian script does not indicate vowels. Moreover, the only records of the city's name are carved in stone, and are lapidary in every sense; and no manuscripts on leather or papyrus have been found that might have had longer texts and included vowel signs, such as are used in the Koran to avoid ambiguities. When Timna fell in the catastrophic conflagration evidenced by fire debris found in the excavations all texts on organic materials must have been destroyed. Not that, in any case, much could have survived the intervening centuries, for, as Wendell Phillips noted: 'Bayhan is very dry, so papyrus would not rot, but it also has an active and varied insect population, to which Professor Albright has ascribed the destruction of all papyri.'

Bayhan is the name of the region in which the remains of Timna were found, a single day's journey from the Ma'rib oasis by caravan, but protected by difficult mountains. Until 1967 Bayhan was a princedom, and in the 1950's it had a ruler, Sherif Hussain Ibn Ahmad, who could guarantee foreigners safe access and was also open-minded enough to do so. It is thanks to his influence and tolerant attitude that scholars are relatively well informed about Timna.

The Semitic scholar Walter Müller wrote in the 1970's: 'Our most important source for the history of Qataban are the Qatabanian inscriptions, which are written in the

Timna, excavation work at the temple of the god Athtar (associated with the planet Venus), during the campaign in 1950-51

Old South Arabian alphabet, but in a language clearly different from Sabaic while sharing some archaic features with Minaean and Hadramatic. Although the Sabaean texts in which Qataban is mentioned also make a vital contribution to knowledge of the history of this kingdom, even the approximately accurate dating of many events is still disputed.'

Thus Wendell Phillips wrote after his excavations that 'the most important period in the history of Qataban fell between about 350 and 50 BC', and he conjectured that Timna was destroyed and abandoned in the years around the beginning of our era. Wissmann on the other hand thought that this collapse occurred in the decade between AD 90 and 100. And whereas Phillips believed there to be historical evidence that Qataban was already in existence around 800 BC, Wissmann and other scholars thought that date too early. It would appear that the disputed dates are not essential for a general understanding of South Arabian history.

In 1895 the Austrian savant Eduard Glaser became the first person to draw attention to the almost completely buried ruins at Wadi Bayhan, which he had heard of, but never actually seen for himself. The first European to see them was the Englishman G. Wyman Bury, who managed to visit Hajjar Kuhlan, as the Arabs call

South Gate of Timna after it was uncovered in 1950-51 by Wendell Phillips's team

the former city of Timna, in 1900. Bury copied eight inscriptions from a wall rising out of the sand, but it was to be nearly a quarter of a century before the identity of the site was revealed to the world. In an analysis of all known Qatabanian inscriptions published in 1924, N. Rhodokanakis, an Austrian scholar of Greek descent, demonstrated that it the city that lay beneath the sand hills on the left bank of the Wadi Bayhan must be Timna of the ancients.

This location surprised the scholarly world because it was now apparent that a distance of only 60 or 80 km (depending on the route taken) separated the sites of Ma'rib and Timna. So it seemed that the already mighty Sabaean kingdom had been unable to prevent the emergence of a strong rival on its doorstep, a short distance from the Sabaean capital. In fact such a reading is too strong, since we know little in detail about that period and its history. It may be that Timna was originally a Sabaean foundation, which then grew stronger - at first imperceptibly - and only eventually gained autonomy. Then in the period between 500 and 400 BC it could have taken advantage of a period of Sabaean weakness to become a fully independent state, though the rulers of Saba may in fact have tolerated an independent trading partner beyond the southeast frontier of their state as a buffer against hostile powers in

Hadramawt. These and other questions were the subject of theoretical study up to the Second World War, but the main concern was the deciphering of further inscriptions. The first complete grammar of Old South Arabian was published in 1943 by Maria Höfner.

Then at the beginning of the 1950's came the turn of the practical archaeologists led by the adventurous Wendell Phillips. His team, which included European scholars, employed between 200 and 300 local workers in two campaigns of excavation; in the second phase experienced supervisors and foremen were brought in from Egypt. Their combined efforts uncovered the south gate of Timna, as well as considerable remains of two houses named the 'Yafaan House' and 'Yafash House' after the inscriptions found in them. The remains of a temple dedicated to Athtar, the Qatabanian counterpart of the Roman goddess Venus, were also excavated. Throughout South Arabia this celestial deity was, to our surprise perhaps, masculine. The temple of Athtar proved to be the biggest of the building complexes freed from the sand within Timna. Excavation just outside the city (about 2.5 km to the northwest) uncovered the former cemetery, known to the Arabs as 'Hayd bin Aqil'. Lastly Professor W. F. Albright, the intellectual father of the enterprise, started an excavation for potsherds. In Hajjar bin Hamid twenty cultural layers were uncovered. Albright used the sherds to draw up a pottery index of Qatabanian history.

Qatabanian funerary stele

The campaigns of 1950-51 also revealed remains of a widely ramified irrigation system in ancient Wadi Bayhan. The Belgian epigraphist, Albert Jamme, was taken by a bedouin to rock inscription in Wadi al-Fara which seemed to have been scratched on the stone face at a very early period, before the foundation of a Qatabanian state. These inscriptions were written from left to right, like Greek, Latin or modern European languages. Professor Jamme established that there was a strong similarity between various letters in the script used in Wadi al-Fara and the Canaanite alphabet, from which the Phoenician-Hebrew and the South Arabian alphabets may be derived.

This discovery allows us to assume that Wadi Bayhan, the agricultural area that was the heartland of Qataban, was

27 SHAHARAH A bridge built in the 17th century, when the Ottoman Empire first made inroads into Yemen. It spans a chasm several hundred metres deep and provided a back exit from the refuge of the Imams

29 Al-TAWILAH The little town is called 'the long one' because it is stretched out over several cliffs

28 WADI DAHR Defensive tower built of mud and straw. Until the mid-20th century such towers were maintained all over South Arabia as protection against possible attacks by nomads

30 SHIBAM The most impressive town in the Wadi Hadramawt. Nearly all houses are still built using the ▷ traditional building methods which go back thousands of years

31 AL-HAUTA A town with an architectural style of its own, between Hadramawt and the coast

32 HAJJARAYN A cliff-top town more than a thousand years old

33 JOL Children of semi-nomads
35 TARIM Returning home with fodder for the
livestock

34 JOL Bedouin boy
36 WADI HADRAMAUT Bedouin woman with
face-mask

37 JOL Stones, thorns and arid desolation

38 RHAIL UMR Oasis in the Wadi Adim

39 BIR ALI Crater lake near the sea

settled very early on; but what form of organization the society of that early settle-ment period adopted is still unknown.

The historical sequence can be given - with some degree of certainty - as follows. Until 410 BC Qataban was a dependency of the mighty coastal power of Ausan; then the Minaeans and Qatabanians combined to annihilate Ausan (see page 239ff). Qataban took over a large part of Ausanian territory and what had once been an inland state now extended as far as the shores of the Indian Ocean. It thus became a trading power of the first rank. Whereas previously the Qatabanian state had been able to profit only from the transit trade of the caravans, it now had control of the excellent port of Aden and part of the maritime trade. Qataban thus became so rich that only a short time afterwards - around 390 BC - it was able to shake off Sabaean influence. For nearly 200 years thereafter the Qatabanians remained at a peak of power and prosperity.

At that time Timna would have been almost a big as Ma'rib and the second largest city in South Arabia. Pliny the Elder (AD 24-79) wrote that the Qatabanian capital contained 65 temples within its walls. It could afford such expense because it was powerful enough to control the caravan traffic between Ma'rib and the Hadrami city of Shabwa, thanks both to its military capacity, and to the security and technical improvement of its own communications with Ma'rib. These were carried from Wadi Bayhan across two passes to Wadi Harib: Aqabat Najd Marqad and Aqabat Mablaqah. So important were the roads across these two passes in antiquity that they were paved, and remains of this paving have survived to the present day. Aqabat Mablaqah is particularly impressive: in a single 5 km stretch the road climbs some 350 m in hairpin bends, until, just below the highest point, the gradient proved too steep for the road builders, and they cut through the rock, hollowing out a path 5-7 m wide, 14 m deep and 35 m long. A caravan crossing this point still had, according to Pliny, another '65 camel resting points ahead of it', which the conscientious Roman estimated at 2,437,500 paces.

Later, when fewer camel caravans set out on the long march through the desert, and the maritime trade route between South Arabia and Egypt or Syria (via the pre-sent-day port of Aqaba) began to play an ever more important part, Qataban remained in a fortunate economic position thanks to its control of the coastal zone that had once been Ausanian. But such an advantage could only arouse the envy of neighbours, and this envy grew stronger the more trade was transferred to the sea route. Around the year 120 BC the city suffered a severe setback when two provinces in the northwest of the Qatabanian kingdom - Himyar and Radman - broke away, with Sabaean help. Timna was soon once again the capital of a landlocked state, allied with Hadramawt against the enemies to the north and west. However, when the city fell - the date of this is disputed (see page 190f) - the enemy came from the east, for it was a treacherous Hadramawt that delivered the death blow to its immediate neigh-bour and rival. In fact there were several blows, since the Qatabanian kingdom

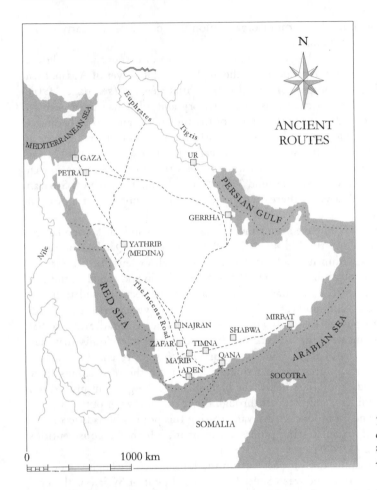

N

ANCIENT
ROUTES

0   1000 km

The most important caravan and maritime routes of ancient Arabia

continued for a few decades after the annihilation of its capital before being completely incorporated by Hadramawt.

The evidence of Timna's destruction is described thus by Wendell Phillips: 'After removing several feet of sand in front of the gate, with only a few ancient objects turning up, [the archaeologists] reached a stratum of heavy burning which contained many artefacts, such as potsherds, beads, bits of inscribed stone, and pieces of bronze and iron. We saw streaks of ashes with layers of clean earth and sand in between, then another layer of ashes with more bits of stone inscriptions, pieces of alabaster rows of beautifully carved ibex heads, and other objects. It was evident almost from the start that the city of Timna had suffered a catastrophic destruction, in which fire played a major part.'

Art and Religion

A few of the Qatabanian art objects that have come to light are the result of chance finds, but most are the fruit of the excavation campaign in 1950-51. Some pieces can be seen in the National Museum in Aden; others were taken - controversially - to the United States by Wendell Phillips.

Among the most notable finds in the 1950-51 excavations was a life-size head of a woman made of milk-white alabaster. She has a young face with a slightly ironic smile playing on her lips - the facial expression has little of the stiffness so character-istic of the majority of old South Arabian physiognomies. The head also aroused interest because it has an almost complete coiffure made of plaster curls (or, accord-ing to some, moulded glass) and the eyes are blue with the remains of lapis lazuli inlay in the sockets. Professor Alexander Honeyman, the archaeologist who discov-ered it, dated the head to the 1st century BC. The unexpected style has caused scholars to doubt the South Arabian origin of the work; it may have been imported from Egypt, for instance, where lapis lazuli was often used as inlay for eyes in this period.

Also reminiscent of Egypt are the two bronze lions excavated in Timna in 1950. These animals, 61 cm high and cast by the lost wax process, are almost mirror images and have an identical inscription on the base, naming two craftsmen who had deco-rated the 'Yafash House', and the king ruling at the time, Shahr Yagil Yuharib. The lions are highly naturalistic in feel; they stand upright raising their right paws as if to strike; each carries on its back an eros wielding a broken arrow in one hand and a broken chain in the other. This symbol of sensual love, popular in Pompeii and else-where, represents Eros taming the wild lion and bridling it with a chain. Professor Albright identified the pieces as copies made c. 150 BC by Qatabanian craftsmen from an original which could have been made in Egypt during the Hellenistic period. The inscribed names helped Albright to improve his South Arabian chronology, but in aesthetic terms, the lions were further evidence of the great intensity of cultural exchange in antiquity .

The third significant find made during the 1950-51 excavations also pointed to for-eign influence. This was the bronze figure of a seated woman almost a metre high with a long inscription on the base, now in the National Museum in Aden. The text identifies the figure as the deceased 'Lady Bar'at', with a vow to preserve her mem-ory. The name of the current king can also be read: he was Warawil Ghaylan Yuhan'im, the son of the ruler whose name is inscribed on the bronze lions of Timna. In Phillips's description : 'The Hellenistic influence was apparent not only in the statue but in the lady herself, for her coiffure was an elaborate coiled and braided affair popular in the Greek world in the 1st century BC. The cut of her flowing robes was also Greek in style, and the modelling of the entire figure was clearly Hellenistic.'

The question in fact is whether there are any examples of indigenous Qatabanian

The gold chain and pendant found in Timna by the Phillips team (now lost)

art. As so often in South Arabia we must turn to the architecture. Brian Doe is succinct in his appreciation of the stonework of the temple at Timna: 'This is a masterly structure. The masonry is well cut with tooled faces, laid dry and bonded in courses of reducing height. This straight wall is joined to the massive irregular blocks of the southern bastioned wall.'

It is unlikely that with architectural achievements of this sophistication, Qataban did not also have have its own distinctive minor arts. Is it possible that all examples of these were destroyed in the fire, or were the minor arts in Qataban used mainly for grave gifts (in which case they would have been taken by grave-robbers over the last 2000 years)? During excavations in the necropolis of Timna, Wendell Phillips and his team found a gold chain with a U-shaped pectoral on which was a chased crescent moon, which like the borders of the pendant was edged with granulations. Around the moon two female names were engraved in Qatabanian script, and in the gap in the pendant hung a small medallion with a woman's head. If any piece deserved a place of honour in the National Museum it was this, but sadly it has disappeared.

In Qataban the moon god Amm was the state deity. 'Amm' means 'uncle' (father's brother). Professor Walter Müller notes: 'Timna as capital is the "city of the tribes of Amm".' The prince, who was first mukarrib and later king, was the most important link between Amm and the 'Children of Amm', that is, the people.

The kingdom's god was not, however, at the apex of the triad of deities. As in the Sabaean kingdom, in Qataban the star god, Athtar, a masculine counterpart to the Roman Venus, took precedence. This was because Qataban's heartland, the Bayhan river oasis, had developed an intensive agriculture dependent on artificial irrigation. Without enough rain even the best irrigation system was useless, so like the Sabaeans for their river oasis Ma'rib, the Qatabanians turned to a fertility god who provided rain. This was Athtar, who consequently enjoyed the greatest respect.

The discovery of the two bronze lions with erotes prompted Phillips to wonder

Qatabanian funerary stele (now in the National Museum, San'a)

whether 'sacred prostitution' could have been practised at Timna. In his account he conjectured that the Yafesh House, in the ruins of which the two lions - symbols of physical strength and sensual love - were found, could have been the location for ritual sexual acts in honour of the god of Venus. In any case a love cult of this kind would only have played a secondary role, since we know from inscriptions that the main acts of worship were sacrifice and prayer.

It is also known that pilgrimages played an important role in the religion. For the Qatabanians, as for other South Arabians, the city of Mecca with the holy Ka'ba would have been of the greatest significance even at this early period. The geographer Ptolemy, who lived in the 2nd century AD, knew of the city which he calls Macoraba, but it is assumed that Mecca played a role long before then. Since it lay on the Incense Road about halfway between South Arabia and the Mediterranean coast, Mecca could combine the worldly with the spiritual, commerce with religion. It is very probable therefore that the Qatabanians went on pilgrimage to Mecca to pay homage to the moon god Hubal and the three goddesses Allat, al-Ussa and al-Manat venerated there. Certainly by the time a new religion came to South Arabia from the region of Mecca and Medina, South Arabian pilgrimages to the north were already an old tradition, though by this stage the Qatabanian state no longer existed - in the 7th century the people of the region, like the Hadramis, were under Persian rule.

We do not know how the conversion of the Himyarite-Sabaean rulers to Mosaic and Christian monotheism in the 3rd and 4th centuries affected the inhabitants of the interior of the former Qatabanian kingdom. No traces of Christianity have been found in Wadi Bayhan, but until the founding of the state of Israel, the little towns and villages southwest of Bayhan were home to several thousand Jews. Like their co-religionists in North Yemen they had been influenced by the Sephardim, though this is not to say that the South Yemeni Jews were themselves immigrants from Spain. They may just as well have been the descendants of those Arab converts who lived in great tribal associations in the region of Mecca and Medina in the lifetime of the Prophet, or they may have arrived in southern Arabia as part of the earlier Diaspora. On the other hand, most of the Jews who used to live in Aden migrated there during the period of British colonial rule.

Visiting Timna

The unification of the two Yemens in 1990 has opened the way for visits to Wadi Bayhan, ending about 20 years of enforced lack of access for foreign travellers. You can travel from Aden to al-Qasab, the main town in Bayhan, and on to ancient Timna (now Hajjar Kuhlan) (about 250 km); but it is more agreeable to follow the ancient caravan route between Ma'rib and Timna. Hans Helfritz travelled this way in 1931 and stayed for three weeks in Harib, and this was the route used by Wendell Phillips in the 1950's.

Ma'rib and Harib (formerly a border town to South Yemen) should now be connected by a good asphalt road over narrow mountain passes (85 km). Until recently this road became a passable track (four-wheel-drive only) at the southern edge of the Ma'rib oasis and near Jabal al-Badi. **Harib** is worth a short visit. The little town has a lively permanent market, where the rock salt mined not far away is traded, and there are some old stone fortifications. However, it is more rewarding to visit the ancient site of **Haribat** (Arabic: Hajjar henu as-Sureir), the ruins of a Qatabanian city, about 3 km outside the town, in Wadi Harib. It seems relatively untouched either by stone-robbers or by mass tourism, thanks to its situation in the formerly restricted border zone between the two Yemens. Although archaeologists have not yet excavated them, the carefully built walls, up to 3 m in height, and the remains of two massive gate houses can be seen. The foundations of the city walls and whole lengths of streets can be made out; the surviving ashlar lower courses of the old houses suggest a well laid out town plan.

For the visitor interested in archaeology Haribat has more to offer than **Timna** itself. Already by the mid-1960's a visiting German journalist could write: 'Many of the laboriously excavated columns, temple steps and walls have been covered by sand again, or been used by the inhabitants of present-day Hajjar Kuhlan for building houses...' In this instance more of the ancient masonry seems to have gone into house building than has been lost to the shifting sands. Nevertheless Timna, now that it can once again be visited, should be of great interest to anyone interested in South Arabian archaeology. The very name has a magical ring to it, not just because of its great history going back around 2000 years, but also because in the 19th and 20th centuries Timna was so strictly protected, first by jealous tribesmen and more recently by a mistrustful Communist government.

The findings of Brian Doe, the former Director of Antiquities in Aden and one of the leading authorities on Timna, can be summed up as follows. The site of the ruins covers an area of about 21 hectares, laid out on a natural

Timna, obelisk of Shahr Hilal Yuhan'im engraved with market regulations

cliff at the northern entrance of the wadi. Timna was a walled city with several gates, apparently four in number: the south gate (in fact to the southwest) and three other gate structures on the southeast, northwest and east sides. The **south gate** is flanked by two bastions. On the massive wall, 3 m above the pavement, is an inscription recording the laws of the city. The masonry shows an archaic method of construction, and appears to date from an early phase in the city's history. The other gates have not yet been investigated. Local people digging for building material have, however, brought to light the bastions of the southwest gate. Here the masonry shows greater skill; the blocks of stone are well cut to size, worked with the hammer and laid in an orderly manner.

Near the town centre is the **main temple**, which was dedicated to Athtar. Its construction probably took place in several stages. From the earliest phase is the massive masonry of the lowest layers, probably the oldest part of the sanctuary. The building was extended in a second phase, datable to the 3rd century BC. Under the kings of the 1st century BC there was a third phase which probably saw the addition of a new courtyard and steps. Yellow and red marble plaques found in the temple courtyard would have been part of the revetment of the interior walls of the temple. In a hole in the sand stood the **obelisk** of the king, Shahr Hilal Yuhan'im, which was uncovered in 1950, and found to carry inscriptions referring to the laws governing trade, market and taxation in the city. The obelisk is currently missing; opinions vary as to whether it has been removed to a museum, or buried again so that it cannot be stolen.

The **Yafaan House** and the **Yafash House**, both excavated in 1950-51 are situated on the west side of the city, the Yafaan House nearer the south gate. The Yafash House has six inscriptions giving information about the succession of some Qatabanian kings, and incidentally allowing epigraphers to trace the development of the Qatabanian script. According to the inscriptions the house itself consisted of several rooms at ground level; an outside staircase led to the upper floor, where there were storerooms and a verandah.

The city **cemetery** lies a little way out of the town. One can see its remains on the west side of a large outcrop of rock. A few Qatabanian buildings of stone and mud-brick masonry stand out. The lowest building at the foot of the rock is thought to a temple of the dead. There is also a shaft about 18 m deep in which many artefacts and an inscription were found.

The People of Wadi Bayhan

After rain the desert valley of Bayhan carries water for a short time from the mountains in the south into the Empty Quarter (Rub al-Khali). It was formerly one of the many little princedoms in this region. The last ruler, bound like so many of his kind by treaty to the British, was Sherif Hussain Ibn Ahmad, the ruler who was so helpful to Phillips and his team. His residence from 1934 to 1968 was in the town of Bayhan an-Nuqub at the northern end of the wadi. The little princedom served the British protecting power as a buffer against its immediate neighbour, North Yemen. When the British were forced to abandon Aden and its hinterland towards the end of 1967, the revolution came to Bayhan too. The septuagenarian Sherif Hussein fled to Saudi Arabia and was sentenced to death in his absence by the rulers of the new people's democracy; he died in exile.

What will happen now? Will the end of communism bring about a revival of the princedom of Bayhan and return an heir of the last reigning sherif to the throne? It seems unlikely that the new, united Republic of Yemen will put the clock back quite so far. The government of the People's Democratic Republic made Wadi Bayhan, together with the stretch of land adjoining it to the east, into the Fourth Governorate, with a population of about 100,000. About 5% of the total population of South Yemen are classified as nomads, but in the Fourth Governorate this figure is 20%. The great majority of the bedouin do not, however, live in Wadi Bayhan itself but further east, where they wander the region from Wadi Hammam in the northeast as far as Wadi Jirdan, and thus come into contact with the provincial capital Ataq and the ancient city of Shabwa.

Former palace of the Sherif of Bay han

The southern part of Wadi Bayhan was settled by people of the Musabein tribe, while in the northern part the Bal Harith tribe predominates. Adjacent towards the northeast, in the direction of Shabwa (formerly Shabwat), is the al-Karab tribe, the bedouin who for long made access to the former capital of Hadramawt almost impossible (see page211).

The al-Karab are also still for the most part full bedouin. They keep dromedaries, goats and fat-tailed sheep, and sell the products of their livestock, hand-woven carpets, and wood which they gather in the desert valleys. Long caravans take the wood to the large villages and towns on important market days. The al-Karab also engage in intermediary trade by bringing modern goods from the coast to the interior - as their ancestors did frankincense. The tents of these bedouin are made of raffia mats and linen; they do not need warm accommodation like the nomads of North Arabia. Nor do the al-Karab have broad, green steppes like those that appear in the north of the Arabian Peninsula after rain. Without sufficient grassland for their animals, they are obliged to procure substitute fodder, so they have accustomed their animals to eating dried sardines and dried shark. The dried fish, bought at the coast, provides adequate supply for their long migrations; furthermore, dried fish has in the course of time become the staple diet for people too. Meat is eaten only on special feast days. Shark, dried sardines, some rice and round flat bread form the main food, eaten with very sweet tea. The caravans, with their load of fish, can be smelt at some distance.

As part of their programme of social reform the government of the People's Republic tried to make the bedouin sedentary. Model villages were built with solid houses, a school and a health post. There were attempts to make use of bedouin expertise with livestock. Agricultural land was farmed as communal property and water pumps distributed the water to the collective fields. Some bedouin do occasionally practice agriculture, but give it up when the conditions deteriorate. They then move on to another region and their houses, which may have only just been built, fall into ruin. It is not easy to distinguish these half-bedouin (colour plates 33, 34 and 36) from their fully sedentary brothers.

Now that the People's Republic no longer exists, the people in Wadi Bayhan once again have more freedom of choice. They will probably use it to dissolve the agricultural collectives. Feudalism is not likely to return, but private ownership of land will, and there will be privately-run farming in Wadi Bayhan. The farmers also have greater freedom of movement than under the authoritarian socialists; but this will not be without limits. The north of the Fourth Governorate opens into the unmarked border region to Saudi Arabia, and not far from the accepted border oil extraction is under way. Oil, now the major influence on the way of life of the people in this region, brings money, but also instability. Consequently, Wadi Bayhan and the adjoining district are still an area on which the state authorities are keeping a watchful eye.

Freya Stark took this photograph of an elderly tribesman of the Beni Himyar in the 1930's. 'The name of the tribe, and of the Jebel Himyar where they live, perpetuates that of the last of the pre-Islamic empires, though in a region far to the southeast of their supposed home. On the man's shoulder is a scaly-tailed lizard (uromastix), which the bedouin use to eat. This one, however, was given to me, and is now a charming pet and very tame, and answers to the name of Himyar.'

Shabwa

The name Hadramawt is mentioned in Genesis and there are legendary accounts of the peopling of the valley by the descendants of Shem, one of whom was a warrior known as 'Death has come' - 'hadara al-Mawt'. Most scholars, however, are agreed that the foundations of a state were laid in Hadramawt around 750 BC. There is as yet no evidence to support Carl Rathjens's assumption that the process had already begun in the period around 1300 BC. Stone inscriptions give us names of rulers of the Sabaean, Minaean and Hadrami states from about 800 BC. In the early period they are identified as priest-kings, but later the rulers of all three kingdoms became secular kings. It is thought that this transition to secular rulership first occurred in Hadramawt, before then being adopted by the adjacent states to the northwest. The impulse for such a change would have come to Hadramawt from overseas, possibly from India.

Wadi Hadramawt proper - called Sariran in antiquity - was certainly the birthplace of the state out of which the easternmost of the South Arabian kingdoms developed. We do not as yet know from which capital the old Hadrami theocratic state was governed. By the time Shabwat (later called Shabwa) rose to become the royal city of the Hadramis, several centuries had passed and the political situation in South Arabia had undergone a number of great changes. The Roman historian, Pliny the Elder (24-79 BC) wrote of the glory of the new metropolis, which he called 'Sabota'. In his *Natural History* he describes the harvesting of frankincense, the incense trade, and also mentions the 'Catabanians' (the people of Qataban - also occasionally called 'Gebbanitae') as the closest trading partners of the 'Chatramotitae' (inhabitants of Hadramawt). According to Pliny Sabota/Shabwa was the pivot of the profitable trade: 'Frankincense after being collected is conveyed to Sabota on camels, one of the gates of the city being opened for its admission; the kings have made it a capital offence for camels so laden to turn aside from the high road. At Sabota a tithe estimated by measure and not by weight is taken by the priests for the god they call Sabis, and the incense is not allowed to be put on the market until this has been done; this tithe is drawn on to defray what is a public expenditure, for actually on a fixed number of days the god graciously entertains guests at a banquet. It can only be exported through the country of the Gebbanitae, and accordingly a tax is paid on it to the king of that people as well... Fixed portions of the frankincense are also given to the priests and the king's secretaries, but besides these the guards and their attendants and the gate-keepers and servants also have their pickings; indeed all along the route they keep on paying, at one place for water, at another for fodder, or the charges for lodging at the halts, and the various octrois, so that expenses mount up to 688 denarii before the Mediterranean coast is reached.'

But what had been happening in the seven centuries that elapsed between the emergence of a Hadrami state and Shabwa's heyday as described by Pliny?

The theocratic princedom of Hadramawt, originally restricted to the great desert valley, had no direct access to the areas where frankincense was produced. The *Boswellia* shrub or tree, which provides the resin known as frankincense, grows in a subtropical climate at an altitude of 600 or 700 m, not in the dry climate of the wadi. Assuming that climatic conditions in South Arabia two or three thousand years ago were not very different from what they are today, we might surmise that most of the Boswellia was to be found further east in the region of Zofar (often written Dhofar, now a province of the Sultanate of Oman), where heavy monsoon rains fall in the hottest months of the year. Similar climatic conditions, though not so intense, predominate in coastal region to the west of Zofar, on the southern Yemeni coast as far as the area around Mukalla. The optimum climate for frankincense production in South Arabia was - and still is - limited to the coastal mountains of Zofar (and the island of Socotra). So it would have been there, a good 600 km east of Wadi Hadramawt, that the fabled Land of Incense actually lay.

Because the producers of frankincense could not export their goods to their customers in Egypt and Syria without the help of the fishermen and semi-nomads of the coastal region further west - since the road going north and northwest from Zofar ran through the most inhospitable desert of Arabia, the Empty Quarter - they had first to transport the merchandise along the coast. The first desert valley they came to that gave access to the interior was the barren Wadi Masilah, which meets the sea near the town of Saihut and begins at the eastern end of Wadi Hadramawt. All incense caravans heading northeast through Wadi Masilah had therefore to traverse the theocratic princedom of Hadramawt - and doubtless pay a heavy tribute there. The caravans further west, passing through Wadi Adam from near present-day Shihr, or from Mukalla through Wadi Duan, on shorter routes from the coast to the north, also could not avoid crossing the upland region of Hadramawt.

The large profits to be gained from transit trade must have encouraged the inhabitants of Hadramawt to extend their area of control along the trade routes. This meant expansion southwards towards the sea, and northwards towards the borders of the Sabaean sphere of influence. We can probably assume that the Hadramis were soon casting envious glances at the region where frankincense was grown. First the coastal region between present-day Mukalla and Saihut came under Hadrami control. But then the kingdom's expansion towards the northwest brought the Sabaeans onto the scene, and in the period between 600 and 450 BC the Hadrami state seems to have been a vassal state of the much more powerful Sabaean kingdom. It was not until about 400 BC that an independent secular kingdom of Hadramawt emerged, and was powerful enough to conquer Zofar, the main area in South Arabia where frankincense was grown.

For more than two hundred years the kings of Hadramawt had three strong neighbours, who were partners and at the same time rivals: Qataban, Saba and Ma'in (the kingdom of Ausan had already been destroyed by the Sabaeans). The livelihood of all four states was based on organizing transit trade with the great powers on the Mediterranean. This meant that merchandise was transported from Hadramawt to Qataban or Saba, and thence via Ma'in, to be sent on the caravan route run by the Nabataeans or other North Arabian peoples. But although they co-operated in business, each state was constantly on the lookout for ways of doing down its rivals - and if possible eliminating one of them altogether. In this power play Hadramawt was long allied with Ma'in, the northernmost of the four kingdoms. For a time there were even caravan roads running between the two states and skirting the Sabaean region. This arrangement led the Sabaeans to take stern action against the two states. Ma'in managed to resist the Sabaean attack successfully, and was even able to gain temporary ascendancy over Saba and relieve Hadramawt from Sabaean pressure. It must have been during this tense period that Sabota/Shabwa rose to become the capital of Hadramawt. The city was situated away from the densely populated wadis, but it had the advantage of a strategic position, a bulwark against the Sabaeans if they attacked Wadi Hadramawt from the west, and at the same time was a good starting point for trade with Saba and with Ma'in, where caravans could gather in numbers large enough to cross the dangerous deserts in safety. Another factor was that Hadramawt now had a new port at Qana, from which an important road ran through Wadi Mayfa'a northwards to Shabwa and from there either to Sabaean Ma'rib or Minaean Baraqish.

Around 120 BC Hadramawt lost Ma'in. The Minaean state was conquered and swallowed up by the Sabaean kingdom from which it had originally sprung. But at about the same time the newly emerged state of Himyar began to put heavy pressure on the Sabaeans. Qataban lost part of its territory to the Himyarite state and saved itself by forming an alliance with Hadramawt. Traffic had clearly declined on the caravan routes to the north, now that the Egyptians and other peoples at the northern end of the trade roads had taken to sailing their boats from the Red Sea into the Gulf of Aden and eastwards as far as the port of Qana. Despite this diminution in overland traffic Hadramawt was able to maintain its position relatively well - since its long coastline meant that it was also a maritime power.

The existence of the Hadrami kingdom was based on a mixture of commerce and warfare. In the period from around AD 100-140 the kingdom reached the zenith of its power, destroying Timna, the capital of Qataban, and later incorporating the whole of the region still held by the Qatabanians. It thus attained its largest territorial extent, which included almost the whole of the area of former South Yemen, as well as Zofar. But this greatness and splendour only brought an intensification of rivalry with the Sabaeans and the Himyarites. Indeed it was only because these two kingdoms were at war with each other that Hadramawt was able to survive for another 150 years.

At sea, too, a powerful new rival to Hadramawt had arisen in the 1st century AD. Carl Rathjens describes the situation: 'Since they were not able to subjugate the southern part of the Incense Road beyond the Nabataean kingdom, the Romans energetically developed maritime traffic in the Red Sea. Under Trajan (AD 98-117) they once again cut through the Suez isthmus from the Nile to the Red Sea, and all along the African coast they established trading posts and colonies which they were able to push forward as far as the Indian Ocean. Thus, probably for the second time in the history of sea navigation, they were able to use the same ships to travel from the Mediterranean to the Indian coast. Understandably, trade on the Incense Road was seriously affected by these political events.'

The Hadrami kingdom, tiny in comparison with the Roman Empire, had to defend its interests against the might of Rome, and it was no real comfort to the people of Hadramawt that the Roman spears were aimed more at the Sabaeans than at themselves. As Rathjens explains: 'The attempts of the Roman Empire, then at the height of its power, to isolate the Sabaean kingdom completely, forced the Sabaeans to push forward and bring the whole of the South Arabian coast into their area of control.'

By the middle of the 2nd century AD serious social tensions had already developed in Shabwa because of the great extravagance of the royal court. In the same century severe earthquakes seem to have affected the Hadrami heartland. Finally, the subjection of the state to the Himyarite-Sabaean kingdom was followed by attacks from the Kinda, semi-nomadic horsemen from central Arabia. In one of these great attacks 30,000 Kinda are said to have entered Hadramawt, where they seem to have established themselves as semi-nomadic feudal lords over a large part of the indigenous peasant population. This irruption of foreign tribes doomed any attempts by local Hadrami princes to regain independence, and was to have very serious consequences for Hadramawt. The Kinda tribes had formed a great confederation in a region more or less at the geographical centre of the Arabian Peninsula. It is described in the history books as a state, but in fact was little more than a fluctuating, unstable concentration of nomad power. The Kinda had migrated to central Arabia from the northern end of the Persian Gulf, and, once Hadramawt had fallen, they moved on further south as far the shores of the Indian Ocean. As a consequence of the invasion the farmers and townspeople of the former kingdom became subject to nomads and a country which was already highly urbanized (the cities of Shibam, Say'un and Tarim in Wadi Hadramawt are mentioned in an inscription at Ma'rib dating from the 4th century AD) once again passed temporarily into the hands of bedouins. The Kinda spoke a North Arabian dialect, which supplanted the South Arabian language and so cut off the original Hadramis from the mainstream of their 1400-year-old culture. The land of Hadramawt, the centre of that culture, was also cut off to a large extent from the outside world since the policy of the Persian governors, who established themselves on the coast towards the end of the 6th century, consisted in playing off the tribes in the hinterland against each other. Hadramawt increasingly became a land of tribal conflicts. At first the Islamicization of the region changed nothing, since even the new religious community promptly split into sects (some of which, however, were famous for their learning). It was not until about two centuries after the victory of Islam that Ahmad Ibn Isa al-Muhajir, an immigrant from Basra on the Persian Gulf, brought new stability to Wadi Hadramawt. This religious man, who claimed descent from the Prophet, was able to impose orthodox Islam as the only faith - and achieved this not by the sword, but by his skilful negotiating and powers

of persuasion. This victory of the spirit over bedouin stubbornness set a trend. The subsequent period saw the emergence of increasing numbers of religious men who sought to create and maintain peace between the tribes, often by word alone, without using armed force. Their authority derived from the fact that they knew the Koran and could claim descent from Muhammad. The activists among the Muslim faithful constituted a sort of aristocratic class, the *sada* (singular: *sayyid*). It was only thanks to this class that some form of urban life survived in Hadramawt through a period of regression to nomadic tribalism and conflict. But crudely stratified as it was, urban culture never managed to achieve an assured supremacy, and suffered some severe blows, such as the invasion in 1809 of the iconoclastic Wahhabis from the north. Right up to the modern period, indeed until the creation of the People's Republic, urban culture remained under pressure from tribal chiefs. The British, who acted as influential advisers to the tribal princes in the 19th and 20th centuries, did little at

Shabwa, the main temple after the French excavation

first to counter the destabilizing selfishness of the tribes, and indeed could have been said to have made use of it. In the 1930's and 40's, however, some British advisers and notably Harold Ingrams, were remarkably successful peacemakers in the region. (As a result, there was for instance communication again between Say'un and Shibam, only a few kilometres apart but estranged since 1857 by the aftermath of a series of bloody wars, sieges and treacherous massacres.) 'Ingram's Peace', as it was known, allowed the peaceful development of this country of petty warring chieftains, its gradual education, and eventually its genuine unity.

Shabwa, the capital of ancient Hadramawt, fell to the nomads very early on. But the royal city had already, at the end of the 2nd century AD, been conquered by the Sabaeans. Henceforth the rulers of the former metropolis remained subordinate to their Sabaean-Himyarite cousins in Ma'rib and Zafar. Now that the city had lost its independence and was declining in importance, its the exposed position on the north-west edge of the kingdom proved disastrous. In its heyday Shabwa had been a bulwark against the bedouins, but now it was unable to defend itself against the rapacious tribes. By the time the Kinda finally dealt the kingdom its death blow, Shabwa had already been devasted several times by bedouin and had long been abandoned. The Arabs gradually forgot about the once splendid metropolis of the Hadramis. Writing about 300 years after the victory of Islam the geographer al-Hamdani, who gives us such vivid descriptions of Zafar, the castle of Goumdan in San'a and other Himyarite sites, is brief when it comes to Shabwa: 'In the region between Bayhan and Hadramawt lies Shabwa, a city of the Himyar.' But he gives us a hint as to the fate of the city: 'When the Himyar waged war with the Madhich, the people left Shabwa and settled in Hadramawt, and Shibam was named after them.'

Other Arab geographers and writers make no further mention of the former capital. However, the name of Sabota had been kept alive in the memory of later researchers from Europe because of the elder Pliny's description of the city with its sixty temples. Even though Adolph von Wrede in the first half of the 19th century had opened up the eastern part of South Arabia to scholarly exploration (see page 20), it was to be almost another hundred years before one of the pioneer explorers, Hans Helfritz, reached Shabwa in 1934.

During the period of British dominance in South Yemen no thorough archaeological survey of Shabwa was made. The protecting power and her protégés, the petty princes, were not able assert themselves against the bedouins and semi-bedouins of the area sufficiently to enable a team of archaeologists to work there for any length of time. In 1938 R. A. B. Hamilton (later Lord Belhaven) was only able to stay a few weeks in Shabwa doing archaeological work, but in that time he uncovered several columns, three or four sites of dwellings or tombs, and the remains of steps. Philby during his visit at least had time to draw a plan, which was later improved by reference to aerial photographs and a visit to the site by Brian Doe.

After initial serious conflicts the People's Republic made efforts to integrate the bedouins into society. There were still more than 100,000 nomads in South Yemen, but their pastures came under the control of the state. Professor Walter Müller, who was there in the mid-1970's, gives this account: 'Shabwa, which lies on Wadi Atf, the lower course of Wadi Irma, on a group of hills, surrounded by more hills, is one of the most magnificent ruined sites in South Arabia. Its area is so extensive that it has room for three villages, Hajyar, Mathna and Maywan, which are lived in by members of the al-Buraik and al-Karab tribes. The rubble of the ancient city provides sufficient building material.'

Over the following decade French archaeologists in Shabwa made some

Saw-tooth wall decoration in Wadi Hadramawt

important discoveries. Among other things they uncovered a building at the main gate of the city which they have identified as an early tower house (see page 214). The archaeologists believe that this large structure is the royal castle of Shaqr.

Visiting Shabwa

Even more than Timna's, Shabwa's attraction for the more adventurous traveller derives in part from the fact that for a century the ruins of the ancient Hadrami capital could be visited only with the greatest difficulties. These were caused by the tribesmen, who lived in three (now abandoned) villages around the site, and often threatened the lives of visitors. Even during the British period archaeologists were unable to stay in Shabwa long enough to make a thorough survey of the site. It was the communist government that arranged for French archaeologists to stay for several years in Shabwa and enabled them to undertake intensive excavations. This seems to have resulted in a lasting change of attitude towards strangers among the local al-Buraik and al-Karab tribesmen. Semi-nomads now camp on the edge of Shabwa, but instead of driving visitors away, they offer them tea and provide open tents for spending the night there.

The great majority of travellers come to Shabwa by the road through Ma'rib, Harib,

Timna and Ataq, where there is overnight accomodation. (The journey from Ma'rib takes about 3 hours; most tourists continue to Say'un in Wadi Hadramawt, which takes another 4 hours. A good bedouin escort is needed.) About 16 km outside Shabwa (to the west of the ruins), on the south flank of **Jabal Uqla**, is a group of rocks of great historical interest. They can be easily recognized by a small stone structure perched on the middle rock, and it is only when one gets within a few metres that it becomes apparent that the smooth sides of the rocks are completely covered with Sabaean inscriptions. These record the names of Hadrami kings and the dates when important works of architecture were founded. The researches of epigraphers suggest that kings and nobles gathered at the rocks on special occasions which were then commemorated in stone. Uqla served in fact as a sort of state archive.

The approach to Shabwa from the east (in a four-wheel-drive vehicle) follows Wadi Ma'shar most of the way. The ruins lie in a hollow which can be traversed by car. The vestiges of Shabwa are scattered over an area about a kilometre long (east to west) and 500 m wide. Most prominent is the lower storey of the temple of the moon which juts out of the sandy ground; it has been uncovered by the French archaeologists. Its carefully worked masonry of hewn stone suggests the prosperity of the ancient city. A processional route must have run through Shabwa from north to south. To the right and left of this street, which is between 9 and 11 m wide, the excavators have uncovered supporting walls, steps, column bases and pedestals for statues. The remains of a large building built on a massive podium, are thought to be the ruins of the royal palace. The foundations of the old city walls and parts of the city gates and bastions have been discovered, but unfortunately there are no notices and explanations on the spot to help the visitor understand what he is looking at. Imagination is thus given a broad scope, all the more so since the site looks as if it has been ploughed up again by bulldozers after the various excavations.

To the northeast of the site (seen from the temple) are some low hills which contain salt-mines. Shabwa was never entirely deserted because of its situation over a dome of salt, one of the most precious commodities. Rock-salt is still mined here and carried by small camel-caravans to nearby trading centres such as Harib and al-Qatn.

Architecture, Art and Religion in Hadramawt

When and why did the South Arabians begin to construct sky-scrapers? Carl Rathjens wrote about this in the 1950's: 'During the height of agricultural development in the Minaean and Sabaean kingdoms the style of domestic architecture that still predominates today in Yemen with box-like tall houses must have already developed. People built upwards instead of outwards because of the mountainous character of the country and the necessity for the population to settle only in natural fastnesses, on mountain summits, ridges and promontories. This was probably the origin of the multi-storey house mentioned in pre-Islamic tradition. Originally found throughout South Arabia, it is still being built today.'

In fact only in the northwest, mainly in the northern part of Yemen, does the landscape have has the mountainous character that Rathjens mentions; such mountain landscape is not found in Hadramawt. Yet it is in Hadramawt that the 'box-like highrise house' is particularly common. It can probably be assumed that the other reasons he gives - the development of defensive architecture in periods of unrest and spacesaving because of the shortage of fertile land - would have determined the emergence of high-rise buildings in the less mountainous areas.

Hermann von Wissmann gives a clearer indication of the defensive nature of the buildings: 'Until about 430 BC the whole of South Arabia seems to have been affiliated, even if only loosely in some parts, to the Sabaean kingdom. The emergence of independent kingdoms of Ma'in, Qataban (Ausan) and Hadramawt (and, much later, Himyar) alongside the Sabaean kingdom, meant that wars were an even heavier burden on the country, which built mountain castles and splintered along feudal lines.'

Wadi Hadramawt, old-style minaret of the al-Hasm al-Idriss near Shibam

In the desert valleys of South Arabia, especially in Wadi Hadramawt, the necessity of building houses that could be defended against attacks continued until the mid-20th century. There was also the fact that in Shibam, for instance, provision had to be made for the short, but often violent flash-floods - walls of water up to 5 m high.

As to the question of dating, Professor Walter Müller states that 'the archaeological evidence points to the existence of multi-storey houses in pre-Islamic South Arabia', since the American excavations at the beginning of the 1950's had revealed remains of ruins of houses with several storeys. Müller also bases his argument on a four-line inscription in the museum at Ta'izz, which probably came from Ma'rib: 'The text speaks of a number of persons building their house from the foundation to the top, with, in its

Wadi Hadramawt, roadside well-house

words, "six ceilings and six floors" besides storerooms, terraces and annexes. There is no doubt that the "six ceilings and six floors" refer to as many storeys, since the Old South Arabian word, which is here translated as "ceiling" and can also mean "roof", is still used in the dialect of San'a to mean "storey". This seems to me to prove the existence of multi-storey buildings already in ancient South Arabia.'

Unlike those in the northwest, the high-rise buildings in ancient Hadramawt were not built of stone throughout. French archaeologists have shown that in Shabwa there were tower-houses with a tall lower storey of stone but the storeys above built of unfired mud bricks. There is also evidence of tower-houses with upper storeys built of wood. This method of building suited - and still suits - the conditions of the country, where there is no shortage of good, malleable mud, but a serious lack of easily-worked stones. The combined wood-and-mud buildings may have been similar to our own half-timbered houses.

Today in Hadramawt almost all buildings (even modern functional buildings such as warehouses and post offices) are built of mud. The **building material** was and is used in two forms: either mixed with chopped straw and employed in a similar way to concrete, or as flat, air-dried bricks which are laid as masonry. More than 2,000 years of practical experience have enabled the architects of Hadramawt to build dwellings of up to eight storeys with a total height of 30 m, employing only natural materials, without any iron reinforcement.

The façades of the houses in Hadramawt are generally plainer than those in the Old Town of San'a, for instance. But South Yemeni craftsmanship does give special care to particular details, such the door-frames and the doors themselves. The same is true of the decoration of the interiors.

The pattern of the Hadramawt house differs only slightly from that of the box-like high-rise house in northwest Yemen. The ground floor consists of a bare room, perhaps 6 m high, giving access to the stables or storerooms, and a steep stairway to the upper rooms. Daylight enters this ground-floor room through the shooting holes placed barely 2 m below the ceiling. These can be reached from a gallery, which can also be used for the defence of the inside of the house, if the enemy has managed to penetrate inside. Proper windows begin only on the first floor, in some houses not until the second floor. Women's rooms and the kitchen are situated in the middle floors (fourth and fifth storeys), and the reception rooms for the men and their guests are right at the top of the house.

The windows of a traditional Hadramawt house do not have glass panes, but are closed with wooden shutters. The wooden frames and shutters are two of the architectural elements on which the local builders concentrate their artistic skill. The same is true of the design of the heavy wooden front doors and their door-frames. Mud and plaster are skilfully applied for the battlement-like tops of the walls, for cresting and applied ornament. More sophisticated architectural design can be seen in mosques, religious schools, mausolea and fountains for ritual ablutions.

The earliest minarets in Hadramawt have a rectangular base, a round shaft and a rectangular upper part on top, from which the muezzin calls to the faithful. This type of minaret is rare now, but one still frequently sees a variant of it, in which the minaret stands next to the prayer hall and, starting from a rectangular base, narrows towards the top. Such towers usually have five bands of ornament formed of mud bricks arranged in a lattice pattern, which run all the way round the building. The first gallery of the minaret is the platform of the rectangular base, which has four stepped and pointed merlons at its corners. Similar merlons surmount the minaret above the second, closed gallery. Just below this gallery will be the tall dome of any mausoleum that may be attached to the mosque.

Hadrami minarets are perhaps the outstanding achievement of the local builders, who have managed to endow the humblest of materials with a genuine sculptural presence. The plainness of the mosque's dome is usually emphasized by two rows of ornamental bands, marking the edges of the supporting box-like structure. If the complex is still used for religious services and burials, it will certainly be kept brilliant white, relieved only by the dark doors and window shutters and the shadows of

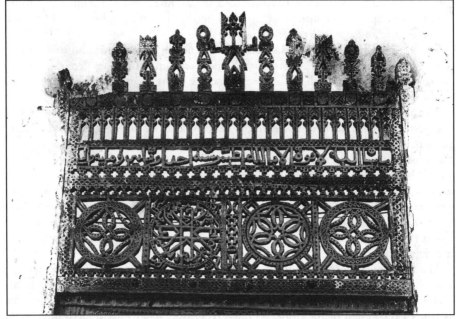

Wadi Hadramawt, ornamental wood carving with Arabic inscription and pagan-looking abstract figures, above the door to the al-Hasm al-Idriss Mosque

the decoration.

Also richly decorated are the water sources attached to the mosques and essential for ritual cleansing. Wells usually have a box-shaped superstructure, which is again surmounted by a high dome. Lattice decoration, pointed crenellation and stylized floral patterns are typical decorative elements. On the domes of wells, and on other domes in the area of the mosque, one often sees stepped shafts ending in a sort of arrow-head (making the domes look a little like German pickelhaube helmets). According to experts these are a very ancient architectural decoration which may have been adopted from Babylon. The lattice ornaments are also perhaps a pre-Islamic development, but since the coming of Islam they can also have a practical function when used in harem windows, enabling the women to follow the bustle of life outside without themselves being the object of curious glances.

The finely carved wooden inserts in the windows are also generally harem grilles. They are a later development dating from the 18th and 19th centuries, when the people of Wadi Hadramawt had again become successful traders and could afford to import expensive woods. It was not only the wood that was imported from overseas –

foreign influences are also detectable in the style. Earlier examples of these wooden inserts still had plain decoration and often only reproduce in miniature the brick lattice decoration of the walls. Later pieces are noticeably lavish: the decoration is dominated by circles, serpentine lines, flower and eye symbols, as well as intersecting lines. The creators of these carvings seem to have been inspired by Southeast Asian motifs. Comparisons can be made with decorative motifs of the Toraya on the Indonesian island of Sulawesi (Celebes) - in the 18th and 19th centuries there were close commercial relations between Hadramawt and the Dutch East Indies, and thousands of Hadramis were at home in either place (see page 232).

The same can be said of the beautifully carved doors, many of which are still fitted with wooden locks which take keys with wooden pins. The ornaments on such doors are Arabian in origin, but have later been influenced, if not overlaid, by ornaments from other cultures, in particular motifs from Indonesia.

A noticeable feature of the larger rooms in a typical Hadramawt high-rise house is a post supporting the ceiling. It almost always has a capital richly carved with flowers and foliage scrolls, wavy lines and circles. Here the foreign influence clearly predominates, and this is particularly evident if one compares the ornamentation of such capitals with other exhibits in the little ethnographical museums in southern and southeastern Yemen (in Aden, Mukalla and Say'un). Unfortunately these museums will remain closed for some time to come as most of their exhibits were looted during and after the fighting in the summer of 1994.

However, the numerous plaster decorations in the interiors of a Hadrami house are mainly of indigenous origin. Some elements are taken from the mosque, such as recesses that resemble prayer-niches, decorative panels similar to the high domes of the mausoleums, or consoles in the style of Koran-stands. The plaster ornaments below the wooden ceilings are richer than in the box-shaped tall houses of the northwest. This is because in Hadramawt the wealthy but politically powerless bourgeoisie were already beginning to live lavishly, while society in the north was still dominated entirely by the tribes and the religious aristocracy.

Visual Arts

It is still not known whether Hadramawt developed any visual arts of its own - other than architecture and architectural decoration. Wissmann thought that there must have been such a visual culture, and put forward the following reasons: 'Despite its position on the trade road, Wadi Hadramawt and the valleys that run off it remained an out-of-the-way land within South Arabia. It was a country of highly developed oasis cultivation, and in this resembled the Nile Valley. The population was relatively dense and isolated, with its own separate, long-established culture, which meant it could reject, retard or only selectively adopt developments which had been taken up in the central regions around Shabwat and Ma'rib, with their close trading relations with Assur, for instance.'

It is difficult today, however, to discover any traces of that 'long-established, separate culture' of Hadramawt, especially any traces of the visual arts. This has much to do with the uncertain provenance of most of the ancient statues and reliefs displayed in all the museums of southeastern Yemen. Not one of the pieces can be indisputably traced back to Hadramawt, and even if the French archaeological excavations at Shabwa bring significant finds, Wissmann's thesis will still not be proved, since, as he pointed out, Shabwa was involved in cultural exchange between the regions much earlier than Wadi Hadramawt itself. So while we can still expect to find antiquities from Shabwa that show the early influence of the high cultures of Egypt, Mesopotamia and Syria, the original Hadrami high culture still has to be sought 10 or 15 m below the foundations of the houses of Shibam, Say'un and Tarim. But any high expectations suggested by Wissmann's comparison with ancient Egypt are surely misplaced. Compared to Egyptian high culture the independent culture of Hadramawt was but a short episode. It seems that the Hadramis' gods were more or less the same as those in the other South Arabian kingdoms, and from this one can probably conclude that, despite some notable differences in details, there was no crucial deviation from the religious ideas then current throughout South Arabia. The pantheon dominated by the celestial deities of the moon, sun and Venus did not provide the same fertile religious basis for artistic achievement that we find with multifarious gods of pharaonic Egypt.

To some extent we can guess what the visual arts in Wadi Hadramawt may have looked like. The raw materials were sandstone from the desert cliffs, clay from the bed of the wadi and wood from the palms. These materials were well suited for the production of reliefs, statues and carvings made to honour the gods, the dead and the powerful. Because Hadramawt was a land of highly-developed oasis-cultivation, fertility cults would have played an important part. The more easily worked materials in Hadramawt could have been used for portraits, which had more detail, greater expressiveness and more variety than the works of the kingdoms further west and north, where granite, alabaster and marble - all more intractable materials and difficult to shape - were used. But just as the materials used in Hadramawt were more easily worked, so they were also less durable - which is one of several factors that may have contributed to the fact that so far no authentic ancient Hadrami art has been discovered.

Freya Stark mentions that in the 1930's the Sultan of al-Qatn had a habit of presenting prominent visitors with archaeological finds: 'he had given to Colonel Boscawen' - who had stayed with him the year before - 'a bronze lion of great beauty, dug up under the cliff.' The piece was surely from a late period when Hellenistic, Roman or Persian influences had made themselves felt. Probably of even later date is the fragment of a limestone frieze in the library of the Friday Mosque of Mukalla mentioned by Brian Doe. It shows two fish lying parallel to each other, a motif that Doe ascribes to Christian influence.

To Wadi Hadramawt

Wadi Hadramawt is the second largest desert valley in the Arabian Peninsula (after Wadi Rum in Jordan). Today its name is applied to a whole province with numerous desert valley, but Wadi Hadramawt proper is about 160 km from the South Arabian coast as the crow flies. It runs for nearly 200 km from west to east, is 10 km wide in place, and has many tributary valleys, such as Wadi Amd, Wadi Duan and Wadi Adim. According to information provided in the period of the People's Republic Wadi Hadramawt has a population of about 350,000.

There are several ways of getting to Wadi Hadramawt: planes fly to Say'un from San'a or Aden. There are three desert routes to Shabwa. The first, and most beautiful, follows the old Shabwa road from Ma'rib across Ramla and Sab'atain, the little desert of Yemen. This was the route of the camel caravans carrying spices and salt. It takes about 8 hours. The second goes from Ma'rib through the al-Abr mountains. You can also follow the classic caravan route from Ma'rib, Harib, Timna and Shabwa, a distance of more than 1000 km; or lastly you can take the port of Mukalla as the starting point for a car journey to the wadi.

We shall deal first with the approach from Shabwa, the ancient capital of the kingdom of Hadramawt. Until the asphalt road link is completed (probably in 1994-95) the visitor will have to make a desert journey first northwards and then eastwards along well-frequented tracks. The first stop (after about 71 km) is a place called **Bir Asaakir** ('Well of the Soldier'), which turns out to be a lone petrol station with a few stalls. From Bir Asaakir the track continues as far as **Haja** (77 km), where a cobbled road dating from feudal times begins. On this hard road we soon reach **al-Qatn**, the first historic and still fully inhabited town of Hadramawt.

Until 1968 al-Qatn was the seat of a sultan of the Qaiti family which ruled Mukalla. On her visit in 1935 Freya Stark found Sultan Ali Ibn Salih to be an educated man interested in the pre-Islamic history of his country. Sultan Ali had arranged excavations in the environs of the town and had come across interesting pieces from ancient Hadramawt. Unfortunately, as we have seen (see page 218), he then gave several finds away to foreign visitors, with the result that important pieces have disappeared into private collections. From the main road today al-Qatn (overnight accommodation) looks like a small industrial town, but inside the town there are still some fine mud houses and several saints' tombs. The architecture of the

Hermann von Wissmann's historical map of Wadi Hadramawt, drawn in the 1930's and improved in ▷
the 1950's, unsurpassed to this day

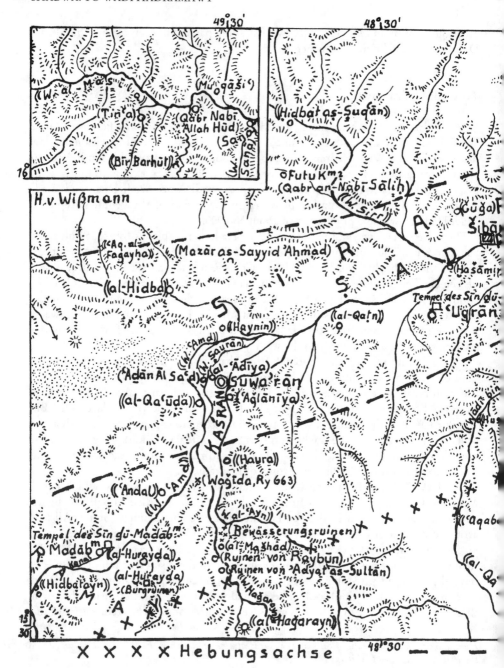

X X X X Hebungsachse

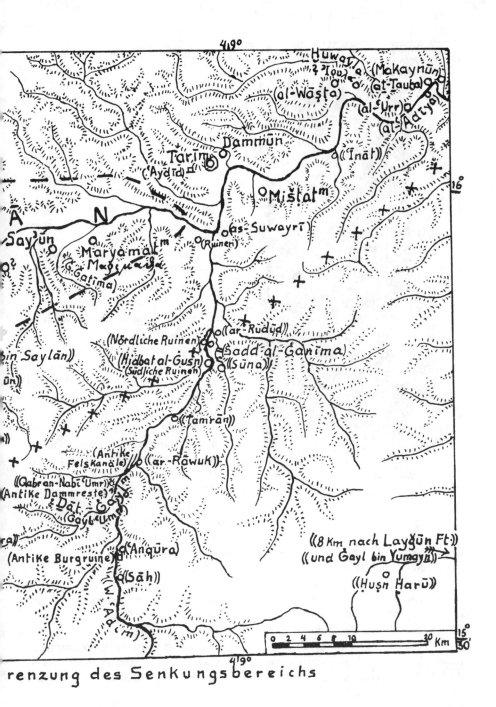

renzung des Senkungsbereichs

221

Mukalla, door of a former merchant's house

main mosque (as the Austrian scholar Eduard Glaser first pointed out over 90 years ago) is based exactly on that of a Sabaean temple, with a plain wall on the entrance side of the court, rather than the arcades of the purely Islamic design (see page 85f).

It was to the fleshpots of al-Qatn that Mrs. Bent and her husband retreated 'with considerable satisfaction' after their dusty reception at **Shibam,** the next large town after al-Qatn (see page 228f.) which we here approach sideways from the west. The famous main front in the wadi faces north. The best photographs of the complete town can be taken in the late afternoon from a hill in the village of Sihayl, which faces it from the southeast.

The traveller coming from Ma'rib, Timna and Shabwa has followed the road once used by the frankincense caravans and still used today for transporting rock salt extracted from the mountains in the desert around Shabwa; columns of camels carrying yellowish brown salt to market in sacks and baskets may still be seen.

On the route from the coastal town of Mukalla one is more likely to come across transports of stinking fish than salt. The bedouins of the hinterland use vast quantities of dried sardines, called *aid,* as animal fodder. The asphalt road to Wadi Hadramawt completed in 1984 turns north at the old airfield (Riyan airport has been moved further east). From here it is about 300 km to Say'un. Southwest of the town the road enters the wadi. Taking this route the traveller misses the old cobbled road and some attractive landscape. If this is not possible otherwise, a trip from Say'un to Adim and Rhail Umr should be requested.

Next we come to the **jol,** which has only become accessible with the new road. Early travellers found the jol the greatest obstacle on the way to Hadramawt (colour plate 37). A jol is a high plateau covered with a wasteland of detritus and gravel. The difficult terrain required great physical effort, and the area was also made unsafe by

Shibam, view of the north side of the town

the presence of bedouins. It was only possible to cross it with the protection of a bedouin escort recognized by all the neighbouring tribes. Leo Hirsch, who travelled from Mukalla to Wadi Hadramawt in 1893, wrote about the plateau in his journal: 'A feeling of isolation crept over me as our tiny caravan... headed into the unknown, and the barrenness and desolation around about weighed heavily on my mind... Low hills, like earthworks, completely flat on the top, cover the Jol for its whole extent; broad stretches have no vegetation at all; and where it exists, it is very meagre, and trees and shrubs are often utterly withered... The numerous wadis which begin on either side of our path clearly show the power of the water flowing down from this plateau by the wildness and depth of the ravines which they have torn into the flat ground.' Mrs. Bent, who followed the same route a few months later, describes it as 'looking as though a gigantic coal-scuttle had been upset'.

The modern traveller is soon compensated for this 'barrenness and desolation' by the beauty of **Wadi Adim**, to which one descends by a gravel road. Palm-trees, fields of cereals and vegetables, white river-bed boulders, yellow sand and reddish brown cliffs combine to create a very colourful spectacle. The villages on the slopes on either side of the wadi are raised up to avoid the occasional flash-floods. The route now follows a narrow cobbled road built with great difficulty in the 1930's to suit the traf-fic conditions at that time. Countless stones were taken from the surrounding fields

223

for the paving, and one can easily imagine how many farmers had to give their labour for the construction of this new thoroughfare, but it was conceived and paid for by native Hadramis, not by any colonial power of foreign development agency.

The paved road soon reaches **Rhail Umr** (colour plate 38), an oasis in Wadi Adim, and a good place for a rest. Here the water of a powerful spring feeds a lake from which a stream runs in the direction of Wadi Hadramawt, later seeping away into the ground. Dense palm-trees line its shores. On the western shore, which is rocky in places, two channels carved out of the rock are preserved. Wissmann identifies them as part of an ancient irrigation system. A little upstream are some ruins set on a hill on the western side of the wadi with a small mosque on its slope. The remains of defensive walls, a gatehouse and several individual buildings can be made out, as well as mud-brick structures. In antiquity this could have been a fortress or a small fortified town, and it was still inhabited in early Islamic times.

From Rhail Umr the car journey to Say'un takes another 2-3 hours. Say'un is a district capital of Wadi Hadramawt. The travel companies bring tourists here to stay at a hotel built in the late 1970's (air conditioning, swimming pool) as a base for excursions to places in the region. (Travellers who are not members of tour parties are at a disadvantage.)

Excursions from Say'un

The great charm of the landscape of Hadramawt lies in its reconciling of opposites. It has a high level of urban culture, but this has not interfered with the world of the farmers and their villages. Agriculture is so much in harmony with nature that for some stretches the primeval landscape has survived intact.

It is difficult for today's traveller, usually restricted by the wishes of a group or the capacities of the official travel couriers, to grasp all the beauty of the wadi. It is a wonderful experience to watch from the cliffs that rise 80 or 100 m on the north side near Tarim as the sun rises, and see the opposite side of the wadi glowing in the reddish gold morning light, while on the floor of the valley, the places eroded by wind, sand and water are usually still under a layer of mist, through which rise minarets, mud castles and the tops of palm-trees.

At many points the floor of the wadi is so flat and smooth that an aircraft could land on it. These are the places were maize and cereals are sown as soon as a flood has passed over. Elsewhere agriculture is practised throughout the year, nowadays using motor pumps to force water from wells sunk 15 or 20 m, or deeper. In the fields women squat nearly all day long, their black headscarves held on by high conical straw hats.

On the cliffs on either side of the valley stone towers stand at regular intervals, and many of the free-standing houses on the valley bottom resemble medieval castles

41 KAWKABAN

42 KAWKABAN   Room in the Kawkaban hotel
40 JIBLA   Interior of main mosque

43 Yemeni gate

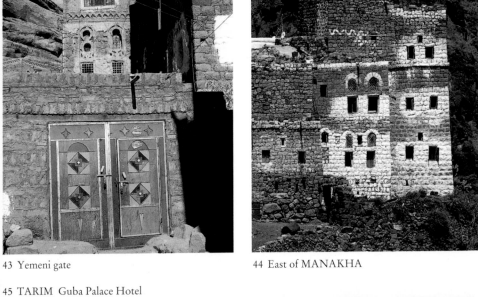

44 East of MANAKHA

45 TARIM Guba Palace Hotel

46 In HUDAYDA 47 In SAN'A 48 In AL-KADAN 49 Buying qat in SAN'A

51 Children in JIBLA 52 Market day in WADI SARDUDH

53 Suq in HUDAYDA

54 In JABAL IRAF   55 Near SAN'A   56 Woman farmer   57 North of WADI
                                          northof ADEN   MASILAH

50 Working in the fields in the
   HADRAMAWT

           58 Near AL-KADAN ▷

59 Market day in SUQ AL-KHAMIS   60 Catching fish off WADI MASILAH

61 Suq in SAN'A

SOCOTRA Desert Rose or Bottle Tree
SOCOTRA Dragon's blood trees
SOCOTRA Frankincense Tree

64 HIGH YEMEN Euphorbia tree
68 HADRAMAWT Moonrise: ▷
66 SOCOTRA Frankincense tree: bark and resin

67 SAN'A Agami lizard

View from the Sultan's palace in Say'un towards the tall houses of the town (photograph by Freya Stark in the mid-1930's)

with their corner towers, embrasures, battlements and archways. These are the defences that survive from the time of the Qaiti and Kathiri families, who had been the main powers in this region for centuries until 1967. They built watchtowers and castles to protect their own and others' caravans against robber bedouin. The defensive structures were, however, directed only against those outside the law, outcasts from their own tribes. True, the fortification also signalled a readiness to fight to the tribes under the leadership of sheikhs - but whenever possible these tribes preferred to enter into contractual relations with the lords of the desert and pay for their security with part of the profits in the form of tolls and duties.

In earlier times the towns were usually built on hills in Wadi Hadramawt, but as they were continually renewed they 'migrated' into the shadow of the cliffs on either side. By moving closer to the rock faces they reduced the opportunities for attacks and strengthened their defensive position. Shibam is one of the few towns in the region which chose a location approximately in the middle of a wadi. Its founders must have felt themselves very strong when they began building their houses in such an exposed position.

Amulets and bridal apparel on display in Say'un Museum

Say'un on the other hand is one of the towns that seek security by clinging to the limestone walls of the wadi. The Arab legend of its foundation claims great antiquity for the city. It is supposed to have been built, presumably in pre-Islamic times, on the site of the castle of a certain Princess Say'un of which there is now no trace. Later the town was occupied by intruders from the northwest. Leo Hirsch first came across accounts which stated that about 10,000 men and women of the Hamdani tribes from near San'a under their leader Emir Badt Ibn Tuarik Kathiri penetrated into Hadramawt in 1494 AD. After lengthy struggles with the natives and with tribal warriors from the mountains north of Aden, the North Yemenis settled in the interior of the wadi. When in the late 1960's the People's Republic did away with the petty princedoms of the region, the dethroned Sultan of Say'un was still a Kathiri.

The massive sultan's palace with its four round towers stands on a hill in the town centre and still looms almost defiantly above the mosques and houses of the Old Town. In its present form it is of fairly recent date, built with the profits of the once flourishing Southeast Asian trade and renovated in the 20th century with the help of British subsidies. Two earlier palaces, which are now beginning to decay, stand in the same precinct. Between them and around them the lively bustle of the market still goes on as it did before. This market and the adjoining streets are the earliest part of Say'un. A few strolls through the narrow alleys will take you back to the world of the Arabian nights.

At the very beginning the town was probably no more than a meeting place for camel-drivers from the desert and enterprising merchants from the coast. Both sides took advantage of the security provided here for a fee by the local sheikh. The business activity at the camping place attracted nomads and caused them to settle in the vicinity. The trading centre became prosperous; houses, palaces, mosques and schools were built. The focus of life here was the market, and it was natural that the main mosque should stand within its precincts, following the precepts of the Caliph Omar (634-644 AD), who declared that the suq and the mosque must agree in all things. This mosque is (according to Lewcock) the most beautiful in all the Hadramawt.

Not far from the suq were the warehouses and accommodation for the traders, and a place where money could be changed. All around was a labyrinth of narrow streets and alleyways lined on both sides with open workshops of the different craftsmen. Business was overseen by an official of the sultan, who checked the weights and measures, set the prices and guaranteed the security of the warehouses. His regulations governed the market, particularly regarding all arrangements connected with foodstuffs and consumer goods. On his rounds the sultan's official was preceded by a weigh-master who carried calibrated scales with standard weights. He was followed by a troop of soldiers, ready to put any miscreant in foot-irons on the spot.

In Say'un - as in other South Arabian cities - anyone engaged in the production or distribution of goods was involved in the organisation of guilds. With the exception of the sultan's high officials and the clergy, every man belonged to a particular guild depending on his craft and trade, every duty and right of which was carefully regulated. The basis for the organization of guilds was passed down by word of mouth from one generation to the next, and there must still be some old men in Say'un today who remember the tradition - although the guilds have since had to give way to state-controlled co-operatives.

The early travellers in Hadramawt used Say'un, the biggest town in the wadi, as a place to recover from their strenuous and dangerous crossing of the desert. Leo Hirsch found Say'un much 'more pleasant' (by which he meant it was cleaner and the inhabitants more welcoming) than the nearby cities of Tarim and Shibam. This is probably true even today, since Say'un has a population of over 30,000 and is the provincial capital in Wadi Hadramawt. Most of the almost 2,000 older houses and fifty or so mosques which Hans Helfritz found in the 1930's are still in use today. Several silversmiths, potters, joiners and basketmakers continue the traditional crafts under changed circumstances. Say'un is a particularly good place to look out for their products.

The **Tomb of Ahmad Ibn Isa al-Muhajir** ('the immigrant') is one of the most interesting monuments near Say'un. A few kilometres outside the city on the road to Tarim, about 100 m to the right of the road, the brilliant white domes of a mosque come into sight, with a whitewashed flight of steps cut into the rock and a second mosque set on a platform. This remained a place of pilgrimage during the communist

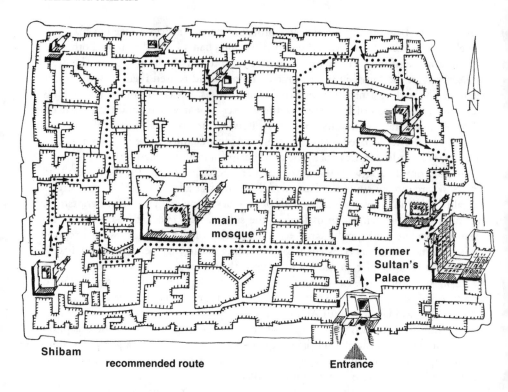

Shibam

recommended route

main mosque

former Sultan's Palace

Entrance

period, but non-Muslims are allowed to visit it. It is the supposed burial place of Ahmad Ibn Isa, the sayyid who re-established orthodox Islam in Wadi Hadramawt about 1200 years ago (see page 292f). Since a sheikha - a holy woman - is also buried near Ahmad Ibn Isa, the sanctuary is particularly popular with women pilgrims. The buildings stand out gleaming white against the brown boulders, and a visit provides an opportunity to become acquainted with the simple forms of Hadrami architecture and ornament.

Shibam, 20 km west of Say'un, is the city in Wadi Hadramawt that all the early visitors (except for Leo Hirsch) found the most spectacular- and today it still makes an unforgettable impression (colour plate 30). Van der Meulen thought on first sight it was a *fata morgana;* Helfritz called it the 'Chicago of the Desert'. Freya Stark who first travelled in Wadi Hadramawt in the early 1930's, approached Shibam from the west: 'And now it looked as if a lower cliff had wandered out into the middle valley: wrinkled and pitted, as we drew nearer, with beehive holes; split like the valley sides with vertical fissures; the top of it splashed with white as by a giant paint-brush; an old and wrinkled city, made of the earth that made the hills around it, built on a mound wherein no doubt lie buried its ancestor cities of the past. This was Shibam, where five valleys like the veins of a sycamore leaf branch out and give an illusion of open sky to the town that lies between them.' Mrs Bent was more down to earth: 'the town of Shibam offers a curious appearance as one approaches; above its mud brick walls, with bastions and watch towers, appear the tall houses of the wealthy, white-washed only at the top, which makes it look like a large round cake with sugar on it.'

The congruence of these wadis that Stark observed also gives the site an obvious strategic importance - indeed it is the strongest point in the whole of Wadi Hadra-mawt. The city is built where it is, on a slight rise, to avoid the danger of flash floods. Stark also noted that no motor road yet led to Shibam, but this was to change soon after her visit, when a cobbled road was built. In the 1990's if you approach Shibam by this road your impression will be similar to Freya Stark's, for, outwardly at least, little has changed in Shibam's appearance since 1934. Now as then, the city has a population of 7-8,000.

Shibam consists of rectangle measuring about 400 by 500 m, surrounded by a wall, and containing about 500 houses. Although built only out of mud and staw, or of air-dried bricks, most of them are about 30 m tall and can be called high-rise buildings. Walter Müller believes that the citizens of Shibam were agreed that they would not to overlook each others' roofs and so decided to restrict the number of storeys of their houses to eight, though the average number is five.

Many of the high-rise houses of Shibam are between 100 and 300 years old. If such mud buildings are given regular maintenance they can attain this great age without any difficulty. Part of the upkeep is regular whitewashing of the roof and upper façade, at least once a year. The whitewash contains a binding material, such as alabaster powder, which not only makes the building impervious to the infrequent rainfalls but also delays the erosion of the air-dried mud bricks by the sun and wind. In 1989 unusually heavy rains caused serious damage to many houses which has not yet been fully made good. The government is therefore increasing pressure for inter-national help to preserve historic Shibam, which in 1984 was added to the UNESCO list of cultural monuments. An objection has been raised to this on the grounds that for centuries the citizens of Shibam had been able to make good the damage caused by repeated rain damage without foreign aid. But one argument for international aid is that in the future this little town will be exposed fairly regularly to an increasing number of tourists, and for their good as well as that of the inhabitants it needs new sanitation systems, for which there are as yet neither the means nor the experience.

It is difficult to say how many generations of high-rise houses Shibam has had on the site. According to the legend of the city's foundation, the people of Shabwa, the capital of ancient Hadramawt, founded Shibam after being driven from their old home. But when did this happen? As far as we know the position of Shabwa became untenable under pressure from semi-nomadic tribes towards the end of the 2nd

century AD. So Shibam may be about 1700 years old. It certainly provided one of the great leaders of the Caliph's armies in the conquest of Egypt and beyond in the first centuries of Islam. Red bricks found in the structure of the mosque suggest that it may partly date back almost as far as that, to the 10th century, but its variety of styles attests to many rebuildings.

There is now a hotel in Shibam, the Universal Guest House, near the main gates and on the old walls.

Tarim, 'the hope of all the Hadramawt', about 33 km east of Say'un, can be reached by an asphalt road completed in 1988. The city is still bordered by a semicircular fringe of palm-trees and so retains the appearance that Helfritz recorded during his pioneering journey in the early 1930's, although the fringe has become somewhat thinner in the course of time.

In antiquity the name of the settlement on the site now occupied by Tarim was written in Sabaean with the letters ALMD - but not much more than this name has survived. On the other hand a large part of Tarim dates from its Islamic heyday - between the 17th and 19th centuries, the period when the cities of Hadramawt were able to assert themselves against the nomads. At that time Tarim was a centre of religious scholarship. Young men came from all over the Arabian Peninsula to study the holy scriptures - the Koran and the collection of Traditions from the time of the Prophet (*hadith*). In the course of time more than 300 mosques and religious schools developed to control the teaching activity. Although the great majority of these places of religious learning are now closed, they could in the future attract funding from the oil-rich Arab states, which could be used to restore mosques and strengthen the role of Islam here.

What were and are still taught in Tarim are the tenets of orthodox Sunni Islam. Orthodoxy suited the spiritual and intellectual attitude of the citizens of this ancient city. Already in the years following the death of the Prophet (AD 632), when many Arab tribes wished to remove themselves again from the new Islamic order and the rest of South Arabia flared up in revolt against the new caliph, Tarim alone in Wadi Hadramawt is said to have stood out for the successor of Muhammad as leader of the faithful and for the true belief in its orthodox interpretation, and the city played an important part in the suppression of the apostates.

In the 19th century, however, this arch-conservative city underwent a remarkable change. Some of its sons went out into the wide world, following the sea routes used

◁ *Wadi Hadramawt, cemetery outside Tarim. 'When we say that we cannot understand how the great leaders of business in Singapore or Java and these men, who played an active part there in education and journalism, can stand this life of inactivity, they answer: "This is the land of sleep and of death. We come here to sleep and towards the end of our lives, so that we may die here."' D. van der Meulen and H. von Wissmann*

Tarim, minaret of the al-Midhar Mosque

by the Sabaeans, Qatabanians and Hadramis about 2,000 years earlier. These routes took them to Southeast Asia, in particular to the island of Java. The able South Arabian traders soon became rich and started second families on Java and other Indonesian islands. In their old age, however, they wanted to enjoy their riches in their old home, and so in the 19th century Tarim experienced a real building boom. New palaces and magnificent villas were constructed, still using the traditional building methods with mud and straw and air-dried mud bricks, but introducing Southeast Asian elements into the ornament and carvings. A new spirit also began to make itself felt throughout the city, influenced by the culture of other peoples. Some Hadramis used the money they had made in the East to improve their native land. The most notable of these was Sir Sayyid Bu Bakr Ibn Shaikh al-Kaf, who used some of the fortune his family had made in Singapore in building roads and introducing the latest technology to Wadi Hadramawt. He was a friend of the British and was knighted by the Queen in the 1950's on her visit to Aden. Freya Stark was one of the many travellers who enjoyed his hospitality in the 1930's. Tradition-bound Tarim at first found it hard to accept this new spirit, but showed itself increasingly open-minded in the following decades. In the 1930's it was even in the vanguard of a reform movement originating from Java, which greatly reduced the influence of the religious aristocracy, the *sada*.

The great al-Midhar Mosque, whose minaret is the most prominent feature of Tarim, is also influenced by Java and 'modernism'. Since the period of the Islamic middle ages it has been repeatedly renewed, and at the beginning of the 20th century it became the symbol of the bourgeoisie which had achieved prosperity in Southeast Asian trade, when the sober building was given a new minaret more than 50 m high. Already in 1939 the Dutch traveller Daniel van der Meulen was saddened by the departure from the local architectural tradition: 'The minaret of al-Midhar is a technical achievement, not an architectural one. The simple lines of the traditional Hadrami minaret have been abandoned and, instead, a thin, square tower has been built, full of windows and ventilation-openings. Decorated bands and corner ornaments have been added and when the tower might have seemed complete a small square room has been constructed on the top of it in order to be quite sure that all height-records have been broken.'

Nevertheless this remarkable tower is built - like almost all buildings in Tarim - of mud bricks. It is worth climbing the 150 steps to the top, for there is a good view over the mosques of the city, including several old ones that are considerably more beautiful than the al-Midhar Mosque. The mosque of Nabi Allah Jarjus commemorates either St Sergius or possibly St George, a reminder of the Christian history of the Hadramawt, which produced famous martyrs and in which many churches were built. These were later converted to mosques, with a rare one, as here, keeping something in its name to remember the past.

Tarim has an old religious library open to the public, with Arabic texts and fine calligraphy which are shown to interested visitors. Also in the city there are beautifully carved doors with decoration that ranges from the dynamic to the severe, and there are many picturesque alleys to explore.

From Say'un to al-Hajjarayn (local pronunciation: Hagrayn) takes about 2 hours by car, passing Shibam and penetrating into the upper course of Wadi Hadramawt.

Beyond al-Qatn we approach the upper (western) end of Wadi Hadramawt. In this part the sandstone cliffs on either side are several hundred metres high in places. On the heights are thought to be the remains of towns from the Sabaean and Himyarite periods, but as yet no systematic excavation has been undertaken. Such excavation would be all the more valuable in view of the fact that the upper course of Wadi Hadramawt changes into a delta of wadis (Arabic plural: *widyaan*), where a very early culture is thought to have existed. A little further south, 20 to 40 km from Hadramawt, a number of ruined sites have been found. For the traveller interested in archaeology an excursion into Wadi Amd to the village of **Huraydha** should be high on the list. A few kilometres northwest of the village are the rubble remains of a sanctuary dating from an early period; detailed research has dated the first phase of the building to the 5th century BC.

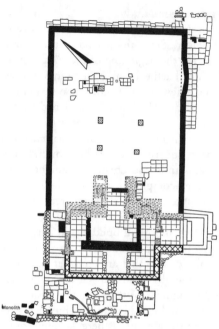

Plan of the Temple of Sin at Madabum, drawn by the British archaeologist Gertrude Caton-Thompson and based on her excavations in 1937

These are the ruins of a temple once dedicated to the moon god Sin. Thanks to the work of the British archaeologist, Gertrude Caton Thompson, the friend and companion of Freya Stark, we know that the original name of the town was **Madabum**. Caton Thompson began her dig here in 1937, the first controlled, scholarly excavation in the whole of South Arabia, and it brought to light inscriptions which gave the name of the place and the religious purpose of the temple.

In Madabum the scanty remains of a paved, elongated platform and stone bases of columns can be seen. Parts of a dividing wall and steps are also visible. It will be noticed that the temple platform was laid on erratic boulders and scree, mixed with plaster mortar. The archaeologists found 21 early South Arabian inscriptions, though none was still in its original location. Nevertheless it was possible to determine from the inscriptions that people first began to honour the moon god on this site in the second half of the 5th century BC. In the period from 100 to 80 BC the buildings seem to have been extended. One reason the remains are so unspectacular today is that even 2500 years ago stone was used only for the substructures in Hadramawt, and the other storeys were built of air-dried mud bricks. Another factor is that around AD 100 the whole region may have suffered a serious earthquake.

On the way to Hajjarayn in the wadi of the same name we pass through **Mashhad Ali** ('Tomb of Ali'). This decaying village is worth visiting for its mausoleum and fine old mosque. The full name of the local holy man whose tomb here used to be a place of pilgrimage was Ali Hassan al-Atas. Around the middle of the last century he moved into a region which had suffered from the struggles between rival tribes, and he proved able purely by the strength of his religious authority to create peace, and even to maintain the peace after his death, for his tomb became a pilgrimage shrine. A bronze dome rises above the tomb, and built into the vaulted entrance to the tomb chamber is a stone relief from the Himyarite period. In the vicinity of Mashhad Ali Leo Hirsch found 'fragments of a light-coloured limestone covered with Himyarite characters' and in a field of rubble in Wadi Raybun, southwest of Mashhad, he thought he could make out the remains of an ancient town and wrote optimistically in his journal in 1896: 'Systematic excavation would bring to light more valuable remains from early times.'

A century after Leo Hirsch's visit to Mashhad excavations were underway. In November 1991 Russian and Yemeni archaeologists could still be seen at work in Raybun, but since then work has ceased and the historic sites have been abandoned again. What remains are some excavated bases, steps, a few columns and even some inscribed stones. Over a wide area tall mounds and many pieces of masonry can be seen. One can only hope that the archaeologists, who seem to have left in the wake of political upheavals, were able to complete a survey of the material.

Al-Hajjarayn (colour plate 32) is one of the daringly placed mountain lairs of the region. It is squeezed onto the upper part of a rock - called Haid Ibn Maimun al-Munneissur according to Leo Hirsch - with its houses clinging to the rock from half-way up right to the summit. Winding up to the gate of the village is a paved path,

Religious procession in Huraydha (photograph by Freya Stark in the 1930's)

235

The mausoleum of Ali Hassan al-Atas before and after restoration

Al-Hajjarayn: the clifftop town is a thousand years old

with cobblestones worn smooth by generations of human feet and donkeys' hooves - so care is needed in the ascent. The path and the narrow alleys of the mountain village are not suitable for vehicles, so all the traffic here is by donkey. The boys of Hajjarayn are remarkably bold donkey-riders, often goading their steeds both uphill and down to a frenzied gallop.

At the highest point in the village there is a cistern which may date from Himyarite times. But the ascent is worth making not so much to see this open basin as to admire the view which extends across mountains and hills as far as Wadi al-Ain further to the east. It takes in a region in which many traces of settlement from the time of the ancient kingdom have been found. The Yemeni geographer al-Hamdani (*c.* AD 900) mentions al-Hajjarayn in terms that indicate that it was a flourishing town in the early Islamic period. Freya Stark discovered part of the village called Dammun - the name of the capital of the pre-Islamic state of the Kinda in Hadramawt (seepage 207). Some old mosques, finely carved doors and the region's last silversmiths are al-Hajjarayn's attractions today.

Wadi Duan, the best preserved and most beautiful part of Wadi Hadramawt, is just a 2 hour drive from al-Hajjarayn.

Important archaeological discoveries were made at the beginning of the 1980's in

Wadi Adim (also written Idim and Idm). The government in Aden at the time had commissioned French archaeologists to undertake research on the spot, and they concentrated on Wadi Hadramawt and its tributary valleys. In Wadi Adim, which opens into Wadi Hadramawt south of Tarim (see page 223f) the archaeologists were able to take a closer look at sites where material had already been found. Thus in Mashqa, known for its pre-Islamic rock temple, they gained new information from the remains of three other buildings. Because of its location large parts of the wood and brick structures on stone supporting walls had remained intact, and it could be shown that the three buildings were tower houses from antiquity. Research is to be continued there.

Aden

Surprisingly perhaps, the great port of Aden was not the capital city of the ancient kingdom of Ausan. According to scholars this was Miswar, which is mentioned in inscriptions, and lies far inland on the edge of the great desert. The identification is not absolutely certain, however, since new evidence has been found to suggest that the upper Wadi Markha (see page 243) was one of the heartlands of Ausan. But Aden was certainly the most important port of the once great trading kingdom, and it is to Aden therefore that we must turn to trace the history of Ausan.

Ausan's greatest period must have been between 600 and 500 BC. Before then the inhabitants of the region would have been suppliers for the caravan trade with the northwest, and, since the African coast was not far away, they probably organized the import of goods from Africa. This intermediate trade made the inhabitants of the coast rich, and riches gave them the power to found a state to protect themselves.

Sailing their boats northwest into the Red Sea and southwest to the east African coast, the Ausanian merchants founded colonies in the areas that are now Eritrea, Somalia and Zanzibar. Some of the outposts were just trading settlements, while others also included conquered territory. But the richer and more powerful these adventurous merchants became, the more they attracted the mistrust and envy of their neighbour, the Sabaean kingdom.

There is no record of the role that Aden played in the heyday of the kingdom of Ausan, but the location of the town in itself allows us to make some conjectures. In the first place, it has a superb natural harbour, the only one in South Arabia. Dominated by a massive volcanic rock, the Jabal Shamsan, 517 m high, the harbour provides shelter from the monsoon winds - the same monsoons that from an early period took Aden's sailing ships to the Indian subcontinent. The Bab al-Mandab, the straits at the southern entrance to the Red Sea, lie a short distance away, and with the right wind the crossing to Africa then took only about 48 hours. A people whose livelihood and wealth depended on trade would only have built a town, harbour walls, warehouses and forts at the best natural harbour available in the region.

Nevertheless, the only definite information we have about the existence of Aden is in connection with the fall of the kingdom of Ausan. A Sabaean inscription tells us that in 410 BC the priest-prince Karib al-Watar of Ma'rib - the first ruler to call himself 'King of Saba' - conquered the state of Ausan including the city of Aden. During this campaign the Sabaeans committed what would now be considered serious war crimes. Not only was the temple of the Miswara (Miswar) fortress destroyed, but most of the Ausanian aristocracy was massacred. According to the inscriptions about 16,000 people were killed after fighting had ceased. Nearly all the towns and villages of the unhappy kingdom were plundered and burned to the ground (including Aden) and 40,000 Ausanians were led away into captivity. Part of the coastal zone of the defeated state was incorporated into the Sabaean kingdom, while another part of the coastline and the interior passed to Qataban.

So around 410 BC Aden was Sabaean, but it was frequently to change hands in the course of the following centuries. For all the rulers, however, the port was indispensable for transit trade between the continents. An anonymous Greek sea-captain who lived in the 1st century AD mentions this in his description of travel routes and harbours between the Red Sea and Western India, the *Periplus of the Erythraean Sea*. Aden is described as 'Eudaimon Arabia, a village on the coast belonging to the same kingdom of Charibael, [which] has suitable harbours and water much sweeter than at Okelis; cargoes from India and Egypt were unloaded there: diamonds and sapphires, ivory, cotton, indigo, cinnamon and pepper, dates and wine, gold, myrrh and frankincense.' Aden played such an important part in the economy at that period that in the *Periplus* the city is given the name of the whole country: 'Eudaimon Arabia' means the same as 'Arabia Felix' or 'Happy Arabia'. (Aden was also known as 'Arabia Emporion', or 'Arabia the Market'.)

Whether this Arabia - including Aden - really was a happy land is an open question. Certainly Egyptians, Syrians, Jews, Greeks and Romans had to pay a great deal of money to the South Arabians in order to acquire the perfumes and spices they so desired, but the unceasing wars between the rival kingdoms and the later military interventions by the Aksumites and Persians must have struck the flourishing trading society repeated heavy blows. This is why busy, prosperous Aden has preserved no remains of buildings from the pre-Islamic period: the city was constantly being conquered and razed to the ground. All that does survive from the early period are the famous tanks, which are drinking-water cisterns.

These tanks, known as the **Tanks of Tawila**, repay close attention. Tawila is the Arab name of a valley which rises towards Jabal Shamsan and squeezes between the rocks at the northern end of the district of Aden called Crater. Under British rule a park was laid out here around the ramifications of the ancient water supply. Basins and overflow gullies, channels and more basins are cut into the mountain, flanked by walled paths and spanned by bridges built of red brick. Seventeen cisterns are arranged in sequence, of which the lowest one collects by far the most water - a maximum of 13 million litres. The whole complex can collect about 45 million litres in a single heavy fall of rain, when the precipitation on Jabal Shamsan is channelled and collected. Today, however, Aden is no longer dependent on these cisterns - the rain-

Aden, general view of the lower part of the Tanks of Tawila

water gathered is used only to water the gardens.

The cisterns, which had been almost filled in with rubbish, were restored from 1859 onwards by the British authorities. Strangely enough, they did not use the opportunity provided by the restoration to make a thorough archaeological study of the site. Consequently the age of the cisterns can only be guessed, or deduced from various other data. It can be taken for granted that such a major work as the hewing of several cisterns out of the solid lava rocks could only be possible in a period of prosperity and stability, which would exclude the time of the wars with Aksumites and Persians. The most likely builders are the Himyarites, whose technological skill has already been seen in their dams and irrigation systems. The high point of Himyarite power over the coastal zone of Aden was around the 1st century AD, so the Tanks of Tawila can be tentatively dated to this period.

Material evidence of Ausan's greatest period was to be seen until recently only in the **National Museum**, housed in the former town palace of the Sultan of Lahej at the edge of Crater. The museum was looted during and after the recent civil war that confirmed the unity of the two Yemens, and among the objects that vanished were two unusually complete statues of kings. These figures had stimulated considerable

241

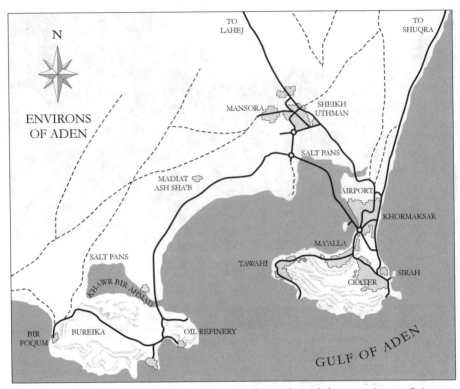

Sketch plan of Aden and the immediate environs. Tawahi was formerly known as Steamer Point

debate among scholars, though no definitive publication has yet appeared and information is scanty. The first, an alabaster statue of Yashduqil Far'am, a king of Ausan, fits the traditional style of South Arabia of the period around 500 BC. Brian Doe, who as Director of the Department of Antiquities during British rule, helped set up the museum, describes it thus: 'A stylized statue which accentuates features and details including the representation of his finger ring, arm band and feet shown encased in thonged, square-heeled sandals. Depicted with a moustache, his hair or wig style is long and at the back is cut with a serrated edge. The left hand may have held a staff.'

This is a fairly crudely carved alabaster statue of the period, with the typical bent elbows and clenched fists of a boxer, though the outsized feet and hands are executed with more detail than is customary. The moustache and the long hair are also unusual. Nevertheless this figure of an Ausanian king can be included without too much difficulty in the long series of South Arabian alabaster statues with almost the same size, posture and form of expression. The same cannot be said of the statue of his successor, King Yashduqil Far'am Sharah'at of Ausan. Despite being very close in time the depictions are fundamentally different, as can be seen from Doe's description of the second statue: 'He is depicted wearing a form of Greek dress, with long hair, or a wig, and a moustache. This is, in all probability, a portrait.' The drapery hanging in folds around the figure and the portrait-like quality, instead of the usual depersonalized facial features, are entirely untypical of South Arabian art. The development that has taken place between the two statues amounts to a new artistic departure.

Since the fall of Ausan occurred shortly after these statues were made, there is no later evidence to confirm such an abrupt change in art. Was it the work of a single Greek artist who had made his way to the court of Ausan, or had the Greek approach to art reached South Arabia, or had there even been an internal artistic revolution in 'Happy Arabia'? We simply do not know.

In any case these two figures of kings are among the very few testimonies from the short-lived kingdom of Ausan, and are in their way remarkable pieces. The 80-cm-high Greek-looking figure of Yashduqil Far'am Sharah'at was, incidentally, found in Wadi Markha, near Timna in the region of the former border between North and South Yemen, far away from Aden. It is only to be hoped that the looters can be traced and the antiquities be restored to the museum.

Many of the other pieces in the Aden National Museum have far less certain provenances. Judging by their style, and bearing in mind the course of archaeological research during the British colonial period, we can guess that the great majority of them must come from the kingdom of Qataban (see page 195). One large alabaster

Aden, Post Office Bay, a picture postcard from the 1930's

fragment that is rather out of the ordinary shows a deer's head bordered with letters and vine leaves. This piece is supposed to have come from Ma'rib and should therefore be classified as Sabaean. Another important alabaster votive panel with a bull's head, of a very high level of craftsmanship, is probably of Qatabanian origin.

The National Museum also had a few fine ancient piece of jewellery: necklaces, arm bands, earrings and brooches. The Yemenis descriptions all read 'Qatabanian jewellery of the 3rd century BC' but Brian Doe avoided giving any precise attribution, stating that the date and origin of the pieces were unknown. In fact, they were probably imported and may have been made in the 1st century AD. Doe added that the pieces resembled Roman jewellery between the 1st and 3rd centuries BC. Those identified as 'golden state seals of the kings of Qataban' do seem to have had that function, since they have legible inscriptions and symbols.

Early Islamic Aden has left as little architectural evidence as the earlier period. The inhabitants of the city probably converted to Islam during the Prophet's lifetime. After his death (in 632 AD), when there was some reversion to the old beliefs and revolts against new Islamic authority in Medina, Aden remained loyal to the banner of the Prophet, and so avoided the devastation of the early Islamic wars. Indeed it was even used as a base for the reconquest of the temporarily apostate Hadramawt.

However, Aden was not to be spared the horrors of war. In the mid-12th century, when the city had been captured by the members of a puritanical sect, an Egyptian expeditionary force came to re-establish the true faith and the authority of the sultan Salah ad-Din (Saladin) ruling in Cairo and Damascus. The Egyptians under Turanshah, a brother of Saladin, took Aden by storm. 'Turanshah plundered Aden and brought more than 80 castles and forts of considerable strength under Saladin's dominion,' is the laconic report of a contemporary chronicle.

Yet, whatever damage the city may have suffered in sieges and looting, neither in the 12th century nor in the centuries that followed did Aden lose its importance as a port and trading centre. This status, which it maintained for nearly 2,000 years, suffered its first serious blow in 1497 when Vasco da Gama dicovered an alternative sea-route to India by sailing round Africa. Aden suddenly found itself far away from the most important trade route. (The situation was not helped by the fact that by this time Aden was already under the authority of the Ottoman Empire, exercised until the mid-17th century by a resident governor.) After the Portuguese navigator's discovery Aden declined rapidly. French visitors in 1708 remarked that 'there are to be seen many fine houses of two stories, and terrass'd on top, but with all, many ruins and decay'd buildings'. By the time Captain Haines, an officer of the Indian Navy, inspected the South Arabian coast in 1835, the once flourishing port had shrunk to a little town with not even a hundred stone houses. Nevertheless it attracted the interest of the colonial authorities in India because it seemed ideal as a coaling station and a base in the struggle against the French naval presence on the

East African coast. In January 1839 under the pretext of punishing the Sultan of Lahej (the ruler of this area, independent of the Yemeni Imam since 1728) for pillaging an Indian ship in 1836, the East India Company took Aden by force and installed administrators. Any revolts of tribes in the country around Aden were quickly put down and usually led to an enlargement of the British-run territory; mostly, however, the British preferred to exercise authority by subtle diplomacy. Aden's economic fortunes changed when the opening of the Suez Canal in 1869 made it the most important transit port on the sea route between the Mediterranean and Asia. It was under control of the British colonial administration in India until 1937, when it became a crown colony. In the Second World War Aden played an important role as an air and naval base. Even after the Empire had broken up, the British were still in the 1960's pouring money into the expansion of the port. Yet already in the mid-1950's Arab merchants and intellectuals (the product of Britain's enlightened educational policies), in alliance with the more progressive rulers in the hinterland (again, the product of generally benign administration that encouraged a sense of nationhood and unity where before had been nothing but warring tribes), had been calling for independence. The British remained intransigent until the Six Days' War closed the Suez Canal; independence followed very shortly after. By now the long, hard struggle had radicalized the liberation movement, and a socialist government was installed that leaned strongly towards the Soviet Union. Up to May 1990 Aden was the capital of the People's Democratic Republic of Yemen (South Yemen). After the unification of the two Yemens, Aden, despite having been declared the 'economic capital of Yemen', was further neglected economically, and its northern suburbs suffered severe damage in the summer of 1994 in the 'battle to preserve unity'.

Tourism in Aden

Until 1990 the territory of the Democratic People's Republic had seen very few independent travellers. The names of these who, during the period of British rule, made their way across the coastal strip on the Gulf of Aden and its hinterland to penetrate into Hadramawt, are still mentioned with respect: Adolph von Wrede, Leo Hirsch, Theodore and Mabel Bent, Harold and Doreen Ingrams, Daniel van der Meulen, Hans Helfritz and Freya Stark. After the Second World War independent travellers still found it difficult to gain access to the two regions of the British Protectorate north and east of Aden; and when after 1956 Yemeni nationalists challenged British supremacy in the region (and direct colonial authority in the port of Aden), the protecting power was unwilling to allow foreigners to travel freely around the country. Shortly after Aden and the regions of the protectorate achieved independence and became a republic in 1967, power struggles, revolutionary troubles and a border conflict with North Yemen prevented any travel in South Yemen. Only from the mid-1970's onwards did the government in Aden open its country - and then only to a very limited extent. The unification of the two Yemens has by contrast given considerable freedom to tourists, whether travelling in groups or independently. They are now only restricted by the fact that there are very few decent hotels and little public transport. The independent traveller, especially the non-Arabic-speaker, may also have quite some trouble finding his way around. On the other hand, any foreigner is now able to take internal flights, buses and shared taxis in all directions without needing a special permit.

For the traveller who already knows northern Yemen, the south (that is, south of Ta'izz) has much that is new, and the first-time traveller will find much of interest in Wadi Hadramawt. However, since unification the tendency has been to push Aden off the tourist routes. For a long time travellers have been able to travel to Wadi Hadramawt by air from San'a, and overland by the two historic desert routes to Shibam and Say'un. There is no need to pass through Aden on the return journey to San'a from Wadi Hadramawt via Mukalla on the main coastal road, since a new road turns off about 175 km east of Aden to the northwest to take a considerably shorter route to the capital. It is true that tours to Wadi Hadramawt are also organized from Aden - but it is not the way most tourists get there, since Aden is much more difficult to reach from abroad than San'a.

Aden will have to work hard if it is to make itself attractive as a tourist destination. The hot and damp climate restricts the period for visits to between October and May, but in the winter months especially (from November to February) Aden and its environs could draw tens of thousands of Europeans to enjoy its bathing, if only enough good-value and well-kept hotel rooms were provided. Sadly, as well as removing much of the cultural interest of the town, the fighting and looting of 1994 reduced the

The Mövenpick Hotel in Aden

Aden, bathing beach near the Gold Mohur Motel

numbers of rooms already available. The local entrepreneurs could easily create clean, protected and sheltered bathing beaches at several places on the two peninsulas in Aden; there are no such beaches on the Red Sea in northern Yemen.

Perhaps Aden can again become a cheap shopping place for swarms of tourists and sailors, as it was under the British until the early 1960's. But it is not enough just to establish the free-trade zone agreed in May 1991; the harbour and airport will also have to be fully integrated into the international traffic between Europe and eastern and southern Africa, and between eastern Africa and the Persian Gulf. But even if that comes about now, the tourist infrastructure will still be a long way from meeting the demands put upon it. Aden's first task before the year 2000 must be to build up a tourist market for its duty-free goods, though the new free-trade zone can never be as it was in the good old days, when thousands of passengers disembarked to go shopping in Aden as the ships stopped there to take on fuel en route for British India.

Visiting Aden

Modern Aden comprises seven districts. Tawahi, Ma'alla and Crater are on the rocky peninsula which was also the site of ancient Aden. Further north lies Khormaksar with some foreign consulates and the airfield. Then come the suburbs of Sheikh Uthman, Dar Sad and Mansora, and finally the industrial suburb of 'Little Aden' (Bureika). Between Mansora and little Aden is Madiat ash-Sha'b, the new administrative centre.

Only three of Aden's interesting monuments date from the Islamic period. First is the free-standing **minaret**, whitewashed and with plaster decoration, that stands near the main post office in Crater (colour plate 11). It used to be part of a mosque said to have been built in the 8th century, which has since vanished. It is worth visiting the **Mosque of Sayyid Abdullah al-Aidrus**, whom legend has made the patron saint of Aden. The mosque, originally dating from the 14th century, fell into total ruin and was rebuilt under British rule from 1859. Although it is used for worship, non-Muslims are allowed to visit it. Lastly the **fortifications** have survived. The oldest date from the 12th century, and they were first built to protect the city from attacks by bedouin from the inland; later the sea front was also fortified. Significant remains of the walls and towers can be seen on the mountains between the districts of Crater, Ma'alla and Khormaksar.

Crater is the oldest district of Aden. As its name indicates, it is built directly in the crater of an extinct volcano. The other settlements that later developed on its outer

Aden, view towards Steamer Point, photographed in 1992

The palace of the Sultan of Lahej (19th-century engraving)

walls have become modern town districts. The appearance of Crater is determined by at least three architectural styles. The houses on the sea front, with verandahs and balconies decorated with carved wooden railings, might be in Calcutta or Bombay. The larger thoroughfares are lined by anonymous concrete buildings, the side streets with stone houses. Near the Post Office is the house where the French poet Arthur Rimbaud lived during his years in Aden; it has recently been restored with French Government money.

The Journey North

Sheikh Uthman is the first place you reach heading north from Aden. Only 15 km from Aden-Tawahi, the former village is now a suburb enlivened by gardens and houses built in traditional style. Despite the proximity of cosmopolitan Aden, the traveller will discover at Sheikh Uthman the first signs of the original South Arabian lifestyle. The exteriors of older houses are decorated with paintings, camels pull carts through the streets, and at the roadside people sell pottery, basketwork, fruit and vegetables.

The town of **Lahej,** 25 km north of Sheikh Uthman has lost its former function as a seat of government. Until 1967 Lahej was the capital of the sultanate from which the British seized the Aden peninsula in 1839. The People's Republic moved the administration of the Second Governorate, in which Lahej is now situated, to al-Hauta in

1967. The palace of the deposed Sultan of Lahej was turned into an agricultural college, which visitors can be shown round. In the gardens and plantations attached to it cotton, cereals, vegetables and a wide variety of fruit are grown.

The environs of Lahej are of archaeological interest, best appreciated at **Subr** on the road between Sheikh Uthman and Lahej. Subr boasts a wide area strewn with red and brown potsherds, from which scholars have concluded that the site was inhabited for a long period and was of some importance as a trading settlement because of its proximity to Lahej. In antiquity the place was probably an assembly point for camel-caravans: large transport columns would be brought together here before the long journey to the north.

Nearly 20 km north of Lahej, near Jabal Tala, is a prehistoric site considered to be one of the most important in Arabia. Stone tools and other traces of settlement have been found that proably date back to the earliest occupation of the peninsula.

Soon after Lahej the road northwards enters **Wadi Tiban**. This is our first encounter with one of the great desert valleys, which from time to time after heavy rainfall carry torrents of water from the Yemeni mountains towards the sea. At the point where the road opens into the wadi stands the interesting **'Palace of the Brides'** (Qasr al-Araaiss), a dilapidated building on foundations constructed of heavy ashlar that suggest a Qatabanian or Himyarite origin (a stone with an inscription seems to support this theory). The mud-built part above dates from the Islamic period. According to popular legend the wedding celebrations of the tribal leaders took place here. From the walls of the building there is a fine view far along Wadi Tiban.

Animal symbolism - often with depictions of panthers or big cats - is mostly found in the highlands of south Yemen.

The 600-year old mosque at Dubayyat

The route also touches the region of the **Radfan Mountains**. Here in 1963, at Habilayn, under the influence of the revolution erupting in North Yemen, the first military action against the British (and the sheikhs who supported them) took place; the now defunct People's Democratic Republic used to commemorate the event as the begining of the revolution.

From the Radfan area the road climbs up to the **Plain of adh-Dhala** at a altitude of about 1300 m. This plateau is again surrounded by mountains, the highest of which, Jabal Jihaf, reaches 2300 m. The landscape is very reminiscent of the southern part of the former North Yemen, which is not far away. As in the highlands of North Yemen, here too qat is grown. In the lower-lying areas the climate is subtropical, and there are citrus trees, pomegranates and papayas. The adh-Dhala region used to be an emirate with its own ruler, whose territory was used by the British Protectorate as a buffer state to North Yemen.

Adh-Dhala itself is now a district capital and the first signs of industrialization are appearing. When walking round the town, which extends over a hill, one should look out for the older houses, built of hewn rectangular and square stones, often laid without mortar. The windows are usually very small and are whitewashed around their outer frames to make them stand out. The façades are also decorated with ornamental strips made of square building stones arranged in lozenge shapes. The old main mosque of adh-Dhala is also well worth a look. Its prayer-hall, again built of hewn stones, is surmounted by twelve small domes, and the stocky minaret is patterned with natural stones in graded colours.

The wider environs of adh-Dhala have not yet been opened up much to tourism. The moderate altitude guarantees a pleasant and wholesome climate, but a short visit will hardly be enough to get to know the natural beauties of the region. An ascent of **Jebel Jihaf** (2300 m), well-known to naturalists for its multifarious flora, can be recommended. This mountain on the adh-Dhala plateau also has impressive examples of the industry of Yemeni farmers. Its terraced slopes are used for growing millet, wheat, oats, onions and vegetables. Instead of a peak Jebel Jihaf has a large hollow flat top, which is also used for agriculture. Numerous springs and, it is said, more than 300 wells are available to the farmers for irrigation.

The town of **al-Awabil** nearby is of interest because it has kept more of the local traditional building style than adh-Dhala itself. Worth seeing here are a saint's tomb in the cemetery at the southern entrance of the town and the stone fort in the centre. Beneath the fort is a large cistern which may date from Qatabanian or Himyarite times. There are also some interesting animal pictures and symbols which are used here - as elsewhere in southern Yemen - to decorate individual houses.

Only about 12 km from adh-Dhala, on a hill below the village of al-Haqfar, stands the **funerary mosque of Jamal ad-Din** with its two domes. Its courtyard reveals it to be an early religious building, and a large cistern belonging to the precinct of the mosque suggests that this was a sacred place in antiquity. Old fragments of columns surmount a wall surrounding the whole complex. In the mausoleum itself, beneath the two domes, are two baldachins with fine carving.

Another place to see near adh-Dhala is the town of **Dubayyat**. Just before reaching

South Yemeni battlements as found in Habban

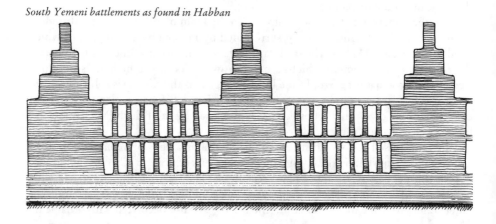

adh-Dhala, the road passes through the village of al-Qafla, at the northern end of which a track turns off to the west towards Dubayyat. The track is suitable for four-wheel-drive vehicles only and the 8 km drive to Dubayyat takes about 45 minutes. The inhabitants are known to be of a conservative disposition. Its most interesting building is what is probably one of the oldest mosques in Southern Yemen.

Estimated to be 600 years old, the mosque has a pillared hall built partly of fired bricks and surmounted by a white dome resting on a structure reminiscent of the stepped pyramid in Egypt. A round minaret built of stones and fired mud bricks with a blunt top stands like a gate-house nearby. Also built of stones and fired mud bricks was the al-Afif Palace which was once one of the town's attractions. Except for a small part of the façade it has since collapsed completely - apparently as a result of heavy rain.

The Journey East

Mukalla is usually visited on the way from Aden to Wadi Hadramawt, but a visit to this sultanate capital on the Indian Ocean can also be made for its own sake. The 622 km journey takes in a sizeable piece of South Arabian history.

Nearly all the early travellers to Hadramawt had to make the first part of the journey from Aden by boat, since the road to the east ended after 60 km and the desert roads were made unsafe by bedouin. Under the People's Republic the first asphalt road all the way to Mukalla was built, with Chinese financial aid. This road runs from Aden for about 50 km through the rich coastal regions. Since independence agriculture here has experienced a boom. Because of the proximity of the capital city much of the overseas aid - mostly from the old Eastern Bloc - was concentrated on this area, where cotton, cereals, tobacco and fruit are grown.

The region forms part of the Third Governorate, formerly known as the Fadhli State of the Protectorate. The landscape is cut through by **Wadi Bana** which opens here into a delta at the Gulf of Aden. In antiquity great trade caravans from the hinterland assembled here, Wadi Bana being an important link on the route to Aden from the Hadrami capital, Shabwa.

After about an hour, just beyond the town of **Shuqra** (where you can rest and explore the market), the road turns north to the interior. It now begins to climb, and crosses extensive lava fields. The black lava stone often forms a stark contrast with the yellowish or white drifting sand eroded from the nearby table mountains by wind and rain. Thousands of years of erosion have left bizarre rock formations throughout this landscape.

Near the town of Am Ayn (about 90 km from Shuqra) the road forks. To the north it runs via Lawdar and al-Baydha in the direction of San'a. To the east the road winds through a varied landscape to the town of **Habban** (about 340 km from Aden) which formerly had a large Jewish population. The school just outside Habban is usually available for overnight accommodation.

A walk around Habban gives a good picture of a South Arabian small town that has largely retained its traditional character. There are several mosques in the old style and many old houses, some of which have the horns of gazelles or ibexes attached to them. Horns are supposed to ward off evil spirits - a pre-Islamic superstition which is still rife, and can be seen on newly-built houses. The new houses, like their predecessors, are constructed of mud-and-straw or mud bricks.

Beyond Habban the road runs for another 30 km through the mountains and then turns south towards the sea, along **Wadi Mayfa'a**. The wadi changes from a narrow, rubble-filled valley between cliff walls to a broad, sandy mouth area as soon as it reaches the coast. About 50 km beyond Habban are the magnificent remains of Mayfa'a, the ancient capital of Lower Hadramawt. The village near the ruins is called Naqb al-Hajar.

Large parts of the city walls of ancient Mayfa'a are extant, built of hewn limestone blocks, almost a metre long on average. The wall was reinforced with bastions at regular intervals, and some of these, too, survive. The location of the North Gate of the city can be clearly seen, while the South Gate opposite must have been the city's most impressive building. Scholars believe it to have been the main entrance into Mayfa'a. The two gate towers still stand to a height of over 10 m; their outer fronts are between 3 and 5 m wide. Three ancient South Arabian inscriptions are set into the walls in the vicinity of the South Gate. According to Brian Doe, the former Director of Antiquities in Aden, the most legible of these reads: 'HBSL son of ŠGB was in charge of the buildings of the wall of MYF'T and its gate in stone and wood and wicker work and the building of the houses which he placed against its wall, from bottom to top. In addition his son SDQYD' heightened the wall.'

Within the wall the city covered an area of about 150 by 300 m. Its houses were built on two hills separated by a depression sloping down to the north, at the bottom of which, near the North Gate, is a well. The well structure included a tall, masonry-clad tower that Doe conjectured was for lifting the water to feed a conduit. The area enclosed by the wall is entirely covered with the remains of buildings, little more than the foundations in some cases, though in others masonry a metre high may still be standing.

The ruins of Mayfa'a lie on a narrow rocky ridge which borders the south side of the wadi. If you follow this ridge upstream along the wadi (which runs southwest-wards) for about a kilometre you come to the remains of a channel cut through here in antiquity to bring water from the valley to the fields to the south of the city. Today this region is no longer under cultivation.

Although Mafya'a was rediscovered about 140 years ago and many archaeologists have worked on it since, the dates of the city's foundation and eclipse have not been fixed with any precision. Very probably Mayfa'a became important when the caravan

Mayfa'a, view through the walls of the ancient city to the neighbouring wadi

trade was at its peak. It was only a day's journey from Qana, the port of ancient Hadramawt and the most important entrepôt for the frankincense and myrrh brought from Dhofar (Zofar) much further to the east. The city and fortress of Mayfa'a, set high on the rocky ridge, dominated the northward caravan route which forked at its foot. One road went to Timna, the capital of Qataban, the other ran over the mountains to Shabwa, the capital of ancient Hadramawt, which was also linked via Ma'rib with the Mediterranean road. The overland traffic flourished in this region particularly in the last three centuries BC. Around the beginning of the Christian era Qana was conquered by the Himyarites. Doe surmises that the defences of Mayfa'a were immediately strengthened. The city could perhaps have held out for quite a long time, but it was now cut off from the world of trade, and so its decline could not be halted.

Qana itself is the next stop on the journey, which now takes us south. Soon after the road reaches the sea again we come to Bir Ali, at present scarcely more than a fishing village, though it is near the end of the new oil pipeline from Shabwa. Just outside Bir Ali is a convenient resting place (camping is possible) on a peninsula extending for about 600 m into the sea with a fine sandy beach and a massive rock called in Arabic **Husn al-Ghurab** (Crow Fortress). This is where Brian Doe finally discovered the remains of Qana. The traveller too can find them by climbing the

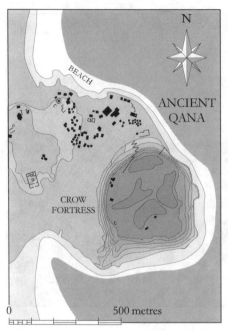

Plan showing the location of old Qana. Rising above the town is the 'Crow Fortress'. The beach is good for bathing

steep - and not very obvious - path up to the plateau on top of the rock. Half-way up you can already make out the plan of the city and the foundations of many buildings. Qana seems to have been divided into several distinct districts. On the east side there would have been smaller residential buildings, while to the north there was a large number of structures with a circular plan. Doe suggests that in the centre of Qana stood tall houses, with lower parts built of ashlar and superstructures of air-dried bricks.

Continuing our ascent to the 'Crow Fortress', we pass two Himyarite inscriptions set into the rock face. They tell us that in earlier times the rock was called Urr Mawiyat, and provide information about the repairs that were necessary following the attacks of the Christian Aksumites in the first third of the 6th century, that is, in the final phase of the Himyaro-Sabaean state. On the plateau of the rock a fortress was built to serve as a look-out and signal post as well as a defence for the port of Qana. Easily recognizable are the remains of the gate-tower (reached up a narrow zigzag path), and there are also cisterns and remains of masonry to see. But the climb is worth making just for the magnificent view of the coast.

Excavations undertaken in 1974 by the Department of Antiquities revealed a temple from the 4th century AD. Brian Doe wrote that Qana merited further research: 'The site of this ancient port deserves detailed investigation for, although much of the foundations of walls are built directly upon exposed rock outcrop, there are many buildings now covered by blown sand which have footings at a greater depth.' Up to about 1991 Yemeni and Russian archaeologists together were staking out fields of excavation and making other preparations for field work. However, following the political changes in their respective countries, the archaeologists have been withdrawn; there have been plans more recently for a combined Russo-German excavation.

A good 3 km east of Bir Ali, on the south side of the road, towards the sea, is an extinct volcano. The easy climb up to the crater is rewarded by a view of the superb

Qana, Himyaritic inscription on the rock of Husn al-Ghurab ('Crow Fortress')

crater lake (colour plate 39). The journey from here to the port of **Mukalla** (622 km from Aden) takes about an hour by car. At the start of the beautiful bay on which Mukalla lies the motor road runs parallel with the old, bumpy camel track through a narrow pass. Just beyond here we pass three large kilns where the lime is burnt for the whitewash that is such a feature of the South Arabian coastal towns.

Mukalla itself is famous for its whitewashed mosques and the equally brilliant whitewashed former merchants' houses in the old town. They make a picturesque contrast with the black rock of Jabal Qara, with a third tone added by the deep blue of the sea. Ongoing industrialization has already brought the first unwelcome marks of modern civilization to the picture. Visitors who have time for a longer tour of the town should look out in particular for the old doors, real works of art with their finely carved rails and copper mounts. The former sultan's palace now houses a small collection of archaeological finds, but also has beautiful views across the bay. In the market the local shops for silver jewellery are worth visiting; you might even find an authentic piece of old silver among the extensive range of standard Arab work.

As far as we know, Mukalla was not one of the early sites of South Arabian civilization; in fact at present its history can be traced back only about 950 years. It probably began as a fishermen's settlement, then became a meeting place for traders,

Mukalla, view from the former Sultan's Palace towards the harbour

fishermen and bedouin. Since at that time there was no longer any overseas trade to speak of, Mukalla remained insignificant for a long time, until around the middle of the 17th century a certain Ahmad al-Kasidi took up residence there as sultan of the coastal inhabitants. Relations with the bedouin of the hinterland - who had to strike a balance between their rapacity and their dependence on the services and quality goods provided by the town-dwellers - were to remain the constant concern of the sultans of Mukalla. In this they acquitted themselves more successfully than their counterparts in the hinterland, and trade began to flourish again. Just as in antiquity all goods passed through Qana, so in the 18th and 19th centuries almost all merchandise was conveyed to the interior of South Arabia via Mukalla. The considerable sums raised in duties and tolls enabled the sultans of Mukalla to maintain a strong mercenary army and so keep the nomads within limits. When in the final colonial phase the British sought to extend their indirect rule in the region, relations with the sultan of Mukalla played an important role in their calculations. However, like the other oligarchies and tribal federations, the sultanate was soon swept away in the left-wing nationalist and revolutionary disturbances which British colonial policy had triggered in Aden.

At present Mukalla is in a state of decay, but the new conditions created by private enterprise mean that its prosperity could improve. The existing hotels would have to be renovated and new hotels built. (The four-star Hadramawt Hotel on the sea front opened in 1993.) There is potential for travel companies using the town as a starting point for overland trips to the Sultanate of Oman, whose western province of Dhofar (Zofar) borders southern Yemen. But so far this has not happened. There are no through roads to the sultanate, nor is there any certainty that the Omani government will allow tourists - whether as independent travellers or in groups - to enter the country by any route other than their own capital Muscat. The possibilities for travel east of Mukalla are still being explored, but in any case the town itself is still worth a visit, though patience and intuition are needed to find the places of interest in the older quarters.

The same is true of **Shihr**, nearly 50 km west of Mukalla on the coastal road. At the moment the town is very run down, but one can still see - if not very clearly - its past greatness. Marco Polo, who visited the region in 1294, mentions Shihr, and when the Portuguese were seeking to secure the sea route to India, which had been discovered by Vasco da Gama in 1497, they soon turned their attention to Shihr, occupying the town at the beginning of the 16th century and managing to hold it for 35 years. In the late 19th century it was from Shihr that the Qaiti clan conquered the neighbouring town of Mukalla and founded the double sultanate that was to survive until 1968. Most of what is picturesque in Shihr dates from the time of the Qaiti sultanate. One of the two town gates, the Bab al-Khor, welcomes the visitor arriving from Mukalla - though for how much longer, it is is hard to tell. Also worth visiting are the remains of the once mighty town walls on the sea shore; but to find more beauty in the crumbling old town requires even greater determination than in Mukalla.

Al-Mahra – The 'Wild East'

After the unification of Yemen the Hadramawt became a great attraction for travellers, particularly for those already familiar with northern Yemen. Until May 1990 the only way to visit the People's Democratic Republic of Yemen had been as a member of a group under constant supervision; but once independent travel became possible in all parts of the country, many Europeans and Americans took the opportunity to explore for themselves not only the legendary Wadi Hadramawt itself, but also many of the tributary valleys, and the high plateau in southwestern Hadramawt, which is crossed only by a few extremely difficult tracks. The crossing of the Jol by minor paths, which the first modern European explorer, Adolph von Wrede, undertook in 1843 at great personal risk, in constant danger of his life, and which even in the 1930's, when Harold and Doreen Ingrams made the journey required great effort, is now regularly offered to more intrepid travellers by travel firms specializing in 'adventure tourism'.

Nevertheless there are other challenges that still await the undaunted tourist. East of both the coastal town of Shihr and of Tarim in Wadi Hadramawt is about 3000 sq. km of almost unexplored desert extending as far as the dangerous Empty Quarter and the western border of the Sultanate of Oman. A large part of this region is the known as the 'Mahra Land', Baylad al-Mahra. When this was the sixth province of the People's Democratic Republic, it was almost completely closed to foreigners, for until 1982 it was the centre of an insurgency movement against the sultan in neighbouring Oman. As Oman gradually opens up to independent travellers and tourist groups on the overland route, this 'Wild East' of the former People's Republic is becoming an increasingly important tourist region.

East of Hadramawt the traveller will find a unique part of Yemen. The Mahra people, who number approximately 160,000, do not speak Arabic but an ancient South Arabian Semitic vernacular. This is thought to be a remnant of the one of the languages of ancient Hadramawt, although it has now of course adopted many Arabic words. Some ethnologists believe the Mahra to be more or less direct descendants of the original inhabitants at the time of the incense caravans. Indeed the 'Wild East' once produced its own incense, for the monsoon winds bring abundant rainclouds at certain times of year (see p. 235), and up to the 1970's frankincense gum was extracted from the wild *Boswellia* trees and bushes, before this laborious task was abandoned for easier and more lucrative work in the oil industry.

Water flows all year round in Wadi al-Masilah, which opens in a broad delta into the sea 250 km east of Mukalla. The course of the wadi begins at the eastern end of Wadi Hadramawt, about 250 km inland. In Wadi al-Masilah many Mahra live as sedentary farmers or semi-nomads; they grow millet and various other crops, keep domestic animals and breed camels. Mahra camels are usually sand-coloured and are famed for their stamina and speed; they are also said to have a sure sense of direction on the steep mountain paths. Camel-breeding is predominantly in the hands of the semi-nomads. During their sedentary periods the semi-nomads live in caves on the edge of the mountains; but they change location following the rhythm of migrations. Nomadism is one of the oldest known ways of life in this region, and the number of nomads and semi-nomads is said to have increased again with the demise of the socialist government that attempted their settlement and full integration.

Other inhabitants of Mahra Land have adapted themselves to living from the sea. Thanks to the abundant rain brought over the coastal mountains by the monsoon winds, the lower levels of the sea are well stocked with plankton, so that the Gulf of Aden is one of the most productive fishing grounds in the world. Descendants of bedouin have long since become fishermen. They use lines to catch sharks and rays, and many Mahra have specialized in catching lobsters. The season lasts from October to June. This specialization is now threatened, for it is difficult under private enterprise to continue to freeze the shellfish on the spot and maintain the cold chain via the markets of Aden to Paris or London.

The majority of the Mahra fishermen are not affected by the consequences of the changes in the economic system, however. They continue to practise the ancient craft of sardine-fishing. The nets stuffed with sardines are immediately emptied onto the hot sand and the catch is dried. The smell is generally pervasive. The end product (called *aid*) is used as a foodstuff for man and beast far inland. Mahra camels will even eat aid in preference to fresh vegetable fodder. In the past the fishermen also used the silvery harvest of the sea as the raw material for another product: by leaving a large quantity of sardines in a pit to rot and diligently stirring the putrid mass, they extracted a fish-oil which was then used for sealing joints in the wooden fishing boats.

The moist-warm climate of the Mahra Land is ideal for various species of palms. These play an important part in house-building in the coastal zone. Posts and roof-supports of the fishermen's huts are usually roughly hewn from palm trunks, while palm fronds are woven to make the outer walls and roof. Rock salt is brought from the interior in hand-made containers made of palm fronds, and is still exported in sailing boats as far as East Africa.

Al-Mahra for Tourists

Scholars are still unsure of the exact route of the Incense Roads from Zofar via Hadramawt and Ma'rib to northern Arabia. It is assumed that initially the sea route was used about as far as the modern coastal town of Saihut and that the caravan then followed a track through Wadi al-Masilah. This seems plausible, for according to old Arabian sources the land route from Wadi Hadramawt through the desert to Zofar took 30 day- or night-marches. The modern travellers should not attempt to cross the border from Yemen to Oman using this route, which is not marked, runs through dangerous stretches of desert, has no resources in case of accidents and breakdowns, and which even with a four-wheel-drive vehicle takes about ten days. The most sensible and safest route is along the coast.

From Mukalla to the Yemeni-Omani border is about 750 km. Construction has begun on a through road. At present the town of Saihut, 280 km east of Mukalla, can already be reached by an asphalt road; a further 200 km of asphalt road is being built to the provincial capital of al-Ghaydah. Another 200 km of road will then be needed to reach the Omani frontier. Although the tracks along the coastal route are difficult for driving and there are few vehicles, hitch-hikers have nevertheless managed to make the trip between Yemen and Oman in both directions.

At present there are hotels only in Mukalla and in the vicinity of the port; anyone wishing to travel further east or northeast must be prepared to stay overnight in the open or in a tent. Fresh fish and drinking water can be found everywhere on the coastal road. Petrol can probably be obtained at each of the five coastal towns on the way to the Omani border. For journeys into the interior of Mahra Land a single four wheel drive vehicle is not enough: it is absolutely essential to take two vehicles if travelling in this almost impassible region, where any breakdown can result in an enforced stop of several days.

The economic situation in Yemen may delay the construction of an asphalt road from Saihut to the Omani border, but technically it is not a particularly difficult project. A greater challenge will be posed by the connecting road, about 100 km long, from the border to the provincial capital of Salala in Zofar. Salala is built by the sea on a broad plain, sheltered on the Yemeni side by three mountain ranges. To blast a sufficiently wide coastal road through the rocky Qara mountains, which fall away steeply on the western side, will be extremely expensive in terms both of money and effort, even if no financial or political problems arise to scotch the current plans.

Socotra

Socotra, known to the ancients as the Island of Bliss, or more commercially as the Island of the Terraces of Incense, has been visited by travellers and merchants from before the time of Alexander the Great (who is said to have stopped here on his way back from India and to have settled colonists here on the advice of Aristotle). In the years of the People's Democratic Republic Socotra was, however, a part of South Yemen that could be visited only by a few foreign specialists. Its riches of frankincense, myrrh and the rich red resin known as 'the blood of the two brothers', cinnabar, are no longer the stuff of international trade.

The island of Socotra itself, together with the smaller islands of Abdul Kuri, Samha and Darsa, form an archipelago off the East African coast almost exactly at the level of the Horn of Africa. Socotra has an area of about 3600 sq. km, and is about 500 km by sea from Mukalla, and about 700 km from Aden. In the Greek shipping manual known as the *Periplus of the Erythraean Sea* (1st century AD), it is described as desert and marshy, and full of crocodiles, snakes and lizards, the latter being edible and reduced down for cooking fat.

It is thought that the Sabaeans took possession of Socotra in about 500 BC. They found an indigenous population, who had possibly also migrated from the South Arabian mainland, though this is by no means certain. According to one expert, 'as research stands at present, we do not know when the first inhabitants reached Socotra or where they came from.' In the pre-Christian period Greek and Indian immigrants came to Socotra in pursuit of the incense trade. Intensive research by two French philologists has shown that Socotri, the unwritten language that predominates on the island, is related to an old southern Semitic dialect, Mahri, which in another form is still spoken by the inhabitants of the province of Mahra in the east of Yemen. Since Socotra was colonized from Mahra in the 10th century AD, it is likely that Socotri does not date from before that time and is not the language of the aboriginal inhabitants. Socotri has always been of great interest to philologists; Mrs. Bent, who visited the island with her husband in 1897, wrote: 'In subtlety of sound Sokoteri is painfully rich, and we had the greatest difficulty in transcribing the words. They corkscrew their tongues, they gurgle in their throats, and bring sounds from most alarming depths, but luckily they do not click.'

As well as their language the people of Mahra also brought Islam to Socotra. Over a long period it gradually ousted Christianity, which had previously been dominant. When Yemen was conquered in AD 525 by the Aksumites, Christians from what is now Ethiopia, Socotra too came under Christian rule. The Greek population in particular seems to have turned quickly to the new doctrine. This led to another influx of Christians from the Byzantine Empire, and also from Ethiopia. For the period around AD 600 there is evidence that the inhabitants were predominantly Christian and spoke Greek. They belonged to the Nestorian church, and their clergy had a bishop subordinate to the Nestorian patriarch, who resided in Persia.

After the victory of Islam on the mainland, Christianity on Socotra came under pressure. In the 9th century Muslims driven from the Euphrates valley settled on the island, but the majority of the population remained Christian. Their faith did not, however, hinder them from pursuing the violent profession of piracy. A cultural decline also seems to have set in, as we can see from Marco Polo's account of the island, which he is supposed to have visited around 1294: 'All the people, both male and female, go nearly naked, having only a scanty covering before and behind... Their religion is Christianity, and they are duly baptized, and are under the government, as well temporal as spiritual, of an archbishop, who is not in subjection to the pope of Rome, but to a patriarch who resides in the city of Baghdad [the Nestorian Patriarch had moved to Baghdad in the 8th century]... The inhabitants deal more in sorcery and witchcraft that any other people, although forbidden by their archbishop, who excommunicates and anathematizes them for the sin. Of this, however, they make little account...'

Christianity on Socotra does not seem to have made any more cultural impact in the years following Marco Polo's visit. In 1480 the South Arabians conquered the island, and in 1507 the Portuguese arrived. Socotra remained in Portuguese hands for only three years before passing once again to the mainland Arabs. Although the island was henceforth to have Muslim rulers, for another 60 years Christian missionaries were allowed to work among the population. A curious eclectic religion emerged, perhaps best described by Padre Vincenzo, a Carmelite. 'The people still retained a perfect jumble of rites and ceremonies, sacrificing to the moon, circumcising, and abominating wine and pork. They had churches called *moqame*, dark and dirty, and they daily anointed with butter an altar. They had a cross, which they carried in procession, and a candle. They assembled three times a day and three times a night; the priests were called *odambo*. Each family had a cave where they deposited their dead. If rain failed they selected a victim by lot and prayed round him to the moon, and if this failed they cut off his hands. All the women were called Maria.' This mixture of Christianity, moon cult and Islam was to survive beyond the 18th century; Islam eventually made some headway, though in the early 20th century people still prayed with their backs to Mecca, and not in Arabic (the universal religious language of Islam) but in their native Socotri.

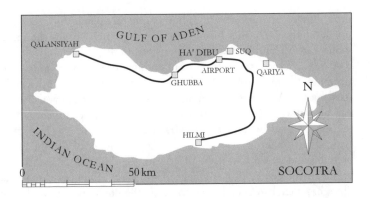

Britain briefly inspected Socotra in 1835 with a view to making the island, rather than Aden, the coaling station for the journey to India, but the lack of a good harbour undoubtedly influenced the decision the other way, despite the better climate and conditions on Socotra. In 1876, however, Britain protected her position by signing a classic friendship treaty with the local sultan, who engaged himself to protect shipping and not to enter into relations with any other power, in exchange for an annual subsidy.

The present population of the island - about 80,000 - has been classified (by the Steins) into three groups: the mountain-dwellers in the interior of the island, the South Arabian traders and craftsmen on the coast, and the fishermen of African origin in the coastal plain. The Steins believe that the mountain-dwellers are descendents of the indigenous population. They mostly use natural caves as dwellings. According to the Steins many Arab traders and craftsmen had taken wives from the mountains and in these mixed marriages both languages, Socotri and Arabic, were spoken. The majority of the fishermen were descendants of slaves from East Africa; Suq known as the 'African colony', and the slave trade continued into this century. Even from this rather backward island more than 10,000 inhabitants made their way as workers to Saudi Arabia and the Gulf Emirates. The money they sent back (until 1990) brought an unwonted prosperity to the island, disturbing the traditional social structure.

Socotra for Tourists

The scanty literature about Socotra, published in Aden, presents the island as potentially a tourist paradise. The scholarly publications of the Steins also suggest that the beautiful flora and fauna, which are basically African in character, make a great impression. The highest mountain on Socotra, Jabal Hajir (about 1500 m) is of enormous botanical interest, with innumerable rare plants and trees growing on its slopes, not least the Dragon's-blood trees, from which comes the cinnabar resin used as violin varnish, and Adenia (see opposite and page 269f; colour plates xx and xx).

As far as we know, no significant architecture from antiquity has survived on Socotra. Near the main town, Ha'dibu, are the remains of a 15th-century fort, which was used by the Arab and Portuguese conquerors of the island. Remains of another fort can be found at Suq, 'buried in groves of palm trees by the side of a large and deep lagoon of fresh water' wrote Mrs. Bent. 'The view at Suq over the wide lagoon fringed with palm groves on to the jagged heights of Mount Haghier rising immediately behind is, I think, to be placed among the most enchanting pictures I have ever seen.' In the centre of the village British archaeologists discovered the remains of a church, which had been last restored by the Portuguese (who left inscriptions there).

It is the people and the natural beauties of Socotra, more than the ruins, that make a trip from Aden or San'a worthwhile. There are two flights a week, one from Aden and one from Mukalla. Visitors can stay three days on the island, though they must be content with very simple accommodation. Food has improved since Captain Saris landed in 1611, when he protested at the high price of goats, adding 'yet are most of them not man's meat, being so vilely and more than beastly buggered and abused by the people, so that it was most loathsome to see when they were opened.' The climate is arduous, and the risk of malaria is greater than anywhere else in Yemen.

Socotra, dwellings at the edge of Ha'dibu, the island's capital

The trees of Socotra

Mabel Bent and her husband Theodore are some of the more unlikely explorers of the Yemen. Restless in their travels in Greece, Africa and Arabia, they did not take on the romantic persona of so many who travelled this area, preferring an almost scientific approach. In their journey to Socotra they took particular notice of the extraordinary vegetation, which has attracted travellers and merchants since antiquity, and now draws scientists from all over the world. These paragraphs are taken from their book Southern Arabia, *published in 1900*

The glory of Mount Haghier is undoubtedly its dragon's blood tree *(Dracaenia cinnabari)*, found scattered at an elevation of about 1000 feet and upwards over the greater part of Socotra. Certainly it is the quaintest tree imaginable, from 20 feet to 30 feet high, exactly like a green umbrella which is just in the process of being blown out, I thought. One of our party thought them like huge green toadstools, another like trees made for a child's Noah's ark.

It is a great pity that the Socotrans of today do not make more use of the rich, ruby-red gum which issues from its bark when punctured, and which produces a valuable resin, now used as a varnish; but the tree is now found in more enterprising countries - in Sumatra, in South America and elsewhere. So the export of dragon's blood from its own ancient home is now practically *nil.*

If the dragon's blood tree, with its close-set, radiating branches and stiff, aloe-like leaves, is quaint - and some might be inclined to say ugly - it has, nevertheless, its economic use; but not so its still quainter comarade on the slopes of Mount Haghier, the gouty, swollen-stemmed *Adenium.* This, I think, is the ugliest tree in creation, with one of the most beautiful of flowers; it looks like one of the first efforts of Dame Nature in tree-making, happily abandoned by her for more graceful shapes and forms. The swollen and twisted contortions of its trunk recall with a shudder those miserable sufferers from elephantiasis; its leaves are stiff and formal, and they usually drop off, as if ashamed of themselves, before the lovely flower, like a rich-coloured, large oleander blossom, comes out. The adenium bears some slight resemblance, on a small scale, to the unsightly baobab-tree of Africa, though it tapers much more rapidly, and looks as if it belonged to a different epoch of creation to our own trees at home.

Then there is the cucumber-tree, another hideous-stemmed tree, swollen and whitish. This tree is found only on Socotra, and is seldom more than 10 or 12 feet in height. It is a favourite perch for three or four of the white vultures which swarm in the island, and the picture formed by these ungainly birds on top of this ungainly tree is an odd one.

To the south of Mount Haghier one comes across valleys entirely full of frankin-cense-trees, with rich red leaves like autumn tints, and clusters of blood-red flowers.

No one touches the trees here, and this natural product of the island is now absolutely ignored. Then there are the myrrhs, also ignored, and other gum-producing plants; and the gnarled tamarinds... Then there are the tree euphorbias, which look as if they were trying to mimic the dragon's blood, the branches of which the natives throw into the lagoons so that the fish might be killed...

Such are among the oddest to look upon of Socotra's vegetable production.

Natural History of Yemen

Geology

Geologically the Yemen is similar to Africa. The Red Sea is part of the Great Rift Valley trough which extends from Mozambique to the Jordan Valley. The volcanic eruptions which caused its formation left a string of craters across Africa and Arabia. The Yemen landscape is spectacular both because of the mountains and deep valleys covered with terraces constructed thousands of years ago, and because of the dramatic colours of the rock formations. North of San'a the Harra, a high plateau where the granite and sandstone are covered with sheets of black lava pierced by the reddish cones of extinct volcanos is strange and impressive. Sulphurous vapour rises from the crater of Hammam al-Issa near Dhamar, and as the name indicates there are a number of hot springs (Hugh Scott recorded a water temperature of 153°F = 67°C at Huweimi).

The country is divided into three main zones: former North Yemen with its narrow coastal strip and steep mountains; the south which is a broad sandy coastal plain; and the desert plateau which falls gradually from the watershed near Yarim (2550 m) to the edge of the desert (1200 m).

The island of Socotra is particularly interesting because of the links with other continents, indicating that (like Madagascar) it was part of the great Palaeozoic land mass known as Gondwanaland which joined up what are now Brazil, Africa, Southern Europe, Central Asia, India and Australia. When a large part of this area was flooded,the high peaks on Socotra were never submerged and certain plants and animals survived there; some of these are unique to Socotra and some (like the crabs and geckos) are similar to species in South America and Polynesia as well as Southern Africa.

The medieval lead and gold mines are probably worked out. Gem stones like agates and carnelians are still found, however, and oil production is increasing (see page 301).

Ecology

The Republic of Yemen is very rich in wildlife. The wide variety of habitats and altitudes, coupled with its location at the meeting of the African, Asian and Palearctic ecological zones, has resulted in the greatest diversity of plants and animals in the Arabian Peninsula, if not the whole of the Middle East.

Flora

The flora of the Yemen is very rich and varied because of the range of climate, soil and altitude. The Tihama is very hot (20° to 40°C) with low rainfall and high humidity; the Escarpments are warm (-5° to +30°) with up to 800 mm of rain; and the Highlands and Eastern Desert (high daytime temperatures and frost at night) have under 200 mm rain and very low humidity. Along the Red Sea Coast the soil is salty and in the mountain basins of the Highlands there are rich, water-retentive loess deposits. Thousands of years of careful cultivation and irrigation on the terrace systems have produced a soil rich in humus and nutrients, but where the terraces are being neglected (because of changing life styles) this soil erodes rapidly. Most of the original forest cover of Acacia trees has disappeared, much in the last 30 years. The old forests have been destroyed by grazing and by the demand for timber and especially fuel wood, which increases with the population and with improved transport facilities. A wide range of plants in Yemen have been used for traditional medicines and in local industries, and several, such as species of Aloe, Juniper and Acacia, are particularly important. On the coast, the fringes of mangrove forest are economically vital as the shrimp stock which supplies the fish populations is dependent on them.

Some 1700 species of flowering plants have been identified and there is more work to be done in this field. About two-thirds of these are tropical African species and most of the rest are Mediterranean. There are certain plants which are of great interest to botanists and geologists because they are endemic in places as far apart as the Yemen, the Canaries and Cape Province and nowhere else.

A visitor to Yemen will be especially struck by two plants - the Bottle Tree and the Euphorbia. The Bottle Tree or Desert Rose, *Adenium obesum*, (colour plate 2X) is a large succulent shrub with grossly swollen trunk and conspicuous pink or crimson trumpet flowers. It can be seen most easily on rocky slopes on the western mountains below 1800 m and is always worthy of a photograph; in Africa, the bark and fleshy parts of the trunk are used for making poison arrows.

Euphorbias are cactus-like plants that grow below the frost line, mostly between 1000 m and 1800 m in the western and southern mountains. The most dramatic species is the candelabra-shaped *Euphorbia ammak*; the latex from its leaves is used as a cure for camel mange and warts.

The strange bottle trees, the balsams and myrrh trees and the aloes grow in the Tihama and up into the foothills. Linnaeus wanted very much to see a cutting of the rare Mecca Balsam tree (*Commiphora opobalsamum*) so he could examine and describe it before he died. Forskål, the botanist who accompanied Niebuhr, had been searching for it unsuccessfully ever since they had arrived in Alexandria in 1761 but it was not until April 1763 in the coffee hills near Bayt al-Faqih that he first saw a tree in blossom and realised it was the Mecca Balsam, the 'crown of the Danish expedition's activity in Yemen'. Forskål wrote excitedly to Linnaeus reporting his find and identifying the family; he enclosed a flowering stalk but as the packet took over a year to reach Uppsala (via India) the blossoms had withered and Linnaeus saw nothing but a bare twig. Poor Peter Forskål had died just three months after his great discovery. The golden coloured resin from this tree, called Balm of Mecca or Balm of Gilead, was highly esteemed for healing wounds in the ancient world and was one of the sources of wealth for Yemen. Resin from Myrrh trees and other members of the *Commiphora* family is still used in perfumery.

The screw pine, *Pandanus odoratissimus*, also called bread fruit trees in other parts of the world, is grown in the wadis of the lower escarpment for its beautifully scented flowers; men wear these flowers, often wrapped with basil, in the folds of their turbans on feast days.

Near San'a the deep gorges of Wadi Dahr and Wadi Hadda have long been famous for their terraced orchards of fruit trees (apple, pear, guava and citrus) but these were all imported. Coffee, too, is thought to have been introduced from Ethiopia in the sixth century AD; it grows at the same altitude (1600-2200 m) as the native qat (a shrub related to the spindle).

The most characteristic succulent plant of the escarpment area is the candelabra tree (see above and colour plate 2X); it is a native that has adapted to desert conditions. The hedges of prickly pear and cactus are imported.

There are many aromatic plants, like jasmine, lavender and thymes and alpines; September, at the end of the rains, is one of the best months for flowers.

The island of Socotra was known to the ancient Egyptians as the Island of Terraces of Incense, and to the Greeks and Romans as the Dioscorides, from the Sanskrit 'Island of Bliss'. It depended for its wealth on frankincense, myrrh, cinnabar and aloes. Frankincense and myrrh are made from the golden resin of two trees and cinnabar comes from the resin exuded by the Dragon's Blood Tree, *Dracaena cinnabari* (colour plate 2X). The aloe is a succulent with flaming poker-like flowers; the sap which is pressed out of its leaves, called bitter aloes, was used for medicinal purposes and the best quality came from Socotra (there is no connection with aloes or eagle wood, a resinous wood from *Aquilaria agallocha*, a tree native to China and the East Indies).

The Dragon's Blood tree (like the aloe a member of the *Liliaceae*) grows in the hills. It starts life looking like a clump of grass, develops a thick trunk surmounted by a tuft of leaves, like a shaving brush, after a year, and then becomes a sort of feather duster before ending up like an umbrella inside out. At this stage it is mature; it produces flowers and fruit and starts to die. The bark is now cut and a clear pale green fluid oozes out. After some days this hardens and becomes tear-shaped gobbets which darken to the red cinnabar used in dyes and lacquers and once used in medicine. Frankincense and myrrh, collected in a similar way, were essential in the procedure followed by Egyptian priests preparing mummies; the demand was once enormous, but has dwindled since the 4th century and *ghi* is now the most valuable export of Socotra.

Richard Porter and Barbara Fyjis-Walker

Fauna

Whilst plants are fairly obvious, mammals are much less so. Although a good range of 55 species occur in Yemen (including Leopard, Striped Hyaena, three species of gazelles and Ibex), it is only the Hamadryas Baboon that is likely to be encountered. A good place to see them is from the Hudayda to San'a road, just after leaving the Tihama on the slopes of the foothills. Over 65 species of reptiles (of which six are only found in southwest Arabia) occur. The most common to be encountered are the Agamid lizards (colour plate XX) which will sit sunning themselves on rocky outcrops from the highland plateau down to the lowland foothills. There are also snakes and chameleons. Over 106 species of butterfly occur, mostly of African origin; the best times to see them are October and May. In the Red Sea the coral reefs support a number of beautiful and interesting fish; the coast south of Mokha is famous for vast stingrays (up to five feet long, and four feet across).

The problem with many wildlife groups in Arabia is that there are no readily available reference books to assist with their identification. This is not so with birds. Yemen is very rich in bird life and of the animal groups, they are the most conspicuous and easily seen. If one includes the island of Socotra (home of the *rukh*, Sinbad's winged mount in the Arabian Nights, and, according to Pliny, of the phoenix), over 360 species have been recorded. Among these are 19 species (13 on the mainland and 6 on Socotra) which are found nowhere else in the world except in some cases neighbouring areas of south-west Arabia. For these so-called 'endemics', Yemen has a special responsibility and, because of them, ranks as probably the most important country in the Middle East for bird conservation.

So why is Yemen so special for birds? There are, in fact several reasons. First, consider the high mountain block of the north Yemen highlands as an island surrounded by the Red and Arabian Seas on two sides, and the sands of the Empty Quarter on the other. After the Ice Age, a number of European or Asian species that were pushed down from the north remained in this isolated island to evolve into the endemics we know to-day.

Second, as mentioned above, Yemen is influenced by three major faunal regions of the world which overlap here, and as a consequence the country has many species representative of each.

Thirdly, because Yemen is positioned at the foot - or funnel - of Arabia, a number of migratory birds become concentrated on their long journey between their breeding grounds in Asia and their wintering areas in Africa.

Finally, there is a spectacular range of habitats, from the mountain plateau and terraces down to the plains of the Tihama and desert, to the biologically very rich coast and its numerous off-shore islands. Each holds its own special bird communities.

The endemic birds - visit to Kawkaban

It is for the endemics that Yemen has a special responsibility and it is to see them that bird watchers will travel from far across the globe. They are the ornithological equivalents of the old city of San'a, Shibam and the temples at Ma'rib.

The endemics are found mostly in the highlands and probably the best and most easily accessible place to see a good selection is the cliffs of Kawkaban, an hour's drive north of San'a. Starting on the plateau and rocky slopes outside the old walled town, there is a good chance in the dawn light of seeing, and certainly hearing, the two partridges: Philby's Rock Partridge and the Arabian Partridge. Like all partridges, they are shy and if disturbed will fly off with a clatter of wings and loud chicken-like calls. They are instantly identified by their grey plumage with striped flanks and bold black and white head patterns. Philby's is the one with the all-black chin and throat.

Then climb down the steep path that leads to the town of Shibam at the foot of the Kawkaban cliffs, which must be one of the most exciting walks for bird watchers anywhere in the Middle East. Moving from the rocky ledges to feed on the open slopes will be Yemen Serins - tiny, active drab birds with tinkling calls. Where Acacia trees start to appear, Yemen Linnets will occur, with grey heads, chestnut backs and broad white wing bars in flight, and also Arabian Serins, similar to the Yemen Serin but darker, more streaked, with a stout bill for cracking seeds. Unlike the Yemen Serin, this is a tree dweller and can often be seen sitting quietly amongst the Acacia branches, gently flicking its tail.

Acacias, especially those with a flaky bark, are the home of another speciality, the Yemen Warbler. This curious bird has caused problems for taxonomists as it does not fit easily into any family. About the size of a slim sparrow and brownish grey in colour, it moves heavily, but unobtrusively, through the branches gently waving its rather long tail or stopping to hang upside down, like a tit, in its search for insects in the bark or leaf litter. Close views show a pale eye in the centre of a dark mask and a flash of apricot on its undertail coverts.

There is also the chance of three other endemics at Kawkaban, but they are hard to see: the Arabian Woodpecker, the Yemen Thrush and the Arabian Accentor. Look for the woodpecker (it is the only species of woodpecker to occur in Arabia) anywhere where there are trees - it is quite widespread in the highlands. The thrush is very shy and a start before dawn is often necessary to catch its flutey song ringing out over the highland terraces. Resembling a female blackbird, it has a powerful yellow bill and when it flies flashes orange beneath its wings. The accentor likes high rocky slopes with low bushes. It is small, brown and secretive, but if a good view is obtained the characteristic white eye stripe will be easily observed. If you are unlucky at Kawkaban then try the upper slopes of the Sumarra Pass.

What about the remaining endemics? The South Arabian Wheatear with its black and white plumage can be found anywhere on the terraces where it is one of the commonest birds. The Arabian Waxbill likes lower slopes especially where sorghum, maize or millet are grown. A mixture of acacia woodland and euphorbias is the home of the Golden-winged Grosbeak, a startling bird with a powerful black bill and bright golden yellow flashes on its wings and tail, especially noticeable in flight. On the Tihama plains amongst the cereal crops the final endemic occurs, the Arabian Golden Sparrow. Flocks of bright yellow males and sandy coloured females descend onto the crops where small boys will rattle tins full of stones to scare them off.

Bald Ibis and Arabian Bustard
Any account should not ignore two species which, although occurring elsewhere in the world, have a special significance for Yemen.

The Bald Ibis is one of the world's rarest birds, with a rapidly declining population that now numbers less than 200, most in Morocco. But a few also occur in Yemen, notably on the marshy land at Ta'izz sewage lagoons where they were discovered in 1985. The big unknown is where they breed. Is it in Yemen or are they migrants from a neighbouring country? Whatever the answer, the wetland pastures at Ta'izz are extremely important to them.

The Arabian Bustard is a bird of the Tihama plains, where it occurs alongside farmers in irrigated agricultural land or grassy savanna amongst Acacia trees. Although it is uncommon, Yemen is in fact its stronghold in Arabia. It is Yemen's largest bird, standing three feet high and with a huge wingspan. It is marvellous to see such a vulnerable species co-existing, unmolested, with the farming people of the coastlands.

Seabirds and Waders
The richness of the Red and Arabian Seas and their muddy shores make Yemen a haven for seabirds and waders. A watch from the coast at Hudayda, Aden, Mokha or Khokha will produce Brown Boobies, Swift Terns, White-eyed Gulls (which are virtually confined to the Red Sea) and a variety of other seabirds, whilst along the shores will be Pink-backed Pelicans, Reef Herons, Spoonbills and a host of wading birds - mostly migrants from their Arctic breeding grounds. Especially exciting are the black and white Crab Plover.

Places to see birds on the tourist track
Saæa
Yemen is not all about rare birds or birds of world importance. The gardens of San'a and other cities can be alive with the songs of Yellow-vented Bulbuls, groups of

White-eyes, or Palestine Sunbirds feeding on the nectar of plants. Out on the open plateau, Red-breasted Wheatears will stand upright in pairs like sentinels of the agricultural fields. Overhead Alpine Swifts search for insects whilst flocks of Black Kites gather to roost at dusk, circling majestically. Brown-necked and Fan-tailed Ravens occur everywhere, and you will never be far from the bubbling call of the Laughing Dove. But, as mentioned previously, a visit to Kawkaban is necessary to see a good range of the endemics.

Ta'izz
In the Euphorbias around the city, look for Golden-winged Grosbeaks, whilst any groups of trees or even telegraph wires will support the hanging funnel-shaped nests of the Ruppell's Weaver. In the crops, Arabian Waxbills and Zebra Waxbills can be found feeding in flocks. On the scrub-covered hills, Black Bush Robins will sit conspicuously on a bush top with tail held erect. The sewage lagoons to the north of Ta'izz are a good place to see waders, ducks and other migrant waterbirds such as the Glossy Ibis.

Zabid
Zabid and its environs are an excellent place to see the typical birds of the Tihama. The open desert areas will have Black-crowned Finch Larks and Hoopoe Larks, while the vegetated wadis will support the unmistakeable turquoise blue Abyssinian Roller, Little Green Bee-eater and the diminutive Nile Valley Sunbird with a tail the length of its body. Black and white Abdim's Storks may nest on the village roof tops, Palm Swifts will search for insects at dusk, when flocks of white Cattle Egrets can be seen flying overhead to their roosting trees.

Aden
The lagoons and shoreline can be very good for a variety of waterfowl, and are one of the best places in Yemen to see the Lesser Flamingo. White-eyed Gulls and Sooty Gulls occur on the beaches, and at sea it may be just possible to find the Socotra Cormorants.

Ma'rib and Shabwa
These ancient towns and the interior desert environs are good places to see a variety of species of larks. Sand Partridges are fairly common, as is the diminutive Namaqa Dove which, with its long tail and black face, is easily recognised. Sunbirds are plentiful, especially the tiny Nile Valley Sunbird. On the bare hillsides, Blackstarts (all grey with a black tail and about the size of a sparrow) will flick their wings and tails, and where patches of trees occur groups of Arabian Babblers can be seen hopping, Long tails erect or flying in follow-the-leader fashion. The new dam at Mar'ib is certainly worth a look for waterbirds.

Socotra

The plant and birdlife of this unique island are fascinating. About one-third of its 800 species of plants are only found on Socotra; and six of the 110 species of birds are endemic too.

Its most dramatic plant, the Dragon's Blood Tree (*Dracaena cinnabari*) is described above, pages 267 and 271, whilst there are also good stands of Frankincense (*Boswellia*), Bottle Trees (*Adenium obesum*) and Cucumber Trees.

Of the six endemic bird species, those most easily seen are the Socotra Rufous Sparrow (occurring in all habitats including human habitation), the Socotra Sunbird (widespread where there are trees and bushes) and the Socotra Cisticola (best seen in coastal dune-scrub near the airport). The others, Socotra Starling, Socotra Bunting and Socotra Warbler are less easily seen. Try the middle-altitude slopes for the Starling (where it occurs alongside the much commoner Somali Starling), coastal scrub for the secretive Socotra Warbler and the higher mountain slopes for the elusive bunting.

Overhead, the near-endemic Socotra Swift can often be seen searching for insects, whilst soaring in the warm air-thermals will be buzzards - those on Socotra are over 2000 km from the nearest known breeding area.

But the most conspicuous of all birds on Socotra is the Egyptian Vulture, which gathers in groups around villages and settlements and is almost fearless of man. The breeding population could well exceed 1000 pairs, making the island the most important breeding area for the species in the Middle East .

Further reading

For more information about the flora of Yemen, consult al-Hubaishi and K. Müller-Hohenstein: *An Introduction to the vegetation of Yemen*, Eschborn 1984; and for birds, R. Porter, Christensen and Schiermacker-Hansen: *Field Guide to the Birds of the Middle East* (published by T. & A. D. Poyser, 1996). The Ornithological Society of the Middle East (c/o RSPB, The Lodge, Sandy, Bedfordshire SG19 2DL UK) publishes a journal, *Sandgrouse*, of which issue 9 contains a detailed report, including check-list of bird species, on Northern Yemen. Issue 17 contains a similar report for Southern Yemen and Socotra.

A delightfully written account of a naturalist's expedition to Yemen is Hugh Scott's *In the High Yemen* (London, 1942).

Richard Porter

Yemeni Silver Jewellery

Yemen has always*een famous for its silver jewellery, though it has undergone a marked decline in quality in recent decades. This decline is almost invariably attributed to the emigration of the Jews in 1948-49, since it was the designs and craftsmanship of Jewish silversmiths that had dominated the market in jewellery and ritual equipment in southwestern Arabia for hundreds of years. Many of the products of the silversmiths' craft were connected with religion, so this meant that Muslim items were in fact made by artisans of another faith. This was the case not only in former North Yemen, but also in the towns and villages in the north of the old Aden Protectorate, which were home to many Jewish silversmiths. Their exodus to Israel was a severe blow to a market extending from Aden to Ta'izz and San'a, and as far as the Najran oasis in Saudi Arabia. Imam Ahmad tried to limit the damage by ordering that the Jewish silversmiths in his domains teach their skills to Arabs before being allowed to leave, but knowledge and skills handed down from generation to generation over the centuries could hardly be passed on to beginners in a crash course. By 1979, according to the Austrian Walter Dostal, who wrote a study of San'a market, only six of the 27 owners of silver shops had undergone a short apprenticeship with a Jewish silversmith. The others restricted themselves to trading in silver jewellery.

Nevertheless the decline of the silversmith's craft can hardly be entirely due to the Jewish emigration. After all, in Ta'izz and Aden there were some Muslim families with a tradition as silversmiths. And in South Yemen, in the region east and north of the port of Mukalla, where no Jews lived, silver jewellery was traditionally made by Arabs, who dealt with the silversmiths of Saudi Arabia and Oman. Today there must be several hundred Muslim silversmiths working in the whole of southwestern Arabia.

At least as big a role in the decline of traditional craftsmanship as the Jewish exodus has been played by permutations in taste and changes in requirements. The whole Arab world - and with it Yemen - has experienced a profound social and political transformation since the beginning of the 1960's. The drastic decline in the number of nomads has led to a decrease in the demand for their particular kind of silver jewellery. In North Yemen the sada (the hereditary religious aristocracy) were stripped of political power, and in South Yemen they were stripped of their property too, so in the united Yemen they now have only a minor role as purchasers of ritual silver jewellery. New standards have been set as a result of the social changes and migrations, together with shifts in taste and, not least, an inflationary glut of gold. Gold is preferred to silver as a way of paying the bride-price and providing financial security for a newly married woman.

Yet it is still worth looking out for silver jewellery in the markets of San'a, Ta'izz, Sa'da and in the tourist shops of Aden, Mukalla, Say'un and Tarim, as well as at the shops of independent dealers in the little towns of Wadi Hadramawt. Some good old pieces can still be found and even some of the pieces made today have an appeal for a visitor used to industrial mass-production.

In the past the silversmiths of Yemen catered for three sorts of customer: the nomads and semi-nomads at the edge of the great desert, the sada, and the property-owning middle classes in town and country. This tripartite division is reflected in the work they produced: to satisfy the tribesmen's demand for jewellery; to provide the aristocracy with status symbols; and to offer in the form of jewellery a suitable means of

A jambiya, combination of leather and silver-work set with cornelians

A jambiya, old silverwork from Ta'izz

Anklet, made by a Ta'izz workshop   *An old container for musket balls*

paying for the traditional marriages.

Silver was always important to the **nomads** and **semi-nomads** of southwestern Arabia. The leaders and junior leaders of the tribes decked themselves out with daggers with hilts and scabbards in chased silver; their wives wanted anklets and bracelets, belts, neck-bands and brow-bands, as well as earrings and nose-rings. Finger-rings were very popular with both sexes, and the possession of silver amulet-holders and amulets seems to have been indispensable to men and women alike.

The **sada** dressed and adorned themselves so that their social status was apparent even from a distance. Besides the turban and white robe, their costume included a special belt and a special dagger. The dagger, usually kept in an elaborately worked silver scabbard, was carried on the right - in contrast to most armed men who wore the curved dagger in the middle, in front of their stomachs. The belt worn by a sayyid could be made of very expensive materials, with silver or gold thread worked into it, and it had a number of articles attached to it, most of them with a ritual significance, including one or two silver flasks for kohl (eye make-up), elaborately worked containers for amulet texts, and sometimes even silver containers for bullets.

The jewellery of the **peasants** and **townspeople** was also made to be worn, but its primary function was as capital for financing marriages. The value of the silver treasure given on the occasion of the betrothal depended on the social status of the bride (though the caste system in Yemen did not allow any great social difference between husband and wife). The marriage agreement usually required that the silver treasure had to supplemented later. But in any case it was the inalienable property of the wife, and her security should the husband make use of his right to divorce her. This explains why bracelets and anklets could often weigh 200 to 250 grammes: their material value counted as much as their artistic workmanship.

Since the departure of the Jews and the revolutionary changes in the social structure the once extensive range of different types of jewellery has noticeably diminished. Some types have disappeared from the market completely, while others are still made, but are only to a low or mediocre standard. Nevertheless some more recently made pieces still catch the eye, and all over Yemen one can find a considerable quantity of old jewellery, which comes into the market piecemeal. Bedouin jewellery is seldom more than 50 years old, because it is the custom in nomad communities for the wife's silver to be melted down after her death and re-made for the next bride. In the urban society of Yemen, however, silver jewellery remains in the possession of the family often for several generations, since it does not belong to the wife as security but is part of the moveable capital of the extended family. Some of it is sold when it is needed, to pay for a pilgrimage to Mecca, for example, or to finance an important business venture.

Since nomad jewellery does not have a long lifespan, our survey of traditional silver jewellery must begin with the special pieces made for the sada.

The numerous silver **attachments for the belt** of a sayyid are hardly made at all today. In North Yemen the members of the religious aristocracy do still dress in the traditional way (see colour plate 4), but they either have to use their own stock of equipment, or else acquire pieces from private collections. The most prominent item on the belt is the *thuma*, the **dagger** which only descendants of the Prophet have the right to wear. The blade was not the most important part (inferior steel usually suffices), but great importance was attached to the decoration of the hilt. Good hilts were carved from a single piece of horn; two silver coins, sometimes even gold coins, were used as decorative covers for the rivets attaching the blade to the hilt, and an ornamental band made of silver wire decorated the area between hilt and scabbard. Often little silver pins were set in the horn hilts. On less expensive pieces simple decorative medallions of bronze or copper were used to cover the rivets. The decoration of the scabbard was mainly the work of the silversmith. He made the separate parts, which were then attached to a leather or wooden case. Even expensive examples almost never had scabbards made entirely of solid silver; they were made of finely ornamented and engraved individual plaques skilfully linked together. Since the thuma is held in a leather sheath under the belt the covered part of the scabbard was left undecorated, though the end was formed of a knob which sometimes had a coral or agate decoration.

The belt of a sayyid is also always decorated with **amulet-containers**. These are either closed capsules, usually containing a verse from the Koran, made either of chased silver plate or decorated with filigree, and firmly attached to the belt. They may also be silver cases that can be opened. A well-to-do man descended from the Prophet used to wear a belt with both kinds. In the case that could be opened he kept religious teachings written on paper in readiness for people to whom he wanted to do

A necklace: silver beads can be bought individually

Ear pendants: these heavy pieces were fastened to a headband

good. Containers for amulets were the pinnacle of Yemeni silversmiths' work. They were executed in various techniques, including filigree which allowed the amulet to appear through the delicate ornament. Granulation was usually applied onto this filigree. The large amulet cases were often made with a technique of layering: fine silver wires, sometimes consisting of two wires twisted together, were soldered onto a smooth silver surface to form geometric or floral ornaments, to which blossoms, a bunch-of-grapes pattern, or rows of little pellets were soldered in the form of granulation, circular and lozenge-shaped silver plaques. Accents were created with balls of differing sizes, which were frequently attached on a circular spiral. This range of forms was often supplemented by stamped or chased elements. The silver treated in this way could be more than 5 mm thick. All such pieces have a stamp on the back with the name of the silversmith.

Containers for kohl are also much sought after by collectors of Yemeni silver. They were made primarily for the use of men. Women did use this eye make-up too, but only men and children are allowed to show themselves in public with blackened eyelids and painted eyebrows. For the sada little flask-like vessels were made, richly decorated with filigree and granulation. Hanging from a little chain was a metal

Necklace: the glass stones and stylized hands show that this is an amulet

pencil for extracting from the flask the graphite-coloured powder (made from the soot of burnt frankincense, and burnt almond shells).

Even simple devices, such as hooks for hanging other objects from the belt, are painstakingly decorated. They are set on **silver rosettes** and from them hang writing equipment, keys and possibly also a cosmetic set (tweezers, ear-spoon and tooth-pick).

The dagger for townspeople, peasants and bedouins is the **jambiya** (plural: janaabiya, pronounced as if 'gambiya'). It is made in various types, materials and price ranges, and there are also regional differences. The jambiya is worn in front of the body and has a scabbard much more curved than the blade. In the highlands of North Yemen this scabbard was always of leather decorated with silver mounts. In Ta'izz, south-wards to Aden, and further east the better pieces had scabbards and hilts of silver. The leather scabbard with silver mounts was often tied together with green bands (green being the colour of the Prophet), a feature that was imitated in the all-silver scabbards in the form of silver rings. There are also janaabiya with semi-precious stones and corals set into the silver mounts; other pieces made do with glass insets. Behind the scabbard of the dagger there is sometimes a smaller knife in its own silver scabbard with a silver hilt. As a rule both pieces were very elaborately decorated, and occasionally a band of Arabic script decorated the knife hilt. The most sought-after material for the hilt is rhinoceros horn. Yemeni demand for this is endangering the survival of the species.

Janaabiya in leather scabbards are still produced in large numbers in the north, but a silversmith will only make an intricate thuma or a high-quality jambiya with silver mounts when commissioned by a wealthy customer.

In the past nomads, farmers and townsfolk - men and women alike - all wanted to equip themselves with **amulet-holders** to ward off evil spirits and and evil influences in the most religiously correct manner. This need still exists today and beautiful amulet-holders continue to be produced by Yemeni silversmiths.

The popular amulet-holder is, however, of a different shape from that worn by the sayyid on his belt. It is cylindrical, 8 to 10 cm long (in some cases 5 to 15 cm wide), and can be opened at the side to insert a rolled-up text amulet. It is worn alone on a chain round the neck or as part of an ensemble of silver and amber balls. The patterns are many and varied. There are examples with very fine, half openwork filigree, as well as pieces set with simple lozenge shapes made of small silver pellets. More modern amulets are decorated only with soldered-on strips of S-shaped silver wire.

Rectangular amulet-holders of solid silver, about 10 cm long and 8 cm high, are among the expensive pieces which in earlier days were traded not only as jewellery but also as a capital investment because of their high material value. They are not a particularly Yemeni speciality, but occur throughout the Islamic world. Only the style of the decoration has a national character. Typical of Yemen is the combination of filigree and granulation, and the patterns of flowers and grapes. Many of the applied geometrical patterns are like those seen on houses, and some may be the pre-Islamic in origin. (Although only a very few pieces have so far been found, it is assumed that silver jewellery was also important in antiquity.)

Coins used as jewellery or as elements of items of jewellery were very popular among all groups of the population. This fashion probably did not appear until the 16th century. Silver coins were already being minted in South Arabia in the 3rd century BC (taking Greek coins as models), but until the end of the Islamic middle ages they had such a high purchasing power that it would have been too extravagant to use them for decoration. It was only after the irruption of the Ottoman Empire into southwestern Arabia and the beginning of the coffee trade that the amount of money in circulation increased considerably with the influx of Turkish and European silver coins. At the end of the 18th century the famous Maria Theresa dollar (or *thaler*) appeared in Yemen, probably in the wake of Bonaparte's invasion of Egypt. Why this silver coin, weighing 28 gram (silver content 83.3%), with a profile bust of a foreign ruler, with much décolletage and an elaborate coiffure, should have become established is still a mystery. Other dollars of equal value, from Venice, Tuscany or Prussia, did not meet with approval - nor did the earlier Austrian dollars with the portrait of Francis I, the Empress Maria Theresa's husband. Throughout South Arabia the Maria Theresa dollar of 1780, although it did not achieve the status of an official currency, was treated as such by the population for almost 200 years. Very early on it was recognized that the coin had had a particular attraction, and the order was given to continue to mint it with the date 1780. In the Austrian capital alone 250 million Maria Theresa dollars have been minted, and from 1935 the coin (used as

Amulet-holder, a religious verse on the front and decorated on the back with an unusual floral pattern

colonial currency) was also minted in Rome, Paris and London, and in these three capitals another 50 million are said to have been produced. Most of these 300 million dollars would have flowed into South Arabia and Ethiopia, where they were reworked into jewellery. Both the Ottoman Empire and, later, the Imam of Yemen tried to counter the Maria Theresa dollar with their own coinage, by circulating silver coins of exactly the same size, and even one or two grams heavier. But even in the independent Kingdom of Yemen the Imam's dollars were less respected than those of the Holy Roman Empress.

Coins were - and are - worn individually as pendants or as part of a necklace in combination with silver balls, glass beads and corals. Large dollars surrounded with silver and glass beads were used for making head jewellery, which was worn suspended from a brow band and hung over the ears to resemble earrings (illustration page 226).

Exclusively **nomad jewellery** was hardly ever made in Yemen, but there are types of jewellery which were preferred by the bedouin and were less highly valued by the sedentary population. One example is the **qaff** (from *qufass*, Arabic for 'glove'). It consists of five finger-rings attached to a central plate by little chains (a very similar type of jewellery is found among the Turcomans of Afghanistan). Generally speaking the silversmiths near the regions where nomads live, that is in Sa'da, Jihana, Ma'rib, the Najran oasis, and in Say'un, Tarim and Shibam, took more account of the nomads' taste than did their colleagues in San'a, Ta'izz, Aden and Mukalla. This resulted in a certain coarsening of the workmanship, particularly of the bracelets and foot-rings. For rings, bracelets and neck-rings cornelian (Arabic: *akik akhmar*) or simple glass was more frequently used; many pieces of jewellery, even simple coin pendants, had little bells attached. These, when they are found on the jewellery of the sedentary people, must be a legacy to the townsfolk and farmers from the camel drivers of former times, who attached warning bells to their beasts.

With townspeople and peasants coral is still very popular as an element of the jewellery ensemble. Since 1987 many corals have come onto the market and the prices have dropped. The silversmiths of Ta'izz formed individual pieces of coral into amulet-holders and kohl-flasks.

The woven silver belts with filigree-decorated buckles, which are now seen more frequently to the east and north of Mukalla, are often attractive.

An interesting speciality of North Yemen, still to be found today, is the chased **hollow silver ball**. Many of these balls are so beautifully crafted that they can be used as pendants on their own. In other cases they are attached in splendid chains. But even in combination with amulet-holders, chain elements, filigreed linking pieces, corals and amber beads, these hollow balls are an important part of a fine jewellery ensemble. It is true of the silver balls, as for so much other Yemeni jewellery, that the finest pieces come from the 1930's and 40's; those made today show a marked decline in quality.

In South Yemen the finest silver jewellery was produced in the little town of the Habban (see page 253), the home until the end of the 1940's of about 300 Jews, many of whom were silversmiths. Since Habban was also a town of the religious aristocracy, who required a great many pieces of ritual jewellery and status symbols, the skilled Jewish craftsmen specialized in these. Since the departure of the Jews Muslim silversmiths have sought to keep the tradition alive.

Glossary

aga - commander of a unit of troops in the Ottoman army.

Almaqah (Ilumquh) - moon god; the principle deity of the Sabaean empire (called Amm and Anbay by the Qatabanians, and Sin by the Hadramis). The Awwam Temple at Ma'rib is dedicated to him.

Athtar - god of the planet Venus, an important deity throughout ancient South Arabia, corresponding to the Phoenician Ashtarte.

bayt - a dwelling unit within a large early Islamic house

caliph (Arabic: *khalifa*) - the successor of the Prophet Muhammad as leader of the community of the faithful; the first caliph after the death of the Prophet in AD 632 (10 AH) was Abu Bakr. Disputes about the succession to the caliphate led to divisions within Islam.

diya - the compensation paid (in accordance with Islamic tribal law) to the relatives of one who has been killed, either by accident or deliberately, as a way of preventing or ending a blood feud.

funduq (Arabic for 'hotel') - in Yemen this is a simple inn with several beds to a room (in rural districts), or a very basic hotel (in towns).

hadith - A tradition relating to a saying or action of the Prophet. The collection of such traditions forms the sunna (qv), which supplements the Koran.

haram (Semitic: found in Sabaean and Arabic) -

1. a precinct under divine protection, a sanctuary; 2. now also used in an Islamic sense, meaning forbidden by religious law. (See also harem)

harem (related to haram, qv) - the room where women spend their time. The only men permitted to enter are very close members of the family

Himyarites - people of one of the ancient kingdoms of South Arabia, which dominated the region from the 3rd century AD.

hypostyle - building supported by rows of columns or piers

imam - Any man who leads public prayers. In the Shi'ite (qv) tradition the Imam is the leader of the community (see also Caliph). In Yemen the Imam was the ruler of the country (until 1962), who was regarded by his Zaydi (qv) subjects as a successor of the Prophet. He had to be a sayyid (qv) and satisfy the fourteen requirements for the post (see pages 152f)

Ismailis - a Shi'ite (qv) sect, which recognizes a different sequence of Imams (qv) and has a distinctive, gnostic interpretation of Islamic teaching. The few remaining Ismailis in Yemen belong the Western branch of the sect.

jambiya (Yemeni pronunciation: *ganbia*) - two-edged, curved dagger, traditionally with a hilt of rhinoceros horn and an elaborate scabbard, worn as a status symbol by all Yemeni men (see page 282)

Karib - Priest-king, a local ruler in the ancient

South Arabian kingdoms. (See also Mukarrib.)

Koran (Qur'an) - The Holy Scripture of Islam containing the revelations made by God to Muhammad

mafraj - In a Yemeni house the living room of the master the household; used as a reception room for male guests (especially for qat (qv) parties); usually at the top of the house.

mahr - bride price, that is, money and silver jewellery left by the bridegroom with the father of the bride as security for his daughter in case she is divorced.

malik - king, the title of South Arabian rulers without priestly powers.

Mamluks - military slaves who overthrew the Ayyubid dynasty and became the rulers of Egypt from 1250 to 1517. They ruled part of Yemen for a period (see page 72).

masjid (whence the English 'mosque') - Islamic place of worship; a large congregational mosque used mainly for midday Friday prayers is called a 'Friday mosque' (*masjid jami*).

madrasa - Islamic mosque school or theological institute with a school and dormitories.

mihrab - Niche in a wall of a mosque indicating the qibla direction (the direction of Mecca), which the faithful face in prayer.

Minaeans - people of Ma'in, one of the ancient kingdoms of South Arabia. Dominant from 4th to 2nd century BC.

minbar - pulpit in a mosque.

minaret - The tower attached to a mosque, used by the muezzin for the call to prayer. Some early Zaydi (qv) authorities disapproved of minarets.

monsoon - a seasonal wind in the Indian Ocean, blowing from the southeast from April to October, and from the northwest for the rest of the year.

mukarrib - Sabaean prince at the head of a federation, an intermediary between the people and the gods. After the 5th century BC the functions of priest and ruler seem to have been separated and the title of the ruler became malik (qv).

Nabataeans - a people of North Arabia with their capital at Petra, whose wealth was derived from the caravan trade on the Incense Road.

propylaeum - Monumental gateway to a religious precinct.

qadi - Islamic scholar who acts as a secular and religious judge

qat - A shrub (*Catha edulis* Forsk.) growing at between 1500 and 2500 m. It is cultivated in Yemen (where it is by far the major crop) for its leaves which have a mild narcotic effect when chewed. Qat-chewing is universal among the male population (and is also practised by women) in most parts of Yemen. It is less common in former South Yemen (see page 82f).

qasr - Arabian palace or castle

qishr - infusion of coffee husks and ginger, a popular drink in Yemen.

Rassulids - dynasty that ruled much of Yemen from13th to 15th centuries AD.

sayyid (plural: sada) A descendant of the Prophet Muhammad. The sada, a religious aristocracy, were formerly of great importance in the High Yemen, where Zaydi (qv) Islam predominates. In Wadi Hadramawt, which is Shafi'ite (qv), the sada were also a significant force. A sayyid often acted as piece-maker between warring tribes.

samsarah - A typical Yemeni type of town

GLOSSARY

caravanserai: a hostel-cum-warehouse attached to a mosque and used by visiting merchants.

Shafi'ites - Sunni Muslims who follow the school of Islamic law founded by Imam Shafi'i in Cairo around AD 800. Most of the population of Tihama and Hadramawt is Shafi'ite.

Sharia (literally: 'way') - Islamic law; an integral part of Islam, contains the ordering of creation as laid down by God and revealed to the Prophet Muhammad.

sheikh - a title of respect given to a tribal leader or holy man.

Shi'ites - Members of the Shi'a (literally: 'party'). Those Muslims who regard the fourth Caliph Ali, the cousin and son-in-law of Muhammad, as the first legitimate successor of the Prophet.

Sin - The moon god in ancient Hadramawt

spolia - Old architectural fragments re-used in new buildings. In Yemen these are usually columns, piers or inscribed stones from ancient temples which have been built into mosques and houses.

Sulayhids - dynasty ruling much of Yemen in the 11th and 12th centuries AD.

sultan - formerly the title of local rulers in South Yemen.

Sunna - collection of traditions concerning the life and doings of the Prophet, as handed down by his companions.

Sunnis - those Muslims who follow the Sunna and, unlike the Shi'ites, recognize Abu Bakr, Omar and Uthman as rightful Caliphs (the *Rashidun*) before Ali.

thuma - A Yemeni dagger with a richly decorated scabbard and brocade belt, worn at the side as a status symbol by the Sada (qv).

Wadd - Moon god, the state god in Ma'in.

wadi - dry desert valley which fills briefly with a torrent after rainfall.

Wahhabis - Members of a puritanical Islamic sect, founded in the first half of the 18th century by Sheikh Muhammad Ibn Abdul Wahhab in Central Arabia; Wahhabism is the state religion of Saudi Arabia.

zabur - Building technique using mud mixed with chopped straw and raised in layers. The best examples are at Sa'da (see page 152f).

Zaydis - Followers of an Islamic sect named after its founder Zayd Ibn Ali. Around AD 1000 they created a state in North Yemen, where Zaydi Islam is still the dominant religion. Although they are Shi'ites (qv), the Zaydis are in many respects closer to the religious outlook of their Sunni (qv) neighbours than to that of their fellow Shi'ites (see pages 125f and 291f).

Practical Information

Contents

Yemen in Brief

Geography

Location: The Republic of Yemen occupies the southwest corner of the Arabian Peninsula. To the west it is bordered by the Red Sea, to the south by the Indian Ocean (Gulf of Aden), to the east by the Sultanate of Oman, and to the northeast and the north by the Kingdom of Saudi Arabia. Parts of these borders (with Saudi Arabia to the north, and with Oman to the east) have not yet been defined in international law. The figures given for the total area of the country therefore vary between 478,000 and 533,000 km², but in any case the Republic of Yemen is the second largest state in the Arabian Peninsula in terms of area, and the largest in terms of population.

Landscape: The former North Yemen is divided into two very different zones: the damp and hot Tihama coastal plain, and the fissured landscape of High Yemen, which rises to over 3000 m. Within each zone there are further regional differences.

The southern part of the country is a flat, mostly sandy coastal strip. To the northwest this area extends as far as the Yemeni highlands, particularly in the region of Dhala, Mukayras and Bayhan. Wadi Hadramawt in the middle northeast of the southern region is a region of its own; in places the valley bottom is 800 m above sea level, and dry desert conditions prevail.

Climate

Roughly speaking the country can be divided into three climatic zones:

The Tihama, the coastal plain (30-50 km wide) between the Red Sea and the foothills, has a tropical climate. The average temperature in this area is about 30°C, often rising to well over 40°C, and seldom falling below 20°C. The Tihama is swept by the monsoon, which brings heavy rains mainly in July and August, when the relative humidity can rise to 90%.

Approximately the same climate prevails in Aden and the coastal region to the west and east of the port. Here it may also rain in the spring.

The central highlands comprise the region between 1000 and 2000 m above sea level. Here the average temperature is only 25°C. On the western side of the mountains in particular there are significantly heavier rainfalls than in the Tihama. This climatic zone contains the most intensively cultivated region in North Yemen.

In spring and summer the monsoon clouds also bring rain to the mountains northwest of Aden. Most of this region, which rises to 2500 m, is rocky and fissured, so despite the precipitation agriculture is only possible in a few places. Larger agricultural regions in the highlands, such as Wadi Tiban and Wadi Bayhan are made possible by the flow of water from the higher northern area. In Wadi Hadramawt too intensive cultivation is practised, using pumps.

The upper highlands, between 2000 and 3000 m above sea level, experience severe cold periods during the winter months (December and January), and two rainy seasons, a minor one in March/April and a major one from July to September. Early morning mist also adds to the moisture. The raw climate at this altitude does not allow the cultivation of tropical plants. Nevertheless there is intensive cultivation right up to the summits of the mountains. On the very intensively farmed terraces the Yemenis grow cereals and other hardy crops, above all qat.

Population

The present population is estimated at between 13 and 14.5 million. It is impossible to be more precise because there is no system of registration, and because there are no exact figures for the hundreds of thousands of Yemeni migrant workers who have returned from Saudi Arabia and the Gulf States.

About 15 % of the population live in towns; 85 % live in the countryside and work in agriculture.

The largest towns are:
San'a   population 800,000 to 1 million
Aden   population approx. 330,000
Ta'izz   population approx. 240,000
Hudayda   population approx. 210,000

Religion

Religions in Yemen: The national religion of the Yemenis is Islam; the Prophet's father had visited San'a and his great uncle was said to have been buried there. Yemen was in some sense the crucible of Islam - its Christian and other population was converted very early on, and it was the source of the great Arab armies and some of their greatest commanders. The Jews (who before 1947 numbered some 70,000 in North Yemen) now make up less than 0.01% of the population; the Jewish remnant is concentrated around Sa'da and Rawdha. About 60% of the population of Yemen belong to the Shafi'ite school of Sunni Islam (concentrated in the coastal plains, the foothills and Wadi Hadramawt); the remaining 40% belong to a branch of Shi'ite Islam, mostly the dominant Zaydi sect (in the northern highlands), though there is also a significant Tayyibi Ismaili minority (around Manakha).

Islam in Yemen
by Sebastian Wormell

Islam (literally: 'submission [to God]') has its origins in the Arabian Peninsula in the early 7th century AD. Its founder, the Prophet Muhammad, was born in the rising commercial and religious city of Mecca. He was a member of the ruling Quraysh tribe, and became a merchant in the caravan trade. Around 610 AD, at the age of about forty, he began to experience revelations from God. These were written down in Arabic and became the Koran, the holy book of Islam. Conflicts with the authorities at Mecca led Muhammad and his followers to leave the city in 622 and move 300 km south to Yathrib, which became known as Madinat al-Nabi ('city of the Prophet') or Medina. The move (*hijra*, literally 'withdrawal') marks the beginning of the Islamic era: Islamic dates are not AD but AH. In AD 630 Mecca surrendered to Muhammad, but the Prophet continued to live at Medina until his death in 632.

Muhammad taught a monotheistic faith related to the Jewish and Christian traditions. The Hebrew Patriarchs and Prophets, and Jesus, were honoured. But there were also links with the earlier Arab religious tradition: in 624 it was revealed to the Prophet that the *qibla* (direction of prayer) was to be Mecca, not Jerusalem as he had taught earlier. A meteoric monolith encased in a simple stone structure at the centre of the *haram* (sanctuary) in Mecca, known as the Ka'ba, had been of religious significance for centuries before Muhammad; now, purged of its polytheist past, it became the focus of Islamic pilgrimage. (In Yemen, too, earlier cults were incorporated into Islam, notably pilgrimage to the tomb of the Prophet Hud in Hadramawt.)

The religious duties of a Muslim – the 'Five Pillars of Islam' – are relatively straightforward:

1. The confession of faith (*shahada*: 'There is no god but God, and Muhammad is the Prophet of God').
2. Prayer (*salat*) five times a day. Prayers must be preceded by ritual ablutions but can be said anywhere, though particularly on Fridays communal prayers conducted by a prayer-leader (*imam*) are held in a mosque (*masjid*), where a wall-niche (*mihrab*) marks the direction of Mecca, and there is a pulpit (*minbar*) from which a sermon can be delivered at Friday noon prayers.
3. Regular giving of alms (*zakat*) for the poor and needy.

4. Strict fasting (*sawm*) once a year during the month of Ramadan.

5. Pilgrimage (*hajj*) to Mecca at least once in a lifetime, if means permit.

As Islam spread across the Middle East and North Africa with the conquering Muslim armies (many of whose finest soldiers and commanders were Yemenis), questions arose about the centre of authority and the legal interpretation of the Prophet's legacy. These led to the development of a body of learned men (*ulama*) who could pronounce on religious questions. One of the leading figures in the ulama was the judge (*qadi*), who had a central role in Muslim society, dispensing justice according to Islamic law (*shari'a*). Descendants of the Prophet (*sada*, singular: *sayyid*) were accorded special respect.

The splits which took place within Islam concerned issues of authority and interpretation. The various branches of Islam in Yemen today derive from these early divisions. The most significant split arose from a disagreement over who was the rightful successor of the Prophet as leader of the faithful (the *khalifa* or caliph). Following the death in 661 of Ali, the Prophet's nephew and son-in-law, many Muslims accepted the leadership of Mu'awiya, a descendant of Ummaya, and founder of the Ummayad dynasty of caliphs, who moved their capital to Damascus. Others thought that the caliphate should stay with the Prophet's close family and supported the claims of Ali's descendants. They became known as the party (*shi'a*) of Ali, or Shi'ites. Those who recognized the full legitimacy of the Ummayad caliphate (and of the caliphs before Ali) became known as Sunni Muslims, because of the emphasis they placed on the *sunna*, the tradition of the Prophet's habitual practices.

Sunnis are divided into four main groups ('the four schools'), based on differing interpretations of the law as revealed in the Koran and the *hadith* (records of the Prophet's sayings and actions). Among Yemeni Sunnis the Shafi'ite school, based on the teaching of Muhammad Ibn Idris ash-Shafi'i (767-820), predominates. Most Muslims in the Tihama coastal plain and Hadramawt are Shafi'ites, and Zabid in the Tihama was a great centre of Shafi'ite learning. There are a few adherents of other schools, notably Hanafis (followers of the teaching of Abu Hanafi) near Zabid; the Rassulid dynasty, which ruled much of Lower Yemen between the 13th and 15th centuries, were Hanafis, and the Ottoman authorities gave them official support. Shafi'ite Islam in Yemen was receptive to the mystical teachings of Sufism. Several notable *sufis* influenced religious life in Tihama, including the famous sheikh Ali Ibn Omar ash-Shadhili of Mokha, who is said to have introduced the drinking of coffee as an aid to prayer. The tombs of holy men proliferated and became cult centres, rather like the shrines of Christian saints. In Hadramawt, too, the burial places of holy men, usually peace-makers between tribes, were venerated.

While Sunni Islam in Yemen is mainstream, the Yemeni Shi'ites are rather unusual. The dominant religion in Upper Yemen is Zaydism, a branch of Shi'ite Islam brought to Upper Yemen in the 9th century by Yahya Ibn Hussain, known as al-Hadi. The Zaydis take their name from Zayd (died 740), a great-grandson of Ali, whom they regard as the rightful successor to the caliphate – or imamate, as the Shi'ites call it. By contrast the 'Twelver' Shi'ites (the dominant religious group in Iran) recognize Zayd's brother Muhammad al-Baqir, and trace a line of succession from him until the twelfth imam, Muhammad al-Muntazar, who they believe has disappeared but will return, while the Ismaili (or 'Sevener') Shi'ites believe that the imamate passed to Muhammad al-Baqir's elder grandson Isma'il (died 760), whose son Muhammad, the seventh imam, was the last visible successor of the Prophet (though some Ismailis later recognized the legitimacy of the Fatimid caliphate in Cairo).

The Zaydis are the most moderate of the Shi'ites. They recognize the legitimacy of the early caliphs, whom the Twelvers regard as usurpers. Furthermore they believe that the imamate is open to any male descendant of Ali and Fatima; the choice depends on a candidate satisfying a number of specific criteria (see pp. 152), in particular scholarship and leadership. This means that in Zaydism the imamate has always remained visible, and it is even possible for two Imams to exist simultaneously. The Imam exercised religious and secular authority over his community. The Zaydis generally have no conflict with their Sunni neighbours, indeed they sometimes call Zaydism the fifth of the Sunni schools. As R. B. Serjeant has remarked: 'It can be fairly stated that geo-political factors really divide the two sects, not differences in religious matters, though these exist.' Zaydis have a longer call to prayer, adding the phrase 'Stand for the best of works', and they adopt different postures for prayer. More significant is a difference in legal practice: the Zaydis still use *ijtihad*, the application of reason to solving individual problems in law by analogy (*qiyas*), while the Shafi'ites believe that since such problems have been solved already by legal scholars in the early centuries of Islam, personal reasoning is no longer required. The Zaydis' main criticism of Shafi'ite religious practice is directed against the cult of the tombs of holy men. There are few such tombs in Upper Yemen and even the graves of past Imams attract no cult.

Zaydism came to Yemen in 898, when Yahya Ibn Hussain, great-grandson of Ali, was invited to take up residence in Sa'da. For over a thousand years (until 1962) Yemen was the home of the only Zaydi state in the world (though in the 9th century AD there had been another Zaydi state in Tabiristan on the Caspian Sea). For periods of its long history the rule of the Zaydi imamate was restricted to a small area of the Yemeni highlands, but the advent of al-Mansur al-Qasim as Imam at the end of the 16th century marked the beginning of a period of expansion, though this was interrupted by the return of Ottoman rule in the 19th century. San'a was not reconquered by the Imam until 1905. Zaydi theocracy came to an end in 1962 with the death of the 66th Imam, Ahmad. Zaydism without an Imam is paradoxical, but Yemenis have taken a pragmatic view, believing that the religious system need not fail just because no suitable candidate has appeared.

'Twelver' Shi'ism is not found in Yemen, but Ismailis still live in the Jabal Haraz region around Manakha. The first Ismailis to appear in Yemen were the Karmatis, a radical communistic sect, whose arrival coincided with the appearance of the Zaydis, but the present Ismaili community, which has played a more important part in Yemeni history than its present numbers might suggest, goes back to the time of the Sulayhid dynasty in the 11th and 12th centuries. Ali as-Sulayhi, a representative of the Fatimid caliphs of Cairo, was able to extend his power over much of Yemen, and his legacy was ably maintained by his daughter-in-law Arwa Bint Ahmad. After the death of the ninth caliph Mustansir in 1094 Isma'ilis were split between those who supported his son and successor Nizar, and those who recognized Nizar's brother, the usurper al-Musta'li. The Yemeni Isma'ilis are Musta'lis or Tayyibis because they recognize al-Musta'li and regard his son al-Tayyib as the last visible Imam. (They are therefore distinct from the Eastern or Nizari Isma'ilis, whose leader is the Aga Khan.) The first *da'i mutlaq* (earthly representative) of Tayyib, was Dhu'ayb Ibn Musa (died 1151), whose tomb is at Huss (Huth). A further split occurred in the Musta'lians in 1591, and today the *da'i* of the Da'wudi branch is based in Gujerat, while that of the Sulaymani branch resides at Najran. Under Zaydi rule the Yemeni Isma'ilis generally suffered greater persecution than the Shafi'ites. Their religion is close to Twelver Shi'ism, except for differences in astronomical calculations and the characteristic Isma'ili distinction between *zahir*, the outer forms of religion, and *batin*, an esoteric interpretation of the Koran with gnostic features. The Isma'ili doctrine of *taqiyya* (dissimulation) has impeded the study of their religious beliefs by outsiders.

The State

Reunification: Until unification was proclaimed in Aden on 22 May 1990 the historic land of Yemen was divided into two separate states:

1. To the west and north, with San'a as its capital, was the Yemen Arab Republic, or North Yemen, the successor to the Kingdom of Yemen under the rule of the Imams.

2. To the south and east, with Aden as its capital, was the People's Democratic Republic of Yemen, or South Yemen for short, the successor to the British colony at Aden and the various sultanates of the British Protectorate in the hinterland of Aden and the Hadramawt.

The division along the pre-1990 borders was at least partly the result of the distinctive religious conservatism of the north, and the legacy of Turkish rule and British colonialism. Nevertheless, the union, though unprecedented, reflects general popular sentiment and on the whole has been welcomed. Now that the border has been swept away a tourist can travel to any part of Yemen from Aden or San'a. In this guide reference is occasionally made to 'North' or 'South' Yemen as a reminder of the differences that still exist.

Recent Political History
by Michael Field

Until 1990 Yemen was never a united country. Its peoples regarded themselves as one, they appeared very similar when seen from the perspective of any of the other Arabian Peninsula countries, and in modern times, from the 1960's onwards, they had aspired to unity. Yet sentiment and broad cultural similarity do not on their own produce a single state. Historically, the Yemenis have been divided between different tribes, and they have been ruled by dynasties and imperial powers which have never quite brought all their territories under one authority. This has been not only a consequence of the country's large area and rugged terrain. It has reflected the fact that within the nation there are strong variations in culture. These have been very relevant to Yemen's recent turbulent political history.

One division is between the tribal people of the centre and north, and the urban people of Ibb, Ta'izz, Aden and much of the rest of the south and east of the country. The cultural frontier is in the region of the town of Yarim, which is well to the north of the pre-1990 political frontier between the Yemen Arab Republic and the Popular Democratic Republic of Yemen.

The northerners, who are Zaydis, members of a moderate Shia sect with strong Sunni leanings, are mostly small landowners. They are settled in little farms scattered across a dry and rather unfertile mountain plateau. They grow sorghum, alfalfa, barley, wheat and qat. A few of the tribesmen are nomadic. Traditionally the rulers in San'a have come from the tribes, but the tribes have always resisted their authority. Until recently no tax could be collected from the tribes, cars more than 30 miles outside San'a carried no registration plates, and everybody in these regions went around armed. Even now smuggling, banditry and the odd kidnapping contribute a substantial part of the tribesmen's income. In the view of southerners the tribes are godless and violent - 'the fang of a cur in a cur's head', as a popular phrase used to have it.

The southerners are Sunnis, members of the orthodox majority of Islam, and followers of the interpretation of Sharia law proposed by the 9th-century jurist, Mohammed bin Idris Al-Shafi'i. This has lead to their being known always as Shafi'ites - though nowhere else in the Muslim world is a people known by the name of this shaikh, or by the name of any of the other three great jurists of early Islam. The people around Ibb, Jibla and Ta'izz live in remarkably rich, green country, which receives a small amount of monsoon rainfall. Traditionally, most of them have been sharecroppers, working on farms owned by a few big landowning families. In Ta'izz, Hudayda (on the coastal plain, which has a southern culture) and Aden, there are, or have been, big trading communities. Further west, in the Hadramawt valley and the port town of Mukalla, live a trading people who have had a remarkable enthusiasm for travel. There are Hadrami communities in many towns around the edge of the Indian Ocean, including Singapore, and there is a very large and rich Hadrami population in the Saudi port of Jeddah. It is partly the money sent home by the Hadramis abroad that has financed the construction of the extraordinary tall houses of Shibam and Say'un. Between the urban areas of the south, in the mountainous hinterland of Aden and in the desert bordering Saudi Arabia, there is a tribal population - but it does not have as strong an influence, culturally or politically, as the tribes do in the north.

In relatively modern times, since the middle of the last century, the traditional cultural divisions have been overlaid by the influence of the different political regimes under which the people have lived. The east of the country and part of the south, around Aden, was ruled by the British until 1967 and then by a nominally Communist regime until 1990. During the British period the cosmopolitan character of the region was strengthened. Aden became one of the richest ports on the Indian Ocean. Both the British and the Communists had a secularising influence. Under their rule the people became relatively well educated. This, together with the south's greater exposure to the outside world (before 1967), has produced a culture that is softer and, usually, less violent than that of the north. It is noticeable that the south is less xenophobic than the north.

The north was ruled until 1962 by an Imamate. This was a hereditary monarchy with religious authority. Both the Imams Yahya (1919-48) and Ahmad (1948-62) governed their turbulent peoples with a very necessary rod of iron - never hesitating to imprison, torture or behead (in public) anyone who threatened public order or their rule. A week after the death of the Imam Ahmad, his successor Muhammad al-Badr, who was an aspiring liberal, was overthrown by a republican coup d'état. The young Imam's supporters rallied the tribes to their cause and the republicans called for help from President Gamal Abdul Nasser of Egypt. The Egyptian army that was sent to the country proved itself thoroughly incompetent. Its soldiers found the terrain difficult - many had never seen a mountain before - and they were frightened of the tribesmen. Their presence caused the Saudis, encouraged by the British and Americans, to back the royalists with money and arms. In 1967, in the wake of the Arab-Israeli Six Day War, the Egyptian forces were withdrawn, at Saudi expense, and three years later the republicans and royalists settled their differences. They had been divided, ultimately, less by ideology than by the competing personal ambitions of their leaders.

A conservative republican government was formed in San'a, but it did not carry great authority. The Saudis continued to finance the tribes because it was part of their policy to keep the government weak. They were very much aware that they had a large Yemeni population, trading and doing menial work, in their country, and that parts of their southern provinces, which they had conquered in the 1920's, were claimed by Yemen. The threat that a strong Yemeni government might pose to them was made more worrying by the fact Yemen's population at the time was bigger, and more war-like, than their own. The Saudi subsidies certainly did not make the Kingdom popular. To this day the Yemenis feel jealous and resentful of the Saudis -

but in their political purpose the subsidies succeeded.

Throughout the 1970's and early 1980's various discontented political factions, sometimes carrying an ideological label but normally representing tribal interests at heart, were in rebellion against the central government. They were supported, in an unholy alliance, by the Communist government of southern Yemen, the Popular Democratic Republic of Yemen. The San'a Government, in turn, backed rebel elements in the south, who were also receiving finance from Saudi Arabia. These rivalries lead to two short wars between the Yemens, in 1972 and 1979. At the end of each of these the rival governments declared that their countries should be united, but neither had an interest in living up to their brave words. Nor did they command bureaucracies capable of bringing about union in a peaceful fashion.

The tribal and north-south rivalries lead to periodic changes in the governments of the north. In 1974 President Abdul-Rahman Iryani was deposed in a coup, and in 1977 his successor Ibrahim Hamdi was assassinated. Hamdi was a brave man, who was not afraid to meet the tribal leaders on their own territories and seemed to be capable of standing up to the Saudis. He was murdered partly because he was believed to be getting too close to the leaders of South Yemen, which offended the tribes and their Saudi backers. At the time of his death it was put about that he was a drunkard and sybarite. To lend credence to these untruthful accusations his killers imported two French prostitutes and murdered them with him.

Hamdi was succeeded by Ahmad Ghashmi, who was not a popular figure, being regarded as too pro-Saudi. He was accused in the demonstrations that erupted in November 1977 of being Hamdi's assassin. He met his own death in June the following year, from a briefcase bomb carried by an envoy from South Yemen. The exact nature of the plot on this occasion has never been explained. Unanswered questions concern the role of the briefcase carrier, who died in the blast, and the link with the deposition the next day of the South Yemeni president, who was duly executed.

After Ghashmi's death the republic's Constituent Assembly, an appointed parliament established in 1977, appointed as President the Deputy Chief of Staff, Ali Abdullah Salih. The new President, whose chances of survival were not rated highly, wore a somewhat haunted look in his early months in power. He surrounded himself by a bodyguard of several hundred men, recruited from his own tribe, the Sanhan, from south east of San'a. Gradually, by a mixture of force and diplomacy aided by the slow development of his country, he was able to extend his authority. In 1982 he finally defeated the southern-backed tribal and disaffected republican opposition, whose members were forced to flee to the PDRY. His authority was strengthened by the fact that he got on well with the then President of the PDRY, Ali Nasser Muhammad. From the late 1980's his Government benefited from a small flow of oil revenues. This made it able to strengthen its army, pay its own periodic subsidies to the tribes and spend some money on development projects.

The south meanwhile had a very different history. The British took Aden, as a colony, in 1839, and later extended their authority to the east, over what became the east Aden and west Aden protectorates. In 1967, after four years of fighting a left-wing independence movement, the British withdrew, handing power to what became the only (nominally) Communist government in the Arab world. This regime preached Communist ideology, seized private property and introduced some Communist social policies, but was not able to transform its country into the socialist paradise of which it spoke because it had no money. It impoverished the once rich entrepôt of Aden by pursuing policies which cut it off from most of the rest of the world. It was more leftwing than the other Arab republics and was treated with suspicion or outright hostility by the Arab monarchies. In the late 1960's and early 1970's it supported a leftwing guerrilla group, the Popular Front for the Liberation of the Occupied Arabian Gulf, that was operating in Zofar, the southern province of the Sultanate of Oman. With the help of the British the Sultanate eventually defeated the insurgency. South Yemen's only real backers were the Soviet Union and, particularly, East Germany.

The regime was much weakened by internal power struggles which erupted into a short civil war in January 1986. The trouble began when the President, Ali Nasser Muhammad, sought to eliminate some radical rivals in the Political Bureau of his Yemen Socialist Party. He summoned them to a cabinet meeting, which he did not attend, and instructed his guards to shoot them. In doing this he was acting partly in self-defence because he believed that his rivals were themselves plotting. As a diplomat in San'a put it afterwards, 'he wanted to have them for breakfast before they had him for lunch'. His stratagem failed. His rivals arrived armed, and with their own guards, and when fired upon shot back. Half of them were killed but the rest escaped. The fighting spread from the party headquarters into the streets of Aden and then into the mountains and villages as the protagonists fled to rally their tribal supporters. At the end of a month of fighting, which left several thousand dead, Ali Nasser Mohammed and his forces were defeated and took refuge in north Yemen.

The PDRY regime was discredited, internally and internationally, by this bloodshed. It suffered a worse blow still in the autumn of 1989 when the Communist government of East Germany collapsed, and the Soviet Union made it known that it was not going to continue to give aid to Third World client states. The regime faced bankruptcy, and perhaps revolution. It was in this context that the occasional talks on unity which the two Yemeni governments had been holding suddenly bore fruit. President Ali Salih visited Aden at the end of November 1989, and after brief discussions with the southern leadership announced that the two countries would be united within a year. Thereafter negotiations on the details of unification were pushed ahead as quickly as possible, partly because the leaders feared Saudi intervention, and the north and south were finally joined, amid popular rejoicing, on 22 May 1990. San'a was made the capital of the new Republic of Yemen.

The union was not one between equals. The north had a bigger population - a very roughly estimated eleven million, compared with two million in the south - and Ali Salih was politically in a far stronger position than his opposite number, Ali Salim al-Baydh. The southern leader and his government colleagues saw a union as offering them the prospect of survival and they were pleased to be able to negotiate half the posts in the new cabinet, including the vice presidency, and more than a third of the seats in a newly appointed parliament, the Council of Deputies. From the point of view of Ali Salih, who became President of the amalgamated state, the deal was over-generous, but he saw that it could be adjusted by means of democratic elections. These would not only look good internationally, they would be bound to result in a reduction of the representation of the single southern political organisation, the Yemeni Socialist Party, and this in turn would enable him to alter the make-up of the cabinet.

Elections were held in April 1993, after much violence, including bombings and assassinations of political figures, and a postponement made necessary by the general state of turmoil. Most unusually, voters were required to write the name of their chosen candidate on their ballot papers, instead of simply marking a name with a cross, and as three quarters of the northern population was illiterate this meant that on polling day most people had to have the polling station officials write their vote for them. There were also allegations of vote buying and the pre-marking of soldiers' ballot papers. Yet after the event the general conclusion was that the result was both plausible and convenient for the President. His own General People's Congress and the conservative, tribal-based Reform Party won almost all the seats in the north and the Yemen Socialist Party, which carried all the southern seats, was reduced to having only a sixth of the seats in the Council.

Once again the President invited the southerners into a coalition government, but he also gave some posts to members of the Reform Party and he redoubled his efforts to control the parts of the southern administration that were still run by the Yemen Socialist Party. After May 1990 the frontier posts between the two parts of the country had been immediately demolished but in many important administrative respects there had been no union. The two leaderships had kept their own armies and security forces, as well as separate airlines, currencies and car registration offices. In the parts of the government that were amalgamated - those affecting the development of the economy - it was quickly noticed that the system was dominated by the northern bureaucracy and the influence of northern businessmen. Government seemed to be biased in favour of the development of the north, even though the south had great potential and the more sophisticated population. The southerners were promised that property seized by their government after 1967 would be handed back to them and that Aden would be redeveloped as a free port, but neither of these things happened. The southerners were angered by the inefficiency and corruption of the northern bureaucracy. It was said in the early days of the union that even though their old government had been brutal, it had at least been honest.

These points of friction lead to a steady deterioration of relations between northerners and southerners at the top of the government. In July 1993 Ali Salim al-Baydh, who was still Vice President, retired to Aden and did not return. Early in 1994 the southern Party moved tanks to the region of its one small oil field. It appeared that it was planning to secede from the Union. Attempts by other Arab governments to mediate failed. There were several minor outbreaks of fighting and at the beginning of May a full scale war broke out when the northerners attacked one of the south's best brigades, which as a confidence-building measure had been stationed in an isolated position well inside northern territory. With this unit eliminated as a fighting force, the northerners were able to take the war into southern territory. The southern defences in the mountains were breached, Aden was besieged and bombarded and the southern leadership fled to Oman. At the beginning of July resistance collapsed.

In the year since the end of the war Yemen has been ruled nominally by a coalition of the General People's Congress and the Reform Party, but in reality power lies with Ali Abdullah Salih, his family, his tribal supporters and the army. The southerners remain disaffected and the authority of the central government is still contested by the northern tribes and, to some extent, by the businessmen of the commercial heartland of the country, around Ta'izz.

The country suffers from a weak administration and a chaotic economy. It has high inflation, seven different rates of exchange and an array of subsidies designed to win popularity for the Government by reducing the prices of foodstuffs and other necessities. The state cannot afford the subsidies, which together with government salaries absorb a third of gross domestic product, but there are vested interests which prevent their being abolished. Ardent supporters of the system are some of the tribes, who smuggle subsidised petrol into Saudi Arabia, where it competes with the local product, itself heavily subsidised. A team from the World Bank and the International Monetary Fund which visited Yemen in the winter of 1993-94 concluded that the Government was virtually incapable of reforming its economy. Much of its advice the regime had rejected in advance. Without reform and the endorsement of its policies by the two international bodies Yemen cannot attract the investment and aid that it needs to develop.

The Economy

At the beginning of the 1990's about 85% of the inhabitants of North Yemen are still dependent on agriculture, but there are signs of a great change in the economic structure of the country. At the end of 1985 President Ali Abdulah Salih announced that the oil reserves of his country in the Ma'rib/al-Jawf field amounted to 300 million barrels, enough to ensure commercial viability. While this does not place Yemen among the oil giants - and Yemeni oil began to flow in a period of world-wide over-production just when prices were falling - it is clear that the exploitation of Yemen's own oil reserves has meant a step towards industrialisation. A refinery for domestic consumption has had to be built in the Ma'rib/al-Jawf basin and a pipeline from there to the Red Sea. In the next phase petrochemical processing plants are to be established. Having its own oil resources also ensures the Yemen's own energy supply and brings in some foreign currency at a time when the contributions from Saudi Arabia and the oil-rich Gulf states, as well as the money brought in by the Yemeni guest workers, fell sharply as a result of the dispute with the Arab monarchies during the Gulf crisis of 1990/91.

In the years since unification oil exploration has progressed a good deal. A large part of the territory has been allocated in concessions, and the hunt for oil continues apace. Since the end of 1987 oil from the Ma'rib region has been exported via a pipeline to the Red Sea, but the pipeline from Ayadh to the Gulf of Aden was completed only at the end of 1991. In 1991 Yemen was producing a daily output of almost 200,000 barrels of crude oil and large quantities of natural gas.

A great deal of the agricultural sector is devoted to qat, and it is not difficult to see why. The bush has an extreme resistance to drought, and so is a viable cash crop on what would otherwise be barren or uneconomical land. Moreover the active ingredient of the drug is an alkaloid so unstable that the leaves should be consumed where possible on the day they are collected. There is consequently not much scope for middlemen in the qat trade, so that the grower will see more for his pains than for many other crops.

However the noticeable decline in the influx of foreign money had already led to restrictions on food imports and the encouragement of agricultural production at home. The government ran a propaganda campaign to reorientate the Yemeni farmers, in particular away from qat, though it remains the largest single crop. Wherever possible the farmers have also tried to grow fruit trees, vegetables or fodder for livestock. Another cash crop, coffee, is making a comeback, and new terraces are being built for it. Further stimulus for the cultivation of higher-value produce are the new roads and tracks built in recent years.

In South Yemen fishing is more important than agriculture as a source of income and food. More than 10,000 people work in the fishing industry on the coast which runs for 1200 km along the Indian Ocean. Serious damage was caused for some time by the government's economic experimentation, when the predominantly self-employed fishermen were forced to join co-operatives. The crisis was only overcome in the 1980's when the government allowed the co-operatives to sell 40% of their catches on the open market. Following the end of socialism in 1990 new forms of ownership have had to be found, though as co-operatives also exist in tribal associations, it is possible that they may survive if they adapt to the new order.

In 1987 South Yemen was able to look back over twenty years of independence from British rule, which had begun in Aden in 1839. The struggle for independence had been very hard, and when the British finally withdrew, the country's economy was in a very bad state, though the British also left a relatively well educated population (especially by comparison with North Yemen), a fine asset in the shape of Aden port itself, into which much investment had been poured, and an experience of unity and peace noticeably lacking in the North. The new rulers soon turned for economic aid to the Soviet Union and set about the socialist transformation of the social foundations of the country. In the course of this radical change there were frequent bloody internecine clashes within the ruling elite. Finally in January and February 1986 unrest amounting to civil war broke out, which led to a change in personnel in the upper ranks of the party and the state. The country and its people suffered badly in these conflicts. Tourism, which was valued as a source of hard currency, was also badly affected. As the economies of the eastern block countries became weaker, they reduced their aid contributions following the unrest, and in 1990 terminated them altogether. It was this that led the South Yemen government to seek refuge in unification, a refuge that proved illusory when the North wiped out any opposition to its plans in the short and decisive civil war.

Chronology

Chronology of Pre-Islamic Yemen

8th century BC: beginning of a Sabaean state; construction of the irrigation system at Ma'rib.

c.740 BC: Sabaeans pay tribute to the King of the Assyrians.

5th century BC: Sabaean military campaigns conducted from Sirwah, the capital city

c.500 BC: construction of city walls of Ma'rib.

c.400 BC: the North secedes from the Sabaean empire; beginning of the kingdom of Ma'in.

c.400 BC: the Sabaeans destroy the kingdom of Ausan; Qataban, a Sabaean vassal state, becomes stronger; secession of Hadramawt from the Sabaean empire.

c.390 BC: alliance between Qataban, Hadramawt and Ma'in against Saba; beginning of a long war between the Sabaeans and the Qatabanians.

c.343 BC: victory of the Sabaean empire over Qataban; for a short time the Quatabians again become vassals of the Sabaeans.

c.320 BC: Qataban becomes strong again and subjugates the kingdom of Ma'in.

c.120 BC: Ma'in is reconquered by the Sabaeans; secession of two provinces of Qataban - Himyar and Radman - which become allies of the Sabaeans; the Qatabanian rump state forms an alliance with Hadramawt.

23/24 BC: South Arabian campaign of Aelius Gallus, the Roman governor in Egypt, who reaches the walls of Ma'rib; unsuccessful siege of the Sabean capital.

c.20 BC: Himyar grows stronger; Himyarites conquer the Sabaean south and the straits of Bab al-Mandab; foundation of the Himyarite capital Zafar.

from 50 AD: Sabaean empire shaken by wars against the Himyarites and by internal strife.

*c.*100 AD: Himyar destroys Timna, the capital of Qataban; fall of the Qatabanian empire.

2nd century AD: end of the traditional dynasty of the Sabaean empire; power is assumed by rulers from the Yemeni highlands; the Ethiopians penetrate South Arabia for the first time.

*c.*190 AD: subjugation of Himyar and Hadramawt by a Sabaean ruler belonging to the new dynasty; the Ethiopians are driven out.

end of 3rd century AD: the whole of South Arabia conquered by the Himyarites.

*c.*319 AD: First recorded break of the dam at Ma'rib; secession of Hadramawt.

*c.*360 AD: Christian missionary activity in the Himyarite empire; churches built at Zafar and Aden.

*c.*400 AD: a Himyarite king converts to Judaism; the Himyarite empire attains its widest extent.

517 AD: persecution of Christians in the Himyarite empire on the instructions of a king attached to Judaism.

525 AD: the Ethiopians attack the Himyarite empire again; in Himyar power passes to Abraha, a Christian viceroy of

Ethiopian origin who learns to act independently.

542 AD: breaking of the dam at Marib; churches built in Zafar, Najran and near Marib.

*c.*570 AD: a Persian army appears in South Arabia; in the Himyarite empire power passes to a governor appointed by the Persian (Sassanian) King Khusrau I.

*c.*628 AD: the Persian governor in Yemen is converted to the new teaching of the Prophet Muhammad - Islam.

Chronology of Islamic Yemen

631: emissaries of the Prophet arrive in San'a and Hadramawt to settle quarrels.

632: the Caliph (successor of the Prophet) Abu Bakr divides Yemen into three provinces each with an Arab governor.

655: appointment of a new governor for Yemen by Caliph Ali.

660: Yemen devastated by troops of the anti-Caliph Muawiya

661: Yemen becomes a province of the Umayyads residing in Damascus.

812: Yemen becomes a province of the Abbasids residing in Baghdad.

819: the religious university of Zabid is founded by Muham-

mad Ibn Ziyad.

897: Yahyah Ibn al-Hussain arrives in Yemen; as Yahyah al-Hadi he becomes the first Zaydi Imam of Jemen and resides at Sada.

1261: Imam Yahyah Ibn Muhammad enters San'a.

1538: conquest of Aden by forces of the Ottoman Empire.

1539: conquest of the coastal strip (Tihama) in North Yemen by Ottoman forces; an Ottoman governor is installed in San'a.

1599: uprising of the Yemenis against Ottoman rule.

1630: Ottoman troops withdraw from Yemen; Imam Kasim al-Kabir enters San'a

1709: treaty between France and Yemen for the opening of a French trading settlement in Mokha.

1762: the Danish Expedition (with Carsten Niebuhr) arrives in Yemen.

1799: the island of Perim at the southern end of the Red Sea is seized by Great Britain.

1804: the Wahhabis from central Arabia attack the coastal plain of northern Yemen.

1832: the Egyptians conquer the coastal plain of northern Yemen.

1839: Aden is captured by the British.

1840: the Egyptians withdraw from Yemen.

1849: Ottoman forces conquer the coastal plain of northern Yemen.

1867: British authority extends to the hinterland of Aden.

1871: an Ottoman governor is installed in San'a.

1891: beginning of a long uprising of the people of the Yemen highlands against Ottoman rule.

1911: the Imam is recognized by the Ottoman Empire as the religious and secular leader of the Zaydi population.

1914: the partition of Yemen is confirmed by an agreement between Great Britain and the Ottoman Empire.

1918: collapse of the Ottoman Empire; the Turks in Yemen capitulate; many Turks stay on in Yemeni service.

1933: war between Yemen and Saudi Arabia.

1934: some territory ceded to Saudi Arabia.

1948: revolt against Imam Yahyah; the Imam is murdered; rebels are defeated by his son Imam Ahmad. Sack of San'a.

1959: the South Arabian Federation (South Yemen) is founded with British sponsorship, formalizing the system of protectorate and treaties..

1962: Imam Ahmad dies; revolution; a republic is proclaimed; the civil war begins.

1965: radicalization of the struggle for independence in Aden; the civil war in North Yemen continues; increasing Egyptian involvement.

1967: Egyptian forces withdraw from North Yemen after the defeat of Egypt in the Six Day War with Israel; South Yemen gains independence from Great Britain.

1969: factional struggles in South Yemen; victory of left-wing nationalists.

1970: the civil war ends in North Yemen with a compromise between the warring parties.

1972: the first border war between North and South Yemen; treaty dealing with the unification of the two states.

1978: Colonel Ali Abdullah Salih becomes President of North Yemen.

1979: the second border war between North and South Yemen; second treaty dealing with the unification of the two states.

1980: Abdel Fatta Ismael, the head of state and party-leader in South Yemen, resigns; Ali Nasser Muhammad takes power.

1986: bloody factional struggles

in the ruling socialist party of South Yemen; Ali Nasser Muhammad deposed.

1987: 25th anniversary of the Revolution in North Yemen; oil exports begin.

1989: a moderate socialist regime is established in South Yemen; earlier unification agreements with North Yemen are resumed; pragmatic rapprochement: shared projects, opening of the border.

1990: Unification of North and South Yemen as the Republic of Yemen; Ali Abdallah Salih becomes President of all Yemen.

1993: Elections concentrate power in hands of northerners

1994: 'War of Unity' between disaffected South and the North, which achieves total victory.

1995: Border disputes with Eritrea over islands in Red Sea.

Further Reading

Bibliography

Smith, G. Rex (compiler): *The Yemens: The Yemen Arab Republic and the People's Democratic Republic of Yemen,* (World Bibliographies Series), Oxford (Clio), 1984

General

Chelhod, Joseph, et al.: *L'Arabie du Sud: Histoire et Civilisation,* Paris (G.-P. Maisonneuve & Larose), 1984-85

Chwaszcza, Joachim (ed.), *Insight Guide - Yemen,* London (APA Publ.), 1992 (2nd ed.)

Daum, Werner (ed.), *Yemen, 3000 Years of Art and Civilisation in Arabia Felix,* Innsbruck (Pinguin-Verlag), 1990 (Published in conjunction with a major exhibition in Munich, this well-illustrated volume contains contributions by experts in all aspects of the Yemen.)

Fayein, Claudie, *Yémen,* Paris (Editions du Seuil), 1975

Field, Michael, *Inside the Arab World,* London/Harvard (John Murray/Harvard UP), 1994/1995

Hämäläinen, Pertti, *Yemen - Lonely Planet travel survival kit,* Hawthorn (Vic)/Berkeley (Cal) (Lonely Planet Publ.), 1991 (2nd ed.)

Pawelke, Günther, *Jemen, das verbotene Land,* Düsseldorf, 1959

Piepenburg, Fritz, *New Traveller's Guide to Yemen,* San'a (Yemen Tourism Co.), 1988 (1st publ 1983)

Richer, Xavier, *Tourisme au Yémen du Sud,* Paris, 1976

Rohner & von Rohr, *Yemen. Land am Tor der Tränen,* Kreuzlingen, 1979

Serjeant, R.B. and Lewcock, Ronald, *San'a - an Arabian Islamic City,* London (World of Islam), 1983

Stone, Francine (ed.), *Studies on the Tihamah,* Harlow (Longman), 1985

Swiss Airphoto Interpretation Team, *Final Report,* Zurich, 1978

Archaeology

Bowen, R. Le Baron and F.P. Albright, *Archaeological Discoveries in South Arabia,* Baltimore, 1958 (Publications of the American Foundation for the Study of Man, vol. 2)

Doe, Brian, *Southern Arabia (New Aspects of Antiquity),* London (Thames & Hudson), 1971

Doe, Brian, *Monuments of South Arabia,* Naples & Cambridge (Falcon-Oleander), 1983

Doresse, Jean, *Ethiopia. Ancient Cities and Temples,* London (Elek), 1959

al-Hamdani, Al-Iklil; *The Antiquities of South Arabia,* ed. and trans. N.A. Faris, Princeton, 1938

Phillips, Wendell, *Qataban and Sheba. Exploring Ancient Kingdoms on the Biblical Spice Route of Arabia,* London (V. Gollancz), 1955

Radt, Wolfgang, *Katalog der Staatlichen Antikensammlung con Sanaa und andere Antiken im Jemen,* Berlin, 1973

Weidemann, Konrad, *Könige aus dem Yemen. Zwei antike Bronzestatuen,* Mainz, 1983

Wissmann, Hermann von, *Zur Archäologie und antiken Geographie von Südarabien,* Istanbul, 1968

Wissmann, Hermann von, *Zur Geschichte und Landeskunde von Alt-Südarabien,* Vienna, 1964

Architecture

Costa, Paolo and Ennio Vicario, *Yemen. Land of Builders,* London (Academy), 1977

Damluji, S.S., *A Yemen Reality: Architecture Sculptured in Mud and Stone,* Reading (Garnet), 1993

Damluji, S.S., *The Valley of Mud Brick Architecture: Shibam, Tarim and the Wadi Hadramawt*, Reading (Garnet), 1993

Varanda, Fernando, *Art of Building in Yemen*, Cambridge (Mass.)/London (MIT Press), 1982

History

al-Azzazi, Mohammed, *Die Entwicklung der Arabischen Republik Yemen*, Tübingen, 1978

Bollinger, Rudolf, *Revolution zur Einheit. Jemens Kampf um die Unabhängigkeit*, Hamburg, 1984

Daum, Werner (ed.), *Die Königin von Saba*, Stuttgart, 1987

Forrer, Ludwig, Südarabien. *Nach al-Hamdanis 'Beschreibung der Arabischen Halbinsel'*, Leipzig, 1942 (repr Nendeln, Liechtenstein 1966)

Graf, S.U., *Abenteuer Südarabien. Öl verwandelt Allahs Wüste*, Stuttgart, 1967

Groom, Nigel, *Frankincense and Myrrh: a Study of the Arabian Incense Trade*, London (Longman), 1981

Halliday, Fred, *Arabia without Sultans*, Harmondsworth (Penguin), 1974

Holden, David, *Farewell to Arabia*, London (Faber), 1966

Ingrams, Harold, *The Yemen. Imams, Rulers and Revolutionaries*, London (John Murray), 1963

Kour, Z.H., *The History of Aden 1839-1872*, London (Cass), 1981

al-Mad'aj, 'Abd al-Muhsin Mad'aj M., *The Yemen in Early Islam, a Political History*, London, 1988

Philby, H. St John, *The Queen of Sheba*, London (Quartet), 1981

Playfair, Sir Robert L., *A History of Arabia Felix or Yemen*, Bombay, 1859 (repr Farnborough 1970)

Serjeant, R.B., *Studies in Arabian history and civilisation*, London (Variorum Reprints), 1981

Shahid, Irfan, 'Pre-Islamic Arabia' in: *The Cambridge History of Islam* (ed. P.M. Holt et al.), Cambridge (CUP), 1970 (vol. 1, 3-29)

Stein, Lothar and Karl-Heinz Bochow, *Hadramawt. Geschichte und Gegenwart einer südarabischen Landschaft*, Leipzig, 1986

Stookey, Robert, *South Yemen - A Marxist Republic in Arabia*, London (Croom Helm), 1982

Stookey, Robert, *Yemen: the Politics of the Yemen Arab Republic*, Boulder (Westview), 1978

Wenner, Manfred W., *Modern Yemen 1918-1966*, Baltimore (John Hopkin), 1967

Wenner, Manfred W., *The Yemen Arab Republic: Development and Change in an Ancient Land*, Boulder (Westview Press), 1991

Society

Dostal, Walter, *Eduard Glaser: Forschungen in Yemen: eine quellenkritische Unternehmung in ethnologischer Sicht*, Vienna, 1990

Dostal, Walter, *Der Markt von Sanaa*, Vienna, 1979

Gerholm, Tomas, *Market, Mosque and Mafraj. Social Inequality in a Yemeni Town*, Stockholm, 1977 (Stockholm Studies in Social Anthropology, 5)

Gingrich, Andre and Heiss, Johann, *Beiträge zur Ethnographie der Provinz Sa'da*, Vienna, 1986

Halliday, Fred, *Arabs in Exile: Yemeni Migrants in Urban Britain*, London (I.B. Tauris), 1992

Kirkam, James, *City of San'a*, London (World of Islam Festival), 1976

Weir, Shelagh, *Qat in Yemen - Consumption and Social Change*, London (British Museum Publications), 1985

Islam

Serjeant, R.B., 'The Zaydis' in: *Religion in the Middle East* (ed. A.J. Arberry), Cambridge (CUP),

1969 (vol. 2, 285-301)

Jewry

Ahroni, Reuben, *Yemenite Jewry: Origins, Culture and Literature*, Bloomington, 1986

Goitein, S.D., 'The Jews of Yemen' in: *Religion in the Middle East* (ed. A.J. Arberry), Cambridge (Cambridge University Press), 1969 (vol. 1, 226-239)

Rathjens, Carl, *Jewish Domestic Architecture in San'a Yemen*, Jerusalem (Israel Oriental Society), 1957 (Oriental Notes and Studies, no. 7)

Photographs

Jenner, Michael, *Yemen Rediscovered*, London (Longman and Yemen Tourist Co.), 1983

Maréchaux, Pascal, *Arabia Felix: the Yemen and its People*, London (Thames & Hudson), 1979

Maréchaux, Pascal and Maria, *Yémen*, Paris (Phébus), 1993

Philby, H. St John, *Sheba's Daughters*, London (Methuen), 1939

Stark, Freya, *Seen in the Hadhramawt*, London (John Murray), 1938

Exploration, Travel and Memoirs

Bent, J. Theodore and Mabel V.A., *Southern Arabia*, London (Smith, Elder and Co), 1900

Botta, Paul Emile, *Relation d'un Voyage dans l'Yémen entrepris en 1837 pour le Muséum d'Histoire Naturelle*, Paris, 1841

Botting, Douglas, *Island of the Dragon's Blood*, London (Hodder & Stoughton), 1958

Bury, George Wyman, *Arabia Infelix, or, the Turks in Yemen*, London (Macmillan), 1915

Fayein, Claudie, *A French Doctor in the Yemen*, London (Robert Hale), 1958

Hamilton, R.A.B. (Lord Belhaven), *The Kingdom of Melchior. Adventures in South West Arabia*, London (John Murray), 1949

Hamilton, R.A.B. (Lord Belhaven), *The Uneven Road*, London (John Murray), 1955

Halévy, Joseph, 'Rapport sur un mission archéologique dans le Yemen', Journal Asiatique (Paris), sér. 6, vol. 19 (1872), pp. 5-98, 129-266, 489-547

Halévy, Joseph, 'Voyage au Nedjran', Bulletin de la Société de Géographie (Paris), sér. 6, vol. 6, pp. 5-31, 249-73, 581-606; vol. 13, pp. 466-79

Hansen, Thorkild, *Arabia Felix. The Danish Expedition of 1761-1767*, London (Collins), 1964

Harris, Walter B., *A Journey Through the Yemen. Some General Remarks upon that Country*, London, 1893

Helfritz, Hans, *Entdeckungsreisen in Süd-Arabien. Auf unbekannten Wegen durch Hadramaut und Jemen* (1933 und 1935), Cologne (DuMont), 1977

Helfritz, Hans, *The Yemen. A Secret Journey*, London (Allen & Unwin), 1958

Helfritz, Hans, *Land Without Shade*, London (Hurst & Blackett), 1935

Hirsch, Leo, *Reisen in Süd-Arabien, Mahra-land und Hadramawt*, Leiden (E.J. Brill), 1897

Hogarth, David George, *The Penetration of Arabia: A Record of Western Knowledge Concerning the Arabian Peninsula*, London (Lawrence and Bullen), 1904

Ingrams, Doreen, *A Time in Arabia*, London (John Murray), 1970

Ingrams, Harold, *Arabia and the Isles*, London (John Murray), 1966 (3rd ed.)

Jourdain, John, *The Journal of John Jourdain, 1608-17*, (ed. William Foster), Cambridge, 1905 (Hakluyt Society, 2nd ser., No. 16)

La Roque, Jean de, *A Voyage to Arabia the Happy... to which is added account of the captivity of Sir Henry Middleton at Moka...*, London, 1732

Meulen, Daniel van der, *Aden to the Hadhramawt. A Journey in South Arabia*, London (John Murray), 1947

Meulen, Daniel van der and Hermann von Wissmann, *Hadramawt, Some of its Mysteries Unveiled*, Leyden (E.J. Brill), 1932

Mittwoch, Eugen (ed.), *Aus dem Jemen - Hermann Burchardts letzte Reise durch Südarabien*, Leipzig, n.d. (1926)

Müller, David Heinrich and N. Rhodokanakis (eds.), *Eduard Glasers Reise nach Marib*, Vienna, 1913

Niebuhr, Carsten, *Travels through Arabia and Other Countries in the East*, Edinburgh, 1792 (repr. Beirut 1965) (but the editions in French and German are earlier and fuller)

Niebuhr, Carsten, *Voyage en Arabie et en autres pays circonvoisins*, Amsterdam, 1776-80

Niebuhr, Carsten, *Beschreibung von Arabien*, Copenhagen, 1772

Niebuhr, Carsten, *Reisebeschreibung nach Arabien*, Copenhagen, 1774-1837

The Periplus of the Erythraean Sea: Travel and Trade in the Indian Ocean by a Merchant of the First Century, tr. and ed. Wilfred H. Schoff, New York (Longmans, Green, and Co.), 1912

Polo, Marco, *The Travels of Marco Polo*, tr. W. Marsden and T. Wright, London (Dent), 1926

Rathjens, Carl, *Sabaeica: Bericht über die archäologischen Ergebnisse meiner zweiten, dritten und vierten Reise nach Südarabien*, Hamburg, 1953, 1955, 1966

Schruhl, Klaus-Dieter, *Saba heißt Morgenröte. Als Arzt in der VDR Jemen*, Leipzig, 1978

Scott, Hugh, *In the High Yemen*, London (John Murray), 1942 (2nd ed. 1947)

Stark, Freya, *The Southern Gates of Arabia. A Journey in the Hadhramawt*, London (John Murray), 1936

Stark, Freya, *A Winter in Arabia*, London (John Murray), 1940

Thesiger, Wilfred, *Arabian Sands*, London, 1959

Varthema, Ludovico di, *Travels*, ed. J.W. Jones and G.P. Badger, London, 1863 (Hakluyt Society)

Wavell, A.J.B., *A Modern Pilgrim in Mecca, and a Siege in Sanaa*, London (Constable), 1912

Weber, Otto, *Forschungsreisen in Süd-Arabien bis zum Auftreten Eduard Glasers*, Leipzig, 1907

Wellsted, James Raymond, *Travels to the City of the Caliphs about the shores of the Persian Gulf and the Mediterranean; including a voyage to the coast of Arabia, and a Tour on the Island of Socotra*, London, 1840 (repr. Farnborough (Gregg) 1968)

Wellsted, James Raymond, *Travels in Arabia*, London, 1838

Wrede, Adolph von (ed. Heinrich Frh von Maltzan), *Reise in Hadhramawt etc.*, Braunschweig (Friedrich Vieweg u. Sohn), 1870

Literature
Serjeant, R.B., *Prose and Poetry from Hadramawt*, London, 1951 and 1983

Periodicals
Arabian Studies

Al-Djambija (Zeitschrift der Entwicklungshelfer und ihrer Angehörigen in Jemen), San'a, 1985

Bulletin of the British Yemeni Society

A-Z of Practical Information

Accommodation

Since 1990 the number of hotel rooms in San'a has been sufficient to satisfy normal demand. Accomodation in Ta'izz and Hudayda may still occasionally be fully booked, particularly at the Islamic weekends (Thursday and Friday).

Aden does not have any medium-quality hotels. Throughout Yemen it may be difficult finding accommodation during European school holidays, in the more temperate times of year (Easter, Christmas, New Year).

in San'a
Sheraton ***** tel. 237500/1/2/3, telex 22 22
Taj Sheba ***** tel. 272372, telex 2551
Sam City *** tel. 76250, telex 2301
Dar al Hamd ** tel. 74864/5 telex 2270
Al Mocha ** tel. 71526 and 72242, telex 2298
Al Ikhwa ** tel. 74026, telex 2350
Iskandar * tel. 72330
Shahara * tel. 78502/3
Al Anwar * tel. 72457 and 75051
Khayyam * tel. 71795 and 75277
Arwa * tel. 73838
Al Zahraa * tel. 72550 and 75148
Al Sharq * tel. 74226

near San'a
Ramada Hadda **** tel. 215214/5
Al Rawda *** tel. 340227/6, telex 2498

in Ta'izz
Marib *** tel. 210350/1, telex 8848
Al Ikhwa *** tel. 210364/5
Plaza ** tel. 220224/6
Al Janad ** tel. 210529
De Luxe * 226251/2

in Hudayda
Ambassador *** tel. 231247/50, telex 5626
Bristol *** tel. 239197, telex 5617
Al Burj *** tel. 75852, telex 5676
Al Ikhwa ** tel. 76195
Al Bahr al Ahmar * tel. 72507
Hudaida tel. 226100

in Aden
Mövenpick Hotel ***** tel. 32947/3; 32911, fax 9691/3; 2947
Gold Mohur ** tel. 32471
26 September ** tel. 22266
Ambassador ** tel. 24431
Al-Hilal ** tel. 23471

in Ma'rib
Bilqis Ma'rib **** tel. 2 66 and 2371

in Sa'da
Al Mamoon *** tel. 2203 and 2459

Banks, Money, Currency
Banks in San'a
National Bank   53753
Banque Indosuez   272801-3

Arab Bank   240921/29
International Bank of Yemen   272920-3
United Bank Ltd.   272424
Currency
US$1.00 = 12 Yemeni Riyals (Official rate)

Clothing

You should pack clothing to provide protection against the sun for head and arms, wool clothing for the evening chill in the mountains and desert, stockings to protect ankles and shins against mosquito bites, and sensible shoes for clambering over ruins and rocks. You should also take into account the customs of the country; this will help ensure your safety and make access to sacred places easier.

Anyone, man or woman, who cannot do without wearing shorts will be out of place in Yemen. The female visitor should equip herself with a multi-purpose cloth which can be worn round her neck in a draughty car and which will veil her hair when visiting a mosque, and protection for the eyes and hair in a sand storm and bright sunlight. Women are advised to wear long, wide outer garmants covering the elbows and legs. It is best to leave armless and close-fitting garments at home.

Costs

How much a visit to Yemen costs will of course be determined by a number of factors. First there is the current exchange rate, which for some time has been unpredictable. In recent years (since about 1986) exchange rate against hard currencies has improved, and inflation has not quite taken away all the money gained.

In the big international hotels of San'a, Ta'izz and Aden prices are given to individual travellers in US dollars. In the five-star hotels (Sheraton and Taj Sheba in San'a, and Movenpick in Aden) prices have been known to reach US$180 a night for a double room. Outside the high season this price can negotiated down. In medium-class hotels the price of a double room is around US$60, and in more modest houses you can still pay US$20-30.

Eating in Yemeni restaurants is still very good value. There are no high prices for public transport - buses and shared taxis. A couple travelling alone should get by with expenses of US$90 to US$100 per day. For two seats in a four-wheel-drive vehicle which leaves San'a for ten days on a journey to Wadi Hadramawt will cost an additional US$600.

Distances

Currently from San'a, along good asphalt roads:

- to Aden	410 km
- to Hudayda	226 km
- to Ta'izz	256 km
- to Sa'da	243 km
- to Ma'rib	173 km
- to al-Baydha	168 km
- to Amran	50 km
- to Hajja	77 km
- to Mokha (via Ta'izz)	363 km
- to Jizan (via Hudayda)	430 km

Currently from Aden, along good asphalt roads:

- to Dhala	155 km

311

- into Bab al-Mandab   150 km
- to Mukalla   622 km
- to Attak (Shabwa)   386 km
- into Wadi Hadramawt   550 km (by air)
- to Socotra   950 km (by air)
- to Sayut   750 km

Embassies

Embassies in San'a:

UK: Haddah Road, PO Box 1267 tel. 215629-30

USA: 26 September Road, Al-Halali Building, PO Box 1088 tel. 75826, 72790, 74407-9

Embassies of the Yemeni Arab Republic abroad:

UK: 41 South Street, London W1 tel. 0171-491 4003/629 9905-8

USA: 747 Third Avenue 8th floor, New York tel. 212-355 3355

600 New Hampshire Avenue, N. W. Suite 840, Washington tel. 202-965 4760

Food

In the last ten years, at least in San'a, international cuisine has become available. In the mid-1970's it was only possible to eat Yemeni food, there is now a large number of restaurants of various nationalities: Lebanese, Vietnamese, Chinese, American, Palestinian, to name but a few. The luxury hotels offer the standard international fare. More widespread refrigeration means that in San'a there is now usually an ample supply of fish. The small Yemeni restaurants are also better supplied than hitherto.

Ta'izz and Hudayda do not have as many international restaurants as San'a but the range of dishes available in the Yemeni restaurants is sometimes greater than in the capital. In small towns and villages you must make do with the local Yemeni dishes; the range may be limited but they are very tasty. A dish typical of Northern cuisine is *salsa* (spices, green sauce and meat) served with traditional Yemeni bread. Bread in Yemen has deep traditions: there are more than thirty kinds with many different flavours.

The best Yemeni restaurants are the *mohbasu,* which are typical of the Ta'izz region, but are now found throughout the country. They serve traditional dishes from the south and all specialize in fish.

Arab cuisine in the southern part of the country shows evidence of strong Indian and Indonesian influence. Aden used to have a large Indian community, and many South Yemenis, particularly the people of Hadramawt, went to work in Indonesia. This led to many mixed marriages and a particular Indonesian-Arabian mixed culture. There were also connections with India. As a result the southern cuisine is generally somewhat spicier than that of the north. In Aden there is also the usual international hotel cuisine, which is greatly enhanced by the abundance of fish.

Getting There and Back

Flights: Yemenia, Al Yemen (both national carriers), Lufthansa; also KLM, Royal Jordanian, Gulf Air, Egypt Air, Ethiopian Airlines, British Airways.

Visas: Visas can be obtained either by contacting the Yemeni embassy in the country of residence or upon arrival in Yemen provided prior arrangements are made through a travel agent in Yemen at least 3 weeks prior to arrival.

Leaving Yemen
Visas for longer stays: A tourist visa can be extended an extra month, longer extensions will require a Yemeni sponsor.
Airport tax on leaving: Check with airline whether included in the airfare.

Getting Around
The network of metalled roads in Yemen had increased to about 3850 km by mid-1992. There are also several hundred kilometres of track intended for ordinary vehicles. For the other tracks a sturdy four wheel-drive vehicle will be needed. However, there is hardly anywhere in Yemen that cannot now be reached by air. This is even true of the former refuges of the Imams, Shahara and Kawkaban, and the legendary ancient sites of Timna and Shabwa. One may turn up one's nose at the apparently unstoppable progress of the automobile, but a journey on out-of-the-way tracks is still very much an adventure.

On the metalled roads there is a lively public bus system. Since the mid-1980's the following towns have been accessible by bus from San'a: Aden, Ma'rib, Sa'da, Hajja, Ta'izz, Hudaya, Mokha, al-Baydha. By changing at Ta'izz or Hudayda you can also reach the towns of at-Turba (south of Ta'izz) and Jizan in Saudi Arabia.

The buses leave San'a twice a day (in the early morning and in the afternoon); there are five buses a day to Ta'izz and three to Aden and Hudayda. Tickets are bought before boarding; there are only as many tickets as there are seats. Except at weekends (ie. Thursdays and Fridays) the buses are not full.

For Ma'rib, Sa'da and Hajja the buses leave from the bus station at Bab Shawb, for Aden, Ta'izz and Hudayda from the one at Bab al-Yemen (General Transprt Corporation, Zubairi Street).

Health
During the rainy season malaria in Yemen extends to an altitude of 2000 metres. **Precautions against malaria should on no account be omitted.** According to information supplied by the World Health Organization chloroquine is still effective in Yemen.

The high altitude of San'a causes problems for some travellers. Irritation of the respiratory tracts and increased tiredness are common. However, gastric and intestinal illnesses, which affect between 20% and 40% of international tourists, seem not to be so frequent in Yemen. Bilharzia, which causes blindness, is caused by parasitic worms that live in still shallow water: you should avoid washing in water from cisterns and springs.

In summer the high temperatures and humidity on the coastal plains along the Red Sea and Indian Ocean mean that the visitor should have a robust constitution.

Since the second half of the 1980's inoculations against smallpox, cholera and yellow fever are no longer compulsory. Nor is it necessary to show the yellow international innoculation pass on entry into the country if one has come from a country affected by epidemics. Malaria innoculations are however strongly advisable.

Hospitals

San'a has four fully equipped modern hospitals where a seriously ill tourist can find help. The best is thought to be the Kuwait General Hospital (tel. 74004/5/6).

There are also modern hospitals in Aden, Ta'izz, Hajja and Sa'da. In most hospitals, besides qualified Yemeni doctors, foreign doctors can also be found.

Holidays and Festivals

Islam uses the Arab lunar calendar, which is said to have come down from antiquity. The division into months according to the phases of the moon means that each year the religious holidays may shift by about eleven days. Ramadan, the month of fasting, lasts 30 days; the festival at the end of Ramadan (Eid al-Fithr) lasts between three and five days; the great festival (Eid al-Adha) at the end of the pilgrimage period four to five days. On such festivals tourist traffic is greatly reduced, and in the days before and after public transport is fully booked.

Other holidays: Labour Day (1 May); Unification Day (22 May); Revolution Day (26 Sep.); National Day (14 Oct.); Independence Day (30 Nov.).

Language
The Arabic Language
by Barbara Fyjis-Walker

Arabic is one of the world's great languages. It is the mother tongue of 150 million people from Morocco to Iraq and it is the second language of many more since it is the liturgical language in all Muslim countries (a combined population of over 400 million). Since 1974 Arabic has been the sixth official language of the United Nations.

Arabic has a vast literary tradition accumulated over thirteen centuries: sensual poetry, elegant, concise prose, philosophy, historiography and early science as well as the wonderfully imaginative stories which are known all over the world.

Although the spoken dialects vary from country to country, Standard Arabic (based on the classical language of the Koran) is understood throughout the Arab world so books published in Baghdad can be read in Rabat or Khartoum (as once in Córdoba) and the radio, television and films continue this tradition of a standard lingua franca.

Although the youngest, Arabic is by far the most important of the Semitic group. (The Semitic languages are classified in two branches: the South Semitic, which includes Ethiopic and south Arabian, the latter now spoken only in Socotra, Mahra and Oman; and the Central Semitic, to which Arabic, Hebrew and Aramaic belong.). One characteristic of the Semitic languages is that words expressing basic ideas have roots which consist of either two or more usually three consonants and from these roots many other related words can be constructed following recognised patterns. For this reason the alphabets associated with these languages consist of consonants only and they do not adapt very well to languages from other groups, although the Arabic alphabet with a few extra letters has been used for Turkish, Malay, Spanish and Slavonic and is still used for Persian, Urdu and Kashmiri (which are all Indo-European languages). The Semitic languages also share grammatical characteristics: verbs do not indicate past, present and future but whether an action has been accomplished or not; one way of forming the plural of a noun is by changing the vowels, as in boy = *walad,* boys = *awlad.* This can follow a number of patterns and is applied to loan words so the plural of cocktail is *cackateel* and several boy scouts are *bayerskeet.*

Arabic script, written from right to left, consists of 28 letters representing consonants; of these, three can also represent the long vowels aa, ee, oo. The short vowel sounds can be shown by marks above or below the letters, but this is only done in Koranic texts (to avoid possible errors or ambiguity), in some poetry and in childrens books. There are no capitals, but most of the letters have different forms depending on where they come in a word (see table page 317). This alphabet dates back to the 4th century AD and took its present form 300 years later. The script was traditionally held to have been divinely bestowed and therefore perfect so there has always been strong opposition to change. Moreover, because representations of Nature were forbidden calligraphy became an important art. The writing represents the sounds of Arabic so well that it is very efficient. Scribes can take down speeches with no need for shorthand, but as there are no vowel signs it is difficult to read a passage aloud without first reading it through to grasp the meaning. The word 'tomato' would be written 'TMT' which leaves plenty of scope for imagination, and for misunderstanding, particularly as only the vowels show whether a verb is active or passive: thus 'he hits' and 'he is hit' are spelt in the same way and only the context will indicate the meaning and pronunciation.

Although our system of writing numbers came from the Arabs who brought the ideas of place value and of a sign for zero from India, the actual numerals have become different over the last 1000 years (see page 317).

On the island of Socotra there are still about 6000 people who speak one of the few remaining languages of the South Arabian subgroup, which is Semitic but nearer to Ethiopic than to Arabic. These languages used to be spoken all over South Arabia but have been replaced by Arabic and are now only spoken by fewer than 15,000 people along the south coast of Arabia (see page 260) and on some of the islands. The Arabs call them 'the languages of the birds' but strangely the Socotri people have no word for their own language (graphically described by Mrs Bent on page 263). The townspeople (who generally speak Arabic as well) sometimes find it difficult to understand peasants from the mountains because they have a larger vocabulary, some of which is very specialised, like the verb that means 'to trim a camel's eyelash'. Body language is important in Socotra; a useful gesture is to stick one's tongue out, meaning 'I do not understand.'

For English speakers the pronunciation of Arabic is not difficult. There is a difference between the pairs of letters :

s as in sin	s as in sad
d as in dear	ḍ as in double
t as in tin	ṭ as in utter
kas in kind	q as in cutter
h as in hear	ḥ as if clearing the throat

We have not indicated these 'heavy' sounds in the text, but they are shown here because the corresponding Arabic letters look quite different.

The consonants
kh as in Scottish loch and
gh as in a strong French r
present no difficulty, but the 'ayn, transliterated as ('), is strange to English ears. It is a strong guttural sound from far back in the throat sometimes described as hawking.

One of the short vowels which is not usually written in Arabic is the hamza, transliterated as ('); it indicates a glottal stop or short hesitation as when a cockney pronounces the tt in bottle as bo'ol.

The Arabic word for 'the', al, is modified to ad, al, an, ar etc. before the letters d, l, n, r, s, t, z, dh, th.

The Arabic Alphabet

Arabic name	full form	other forms	English symbol
alif	ا	ـا	a
ba	ب	ـبـ	b
ta	ت	ـتـ	t
tha	ث	ـثـ	th
jim	ج	ـجـ	j
ha	ح	ـحـ	h
kha	خ	ـخـ	kh
dal	د	ـد	d
dhal	ذ	ـذ	dh
ra	ر	ـر	r

zay	ز	ـز	z
sin	س	ـسـ	s
shin	ش	ـشـ	sh
sad	ص	ـصـ	ṣ
dad	ض	ـضـ	ḍ
toh	ط	ـطـ	ṭ
zoh	ظ	ـظـ	ẓ
'ayn	ع	ـعـ	'
ghayn	غ	ـغـ	gh
fa	ف	ـفـ	f
qaf	ق	ـقـ	q
kaf	ك	ـكـ	k
lam	ل	ـلـ	l
mim	م	ـمـ	m
nun	ن	ـنـ	n
ha	ه	ـهـ	ḥ
waw	و	ـوـ	w
Lam alef	ﻻ	ﻼ	la
ya	ي	ـبـ	y
hamza	ء	ء	'

Numerals

0	٠	sifr
1	١	wahid
2	٢	ithnayn
3	٣	thalatha
4	٤	arba'a
5	٥	khamsa
6	٦	sitta
7	٧	saba'a
8	٨	thamania
9	٩	tisa'a
10	١٠	'ashra
11	١١	hida'sh
20	٢٠	'ashrin
21	٢١	wahid wa 'ashrin
22	٢٢	ithnayn wa 'ashrin
30	٣٠	thalathin
40	٤٠	arba'in
50	٥٠	khamsin
100	١٠٠	miya
1000	١٠٠٠	alf

Essential Words

yes	aywa (or na 'am	week	usboo'
no	la	month	shaher
please	min fadlak	year	sanna
thank you	shukran	morning	sabah
not at all	afwan	midday	adh-dhur
sorry	mite'assif	afternoon	ba'd adh-dhur
never mind	ma'alesh	night	lail
hello (greeting)	salam alaykum	hour	sa'a
hello (response)	wa 'alaykum as-salam	half hour	nuss sa'a
welcome	ahlan wa sahla	once	marra
you	inta	twice	marratain
me (*or* I)	ana	slowly	shway-shway
do you speak	ti tekekkem	hotel	funduq
English?	inglaisi?	room	ghurfa
please speak slowly	tekellem ala mahlek	key	meftah
goodbye	ma'a as-salama	blanket	bataneeya
go away	imsh	bathroom	hammam
who are you?	min inta?	toilet	tuwalait
what's your name?	aysh ismak?	gents	ar-rijal
my name is	ismi	ladies	an-niswa
how goes it ?	kaif al hal?	soap	saboon
so so	ya'ni	toilet paper	warek tuwalait
why?	laish	restaurant	mat'am
where is?	wayn?	water	may
how much?	kem?	soft drink	asir
is there?	fi?	coffee	qahwa
is it possible?	mumkin?	tea	sha'i
when?	mata ?	milk	haleeb
now	hal	hot	sukhna
never	abadan	cold	barid
today	al yom	sugar	sukkar
tomorrow	bukra	bread	khubz
yesterday	ems (*or* embareh)	butter	zibda
Sunday	yom al-ahad	jam	mrabba
Monday	yom al-ithnain	olives	zaitun
Tuesday	yom ath-thaletha	salt	mileh
Wednesday	yom al-arbi'a	pepper	fil fil
Thursday	yom al-khemees	soup	shuorba
Friday	yom al jum'a	meat	laham
Saturday	yom es-sebt	chicken	dajaj
		fish	samak

317

eggs	bayda	I am ill	ana marid
rice	ruz	pharmacy	saydali'ya
vegetables	khudrawat	hospital	mustashfa
cheese	jibna	car	sayyara
orange	burtugal	bicycle	dejarra
apple	tiffah	bus	bas
banana	mawz	bus stop	mehatta al-bas
fruit	frutta (or fawaki)	airplane	tayira
dessert	hilwa	airport	matar
the bill please	al hisab min fadlak	ticket	tedhakir
market	suq	suitcase	shunta
how much ?	bi kam ?	passport	jawaz saferi
money	fulus	customs	jumruk
I have no change	ma endi fekka		
good	tammam (or kwayyis)		
not good	mush tammam		
finished	khalas		
a little	shwayya		
expensive	ghali		
cheap	rakhis		
cigarettes	sajayir		
matches	kabrit		
post cards	kuroot bareed		
post office	maktab al barid		
stamps	tuwabi'		
information office	maktab al isti'lamat		
which way to?	wain at-turiq ila?		
straight on	mustageem		
to the right	al-yamin		
to the left	ash-shimal		
is the place far?	al-mukan ba'eed?		
tourist office	maktab as-siya'ha		
mosque	jami' (or masjid)		
old city	madina gedeema		
gate	bab		
garden	bustan		
museum	medhaf		
tomb	magbera		
may I take a photo?	mumkin sura?		
it is not allowed	mamnoo'		

Opening Times

Friday is the day of rest when public offices, businesses and most shops are closed. However, in the suqs of Aden, San'a, Ta'izz and Hudayda many shops stay open until shortly before the midday prayers. There are also many Friday markets in towns all over the country.

On weekdays public offices are open from 8 am to 1 pm and from 4 pm to 6 pm, and private shops from 8 am to 12 noon and from 4 pm to 8 pm. During Ramadan these hours are much reduced.

Photography and Film

Yemen is still a most attractive subject for photographers, with its combination of the picturesque and a very fine light. Yemeni men are generally open and do not mind being photographed by tourists. With women on the other hand some caution is recommended, and permission should be asked wherever possible.

Recently, military personnel have been quick to confiscate cameras if they see any infringement of secrecy regulations.

In general travellers should avoid photographing in border regions and anywhere where there is a military presence.

Colour and black-and-white films can be bought in San'a, Aden and Ta'izz at prices only slightly higher than in Europe. Film processing facilities are available in Yemen.

Post

The Yemeni postal service is reliable and efficient. A notice in the main post office in San'a shows the closing times for outgoing airmail. If you time it right an air-mail letter to Europe will take only three to four days. On average outgoing and incoming post takes a week. There are fewer international flights from Aden, so post from there takes about two days longer.

Since there are no postmen in Yemen a foreigner who is temporarily resident there will have to get a post box number. These have now become difficult to get hold of.

Shopping

Modern industrial goods are almost always more expensive than in Europe and the choice is smaller. There are still however many traditional handicrafts, usually to be found in the markets which will interest many tourists.

The Yemenis are famous for their silver jewellery (see section page 277). A few dozen silversmiths still make silver balls, chains, bracelets, rings and cosmetic containers according to current models. The workmanship of these new pieces is not as fine as of those made 100 or even 50 years ago, but older pieces are still obtainable. Many Yemeni families now seem to be prepared to get rid of their silver and acquire gold instead. Prices are not prohibitive.

The new freedom of trade in the southern part of the country has meant that silver jewellery has come back on the market there. In Say'un much silver jewellery and much copperware has emerged. However many of the older pieces are liable to have had patination removed in a cleansing bath, and new pieces that have come onto the market are not of the same quality as the old. Recently some shops in Aden-Crater have been offering good pieces at significantly lower prices than comparable jewellery in Ta'izz and San'a.

Pottery and ceramics, such as incense-burners, ashtrays, drinking bowls, candle-holders and ladles, are to be found at every weekly market. From the Sada region come stone pots in various sizes, which still have a place in traditional Yemeni cookery. These pots are chiselled out of stone blocks broken in the mine. The high prices are commensurate with the effort involved. But if you can bring one of them home with you - there are small ones available - you will have a fine example of craftsmanship going back to the Islamic middle ages. Wickerwork (baskets large and small, mats, fans, decorative strips, hats and bags) is also found at markets, particularly in the Tihama, where it is also worth looking out for textiles. In the little towns of the coastal plain a few weaving workshops making curtains and hangings, as well as the monochrome

Tihama kelims, seem to have survived. Products of traditional blacksmithery should also be of interest to some collectors; rustic scissors and knives, little sickles for harvesting qat, massive keys and simple locks are always available. The Tihama markets also offer examples of leatherwork and woodwork.

Telephones

Telephone calls from San'a to foreign countries function very well thanks to modern satellite connections. Calls will of course be cheaper from the main office of the Cable and Wireless Co. than from hotels. Telephone services between towns in former North Yemen are also satisfactory, far more so than with towns in former South Yemen. Foreign calls from Aden still have to be made through slow manual connections.

International code for Yemen: 00 967
Local codes:

San'a	01
Aden	02
Hadayda	03
Ta'izz	04
Sal'da	051
Mukalla	0952
Ma'rib	0630
Say'un	0984
Hajja	07

Tipping

The mainly Asian staff of the larger hotels expect tips of 5-10%. It is also usual to give drivers of rented cars about a 10% tip after longer tours. In general, however, Yemenis are far less concerned about tips than Egyptians, for example. In local restaurants it is not necessary to add a service charge or any other extra sum to the bill. Taxi drivers usually give a price which includes the tip. In rural districts tips are not usual; a price will be given for any service required.

Travel Agencies

There are more than a dozen modern fully equipped travel agents in San'a.

Universal Travel & Tourism is the largest tour operator, tel. 272861/2/3, fax 272384, 275134

Yata (Yemen Arab Tourism Agency): tel. 224236 /224277 / 231797

ABM tours in San'a, tel. 270856, fax 274106

Al Mamoon Travel & Tourism: tel. 276299, fax 240984

Mareb Travel & Tourism: tel. 272435, fax 274199

Arabian Horizons for Tourism: tel. 275414, fax 275415

and many other small tour operators in the country.

Travel Restrictions

Permits to visit certain parts of the country are no longer needed. Travellers are strongly advised to find out from residents or travel agents/tour operators who know the country whether particular roads or whole districts are considered unsafe.

Photographic Acknowledgements
Colour plates
Dr. Ursula Braun, München-Geiselgasteig 30
Norman Dressel, Frankfurt 33-38
Günter Heil, Berlin 9, 12, 28
Fritz Kroler, Illertissent-Au 3
Angela and Peter Wald, Köln 1, 2, 4, 5, 6, 8, 10, 15, 17, 18, 19, 21, 22, 25, 27, 29, 32, 56, 57
Edith Wald Köln 7, 11, 13, 14, 16, 20, 23, 24, 26, 31, 39
Richard Porter 40-55, 58-68
Black and white plates
Monica Fritz
Text Illustrations
Catalogue of the Islam Festival, London 1976 79
Ursual Clemeur, Köln 37 (after an Ethiopian publication)
M. Neol Desverges *Arabie,* Paris 1847 15, 16, 182, 249
Monica Fritz 93
Thomas Gosciniak, Köln 278 (both), 279 (both), 281 (both), 282, 284 (both)
S. U. Graf, Schwaig 192, 199
Walter Harris, *A Journey through the Yemen,* London 1893 Frontispiece, 14, 17, 65, 178
Günter Heil, Berlin 46, 119
Hans Helfritz, Ibiza 47
Eugen Mittwoch (ed.) *Aus dem Jemen - Hermann Burchardts letzte Reise durch Südarabien,*
    Leipzig (n.d.) 23, 97, 101, 167, 225
Wendell Phillips, *Kataba und Saba,* Berlin and Frankfurt 1955 25, 40, 41, 190, 191, 196
Wolfgang Radt, *Katalog der Staatlichen Antikensammlung von Sanaa und anderer Antiken im
    Jemen,* Berlin 1973 44, 48 (below), 107, 197
Carl Rathjens, *Sabäica,* Hamburg 1958 87, 117
Heinz Schmitz, Köln 75, 88 (both), 98, 107 (above), 110 (both), 111, 112, 113, 114-5, 118, 120, 121,
    134, 136, 137, 138, 140, 144-5, 147, 153, 168, 171, 175, 180
Freya Stark, *Seen in the Hadhramaut,* London 1938 20, 202, 213, 235
Dr. Lothar Stein, Leipzig 266
Angela and Peter Wald, Köln 47, 54, 63, 76/7, 96, 99 (left), 141, 143, 150-1, 154, 155, 156, 163, 176,
    177, 211, 213, 214, 230, 232, 233, 236, 241, 255, 257, 258
Edith Wald, Köln 27, 35 (both), 42, 48 (above), 53, 58, 64, 66, 69, 70, 74, 78, 80, 82, 83, 91, 92, 95,
    96 (right), 106, 126, 128, 129, 130, 131, 132, 142, 158-9, 161, 164, 165, 183, 201, 208-9, 216,
    222, 223, 226, 236 (below), 248, 250, 251, 252
Hermann von Wissmann, *Zur Archäeologie und antiken Geographie von Südarabien,* Istanbul
    1968 220-1
Maps
Ted Hammond, St. Albans, except for inner front cover
Karl-Heinz Bochow, Leipzig 258
All other illustrations are from the author's and publishers' archives.

Index

Figures in **bold** refer to principal entries
Figures in *italic* refer to illustrations

PALLAS GUIDES
LANDSCAPE PEOPLE ART ARCHITECTURE

Uniform with this volume in the Pallas Guides series:

POLAND
This hefty item is a cultural treasure *Polish American Journal*

WALES
Certainly the best book on the country *The New York Times*

EAST ANGLIA
A stunningly good guide *Mail on Sunday*

CZECH AND SLOVAK REPUBLICS
Superb *Traveller*

Forthcoming:

TIBET ISRAEL ANDALUCÍA PAKISTAN

And in the Pallas for Pleasure series:

VENICE FOR PLEASURE
J. G. Links
Not only the best guide to that city ever written, but the best guide
to *any* city ever written
Bernard Levin in *The Times*

FLEMISH CITIES EXPLORED
Derek Blyth
An essential companion *The Sunday Correspondent*

MADRID OBSERVED
Michael Jacobs
He has a gift for finding exotic corners in a familiar city and of resuscitating
the forgotten with colourful intensity *Times Literary Supplement*

For more information, please contact
Pallas Athene, 59 Linden Gardens, London W2 4HJ

You close your laptop
A taste of Brie. A sip o
back and hope you wo

UKCDP1

d adjust your footrest.
Bordeaux. You lean
t be arriving too soon.

That depends on how
far you're going.

The fact that Lufthansa flies to 220 global destinations comes as a surprise to some. Perhaps we've been too busy with our award-winning service to tell everybody that we are one of the world's largest airline networks. A network that can offer you fast and convenient connections to anywhere. A network that offers rewards with Miles and More, one of the world's leading frequent flyer programmes. And above all, a network that makes you feel at home, however far you're going. So call Lufthansa on 0345 252 252 and we'll tell you the full story.

Lufthansa

DISCOVER YEMEN